MEDIEVALISM AND THE QUEST FOR THE "REAL" MIDDLE AGES

BOOKS OF RELATED INTEREST

MEDIEVALISM AND THE QUEST FOR THE "REAL" MIDDLE AGES

edited by

Clare A. Simmons

Routledge
Taylor & Francis Group

LONDON AND NEW YORK

First published 2001 by
FRANK CASS AND COMPANY LIMITED

Published 2014 by Routledge
2 Park Square, Milton Park, Abingdon, Oxfordshire OX14 4RN
711 Third Avenue, New York, NY 10017

Transferred to Digital Printing 2005
First issued in paperback 2014

Routledge is an imprint of the Taylor & Francis Group, an informa business

British Library Cataloguing in Publication Data

Medievalism and the quest for the 'real' Middle Ages
    1. Medievalism in literature 2. Middle Ages in literature
    3. Medievalism 4. Middle Ages 5. Literature – History and
    criticism
    I. Simmons, Clare A., 1958-
    809.9′3358

ISBN 978-0-714-65145-3 (hbk)

ISBN 978-1-138-87816-7 (pbk)

Library of Congress Cataloging-in-Publication Data

A catalog record for this title is available from the Library of Congress

This group of studies first appeared in a Special Issue of *Prose Studies*
(ISSN 0144-0357), Vol.23, No.2 (August 2000),
[Medievalism and the Quest for the "Real" Middle Ages].

Contents

Introduction

CLARE A. SIMMONS

For a long time, Medievalism, the later reception of the Middle Ages, had a reputation as an aberration from scholarly Medieval Studies, conjuring up images of Victorian flourishes, medieval reenactments, and quasi-Arthurian swords and sorcery. The articles in this issue represent a range of the possibilities of Medievalism.[1] These include not only the traditional concerns of Medievalism, namely, direct or indirect commentary on politics, religion and aesthetics; but also Medievalism's new implications for gender studies and for understanding how scholarly disciplines come into being. I propose here to present a brief overview of Medievalism, focusing on its uses in English prose writing,[2] and then to examine recent developments in its theoretical applications, particularly its implications for the field of medieval studies at a time when the "authenticity" that once divided medieval studies from Medievalism no longer seems a scholarly possibility. Much of the information in the first section of this overview will probably seem familiar to those interested in Medievalism, and much of the second to those in medieval studies; my goal here, though, is to trace division and synthesis between the two.

I

In 1853, John Ruskin used the word "mediaevalism" or "medievalism" to describe his own generation's enthusiasm for the medieval (itself a nineteenth-century term; earlier, the phrase Middle Ages was used). In a lecture justifying Pre-Raphaelite art, Ruskin referred to what he called a "Trinity of ages," or Classicalism, Mediaevalism and Modernism. For Ruskin, these were not merely styles of art; they were inextricably linked to ways of life, as his definitions of their time-periods as pre-Christian, Christian and post-Christian suggests. Thus although Medievalism might be generally described as the later interpretation of the Middle Ages, from its original usage, the term implied some comparative valuation between epochs.

Within medieval studies, a number of key questions recur, including the quest for origins; the relationship between religion and nationalism; and the model of an ordered or idyllic society. Yet although all of these present a challenge to the notion of an "authentic" Middle Ages, in the later nineteenth century and early twentieth century, the quest for answers to these questions becomes subordinated to a desire for the real, the historical, the documented. Self-evidently, truth-claims can be found in earlier responses to the Middle Ages, but usually in support of a declared or implicit position.

Ruskin nevertheless deserves credit for theorizing an ideological debt to the Middle Ages. His model for cooperative society, expounded in *The Seven Lamps of Architecture* (1849) and *The Stones of Venice* (1851), was the Gothic cathedral, representing craftsmen working collectively, yet with scope for individual expression, towards a common goal, each recognizing and valuing his own role in artistic creation; in this collection, Chene Heady's article usefully rehearses Ruskin's major arguments. Medievalism is hence often seen as only emerging in the nineteenth century as a reaction against increasing technology, mass production, and the reconsideration of traditional values prompted by scientific discoveries that seemed to call into question the historical status of the Bible.[3] Alice Chandler's seminal book on nineteenth-century Anglophone ideas of the medieval calls this a "Dream of Order."[4] Yet the process of comparison of those seeking to define themselves through or against the time from the fall of the Roman Empire to the Renaissance began far earlier: indeed, only if the Renaissance is seen a "rebirth" of classical learning can this time-period be seen as "middle." As Kelly Quinn's article on Samuel Daniel demonstrates, Medievalist works can be found almost as soon as writers and readers are able to identify themselves as *not* part of the Middle Ages. Medievalism comes into play even when artists distance themselves from part of the Middle Ages, such as fifteenth-century writers recreating the Saxon period or the Arthurian era. For example, William Caxton's edition of Thomas Malory's tales of King Arthur had for Victorian readers the status of an authentic medieval text; yet both Caxton and Malory were representing a past England that functioned differently from the England known to their audience.

After Caxton's time, with the coming of the ideas of the Reformation of religion, attempts to return to the Middle Ages were to become not merely problematic, but potentially subversive. For countries such as England where the state endorsed the Reformation, the idea of Middle Ages was so closely associated with the Roman Catholic church that to argue for "medieval" values was frequently to incur the danger of being suspected of Catholic sympathies. Even this, however, was not an insuperable barrier to a selective reading of the Middle Ages. Protestants were not likely to endorse monasticism, yet some, such as John Foxe, argued that the English church of Saxon times was closer to the ideals of primitive Christianity than the papally-dominated church structure imposed by the Normans.[5] In England at least, Medievalism seems to encode desire or mourning for loss, whether it is for the Saxon kingdom, the ordered society of the Middle Ages, or even for an age where romance and chivalry were still possible. Moreover, a

Protestant establishment was able to use medieval myth as well as Catholics where it suited its purposes, obvious examples being the Tudors' claim of descent from King Arthur, and the allegorical chivalric world of Spenser's *Faerie Queene* – which, as Kristin Haugen discusses, some later readers were inclined to read as authentically medieval. And although the antiquarianism of, for example, William Camden was directed more towards the ancient than the medieval past, a work such as his *Britannia* inscribed a value onto British origins and the physical remains that demonstrated them.

The English Civil War period continued the question of whether a reformation of church and government was a return to classical ideals (a recreation of the Christian church under the Romans, and to Greco-Roman models of government), or to an earlier stage in England's national history, as in the case of Gerrard Winstanley and the Diggers, the subject of a recent Special Issue of *Prose Studies*.[6] Lord Macaulay's characterization of the expulsion of the last Stuart king James II as the triumph of progressive modernity may be largely his own invention, yet distrust of Roman Catholics as un-English was certainly linked to conceptions of modernity. For much of the eighteenth century, Britain was at war with Roman Catholic nations, and at least superficially, as British national identity began to emerge as consciously opposed to France, and antimedievalist.[7] That eighteenth-century British culture is still often called "Augustan" and "Neoclassical" would suggest that in the debate over whether Classicism or Medievalism was the superior model to follow, Classicism prevailed: in Swift's 1697 *Battel of the Books*, for example, the "Ancients" (classical works) and "Moderns" (post-classical works) are represented in conflict, greatly to the disadvantage of the latter. Nevertheless, antiquarian bibliophiles from Elizabethan times until the early eighteenth century were not only interested in classical books, but worked to preserve what they could of early English manuscripts. Matthew Parker, Sir Robert Cotton, and Robert and Edward Harley all amassed collections of medieval materials that remain a significant part of our knowledge of medieval England to this day.[8]

Moreover, Non-Jurors, those members of the clergy who refused to pledge allegiance to William III and Mary, formed the nucleus of a new wave of scholarly Medievalism. George Hicks, for example, published a study of early remains that included an Anglo-Saxon grammar, comparative vocabularies of Anglo-Saxon and Gothic, excerpts from Anglo-Saxon writings, and the first bibliography of Anglo-Saxon works, compiled by Humfrey Wanley. Others, such as Anthony à Wood, began the antiquarian pursuit of collecting and printing medieval works that had hitherto only been available in manuscript sources. Medievalism and antiquarianism are not automatically synonymous: antiquarianism's pursuit of the past *as* past does not necessarily privilege the medieval over the classical, or imply a commentary on the present. Yet although antiquarian retreats into the past might at first sight seem a deliberate avoidance of current politics, such attempts to escape from the contemporary world obliquely suggest that the antiquarians placed a value on the national past that the present had lost.

A revival of interest in Gothic aesthetics began as early as the 1750s, when architects such as Batty Langley published pattern-books of Gothic architectural features, and a selective reading of "good" survivals from the medieval past became possible.[9] Historians reminded English readers that English law emerged during the medieval period. In a passage that Mark Schoenfield describes as replacing "a historical antagonism with an image of harmony," Sir William Blackstone observes that

> We inherit an old Gothic castle, erected in the days of chivalry, but fitted up for a modern inhabitant. The moated ramparts, the embattled towers, and the trophied halls, are magnificent and venerable, but useless. The inferior apartments, now converted into rooms of convenience, are chearful and commodious, though their approaches are winding and difficult.[10]

Central to Blackstone's reading of English law is a sense of continuity, so that modern law is ultimately derived from the laws of the ancient Goths. About this time, though, the word "Gothic" began to apply to more than architecture and law. Horace Walpole, the high priest of the English Gothic revival, initially presented the first Gothic novel *The Castle of Otranto* (1764) as "A Gothic Story" translated from a medieval source, and some critics revised their opinion of it when they learned it was Walpole's own invention.[11] Yet although for Walpole as for many of his contemporaries "Gothic" meant "medieval," the Gothic narrative genre's anti-Catholicism frequently manifests itself as anti-Medievalism, portraying monastic life and medieval castles and abbeys as places to be dreaded, rather than as relics of an age from which the present could learn.

The Gothic novel emerged about the same time as the French Revolution, which itself was anti-medieval in rejecting the traditional relationship between king, church and subjects that had prevailed at least since the time of Charlemagne. Instead, Revolutionary self-presentation tended either to reject history entirely, or to adopt classical models inspired by the Athenian and Roman Republics.[12] At a time when France itself had rejected the medieval connotations of the Roman Catholic Church, British writers were adapting medievalist images to explore their own ambivalence about class. Fred Botting notes, though, that the persistence of these images may imply an intellectual rejection of the medieval, yet at the same time they still fascinate, and that this fascination may itself be political:

Old castles, knights, and malevolent aristocrats seem to fit into an enlightenment pattern identifying all things Gothic with the tyranny and barbarity of feudal times. Rational distancing and disavowal of past forms of power, however, is belied by the continued fascination with the architecture, customs and values or the Middle Ages .[13]

Medievalism also plays an important role in non-fiction prose of the American and French Revolutionary period. The appeal to natural equality in the American Declaration of Independence is ahistorical, but as Reginald Horsman has shown, Thomas Jefferson and Benjamin Franklin were both attracted by the idea that they were reviving a free Saxon government.[14] Similarly, when Edmund Burke lamented in his *Reflections on the Revolution in France* that "the age of chivalry is dead," radical critics such as Catherine Macaulay and Thomas Paine immediately challenged Burke's conception of the Middle Ages, and argued that progress was hobbled by appeals to historical precedent. The apparent ahistoricity of their claims, however, is belied by the fact that while rejecting Burke's love of tradition, they reconstructed their own selective pasts. Paine drew pointed parallels between George III and William the Conqueror; Macaulay declared an end to "historical precedent" as a basis for government, yet called her own "Alfredhouse" and placed a bust of King Alfred over the door.[15]

Yet Burke had established some important precedents for medievalism. First, he detached ideas of the medieval from Roman Catholicism, and instead substituted a vague sense of pious veneration for tradition. Second, he drew larger gender implications from the medieval than before, encouraging a nostalgia for an age in which women were not political beings, but treated with chivalric respect. And finally, he suggested that for Britain and France, and, by implication, other nations also, national identity was rooted in medieval history, and that a rejection of that past was a loss of part of the self.

This conservative elegiac was most ably taken up by Sir Walter Scott. Not merely in romances with medieval settings such as *Ivanhoe* but also in prose works such as the "Essay on Chivalry" and in the extensive historical notes that he wrote to his poems and novels, Scott presented a recoverable Middle Ages, one that was different from the present, but not threatening to it. Although Scott's view of the Middle Ages was not entirely one of idyll, even *Ivanhoe* depicting a "condition of England" that was in many respects "wretched," it seemed idyllic to future generations, as in Carlyle's use of *Ivanhoe* in *Past and Present*, and the strong American interest in chivalric values in the later nineteenth century. Chivalric extremes are represented by Kenelm Digby's *The Broad Stone of Honor* (1822), and the "Young England" movement that assumed that Britain could be saved from the miseries of industrialism by a benevolent paternalism.[16]

Digby's interest in the medieval past seems to have inspired his conversion to Roman Catholicism. When Roman Catholics finally gained equal voting rights in 1828, the sense that to be Roman Catholic was to be unpatriotic began to wane, and critics of the current "condition of England" began to look for new social models in the Middle Ages. The passing of the New Poor Law in 1834, after which the able-bodied poor only qualified for assistance if they entered the workhouse, implied that poverty was a social aberration, rather than having a role in a divinely-appointed order. Utilitarianism, Jeremy Bentham's materialist-based philosophy too often crudely interpreted as "the happiness of the greatest number," was often seen as emphasizing the needs of the majority at the expense of a minority. Hence whereas Britons had traditionally imagined the Roman Catholic past as a time of oppression, some commentators now envisaged the Middle Ages as more compassionate than the England of the 1830s.

An even more influential convert to Catholicism was John Henry Newman. The Oxford Movement, begun in the 1830s, was a group of scholars who met to study the traditions of the Christian church, originally with the purpose of defending the principles of the Church of England. Their members wrote a series of *Tracts for the Times* covering a range of theological issues, until in the notorious Tract XC (1841), Newman argued that the Thirty-nine Articles of the Anglican church could be interpreted as compatible with the doctrines of Roman Catholicism. The resulting controversy drove Newman from the Church of England to Roman Catholicism; some of the other Tractarians followed him, but others, such as John Keble and Edward Pusey remained within the established church while voicing approval of many of the medieval rites inherited from the Roman church.

The medieval church was a particularly strong influence on the decorative arts of the early Victorian period. In 1836, the architect Augustus Welby Northmore Pugin, who had recently converted to Roman Catholicism, produced a series of engravings called *Contrasts; or, a parallel between the noble edifices of the fourteenth and fifteenth centuries and similar buildings of the present day, shewing the present decay of taste*. The title may appear to be self-explanatory, but Pugin's illustrations show not just the aesthetic superiority of the Gothic Middle Ages, but also their moral superiority in functioning as a truly Christian society. One illustration, for example, contrasts the kindness shown by medieval monasteries to the poor and sick with a present-day workhouse, shown as Bentham's panopticon; whereas the monks of the past gave the poor Christian burial, the bodies of the poor in the 1830s are shown as given up for dissection. Pugin's championing of the Gothic as a truly English artform was enormously influential. In the eighteenth century, many had proposed replacing the medieval Parliament buildings with neoclassical designs.[17] Yet when the Houses of Parliament burned down in 1834, the decision was made that the buildings would be replaced by a Gothic or Elizabethan design that proclaimed the richness of England's cultural heritage and legal traditions. The principle architect of the exterior was Sir Charles Barry, but Pugin was responsible for much of the Gothic decoration.[18] He was to go on to design or remodel many churches, public buildings, and houses. One of the oddest emanations of this desire for the medieval was the remodeling of buildings that dated from the Middle Ages, such as Windsor Castle and Arundel Castle, to conform with Victorian ideas of what a medieval castle should look like.[19]

As a result, Medievalism could unintentionally lapse into absurdity. Probably the most bizarre manifestation of medievalism in the early years of the Victorian period was the Eglinton Tournament of 1839, which has been well described by Mark Girouard in *The Return to Camelot: Chivalry and the English Gentleman.*[20] The young Lord Eglinton invited the "very elite of the most elite" to participate in a lavish and authentic recreation of a grand medieval tournament at his estate. Aristocrats gave themselves knightly titles and arrived with full armor and equipment. Extravagant parades, pavilions and jousting were planned; unfortunately, on the day of the tournament, torrential rain reduced the fields into a sea of mud, and the celebration was abandoned, to the general amusement of the popular press. Some jousting did follow the next day, but this attempt at a serious recreation of the knightly world of the Middle Ages contributed to the common association of medievalism with elitism and quixoticism.

Another powerful and more earnest example of the use of medievalism in the period before the Pre-Raphaelites is Thomas Carlyle's *Past and Present* (1843). At a time of considerable economic hardship, especially in Ireland, Carlyle was pondering what he called "the Condition-of-England Question" when he came across a Camden Society edition of the Chronicle of Jocelin of Brakelond. The Camden Society is a good example of a growing in interest in historical publishing after the founding of the Roxburghe Club in 1814. Formed in 1838 to publish documents illustrative of English history, it provided a new window on the medieval world, and Jocelin's chronicle, recounting life in the monastery of Bury St. Edmund's in the early thirteenth century, depicts the triumphs and failures of both ordinary and exceptional people. For the purpose of *Past and Present*, that this is a real, documented past and not a novel is important: "this England of the Year 1200 was no chimerical vacuity or dreamland," and Abbot Samson proves a "true Governor." Yet although Carlyle chooses to contrast the story of Abbot Samson with that of present-day English policy, he is less interested in the religious aspect than in a man who ruled by force of character. For Carlyle, that in the medieval world "might" made "right" is a virtue, and the strength of character and rule demonstrated by Samson suggests a way out of the present "Condition of England."

In France also, scholars such as Francisque Michel tried to recapture the past through the recovery of medieval documents. Reacting against the pointed anti-Medievalism of the French Revolutionary period, under the Bourbon restoration of the 1820s and the July Monarchy from 1830 onwards, French writers and artists drew on France's historical traditions in the reframing of national identity.[21] After Notre Dame had suffered damage during the Revolutionary era (symptomatic of that time's contempt for the medieval) Eugene-Emmanuel Viollet-le-Duc undertook its restoration to more than medieval splendor. Sarah Hibberd and Elizabeth Emery's articles on French Medievalism suggest that restoration, not just of buildings but of lineages and traditions, is a key theme in national desire for the past.

Medievalism, however, represented for France more of a wish for continuity than its achievement, as demonstrated by the revolutions of 1848. In a year of revolutions in Europe, the most extreme political action in Britain was the last thrust of the Chartist movement. The range of uses of Medievalism in Victorian Britain is amply demonstrated by the fact that not only the traditionalists who opposed them appealed to the medieval past, but also the Chartists themselves. In claiming a vote for all men over the age of 21, some Chartists argued that this was not an attempt to achieve a state of society that had never before existed, but rather to reclaim the ancient rights of Britons. The very name "Chartism" recalls Magna Carta, or the Great Charter, signed by King John in 1215. The Chartist rally planned for London in 1848, however, was weakened by the government's appointment of a huge number of special constables to control the crowd, and after that, Chartism rapidly disappeared, or merged into socialism.

The same year, a different kind of revolution was effected by a small group of English artists. William Holman Hunt, John Everett Millais, Dante Gabriel Rossetti and a few others united as the Pre-Raphaelite Brotherhood; as their name suggests, they sought inspiration from medieval art, rejecting the art that followed as not being compatible with "truth." Much of the subject-matter of Pre-Raphaelite art was medieval or Medievalist. The self-styled Dante Gabriel Rossetti (his given name was Gabriel Charles Dante Rossetti) and his friends painted many works based on the poetry of Dante, the Arthurian cycle, and other medieval stories. Even some paintings on Biblical themes, such as Rossetti's 1850 *Ecce Ancilla Domini!*, are influenced by medieval styles and almost resemble illuminated manuscripts.[22] Framing and related texts thus become an important part of the entire work. For example, Rossetti's *Blessed Damozel* (1875–78) illustrates Rossetti's earlier Dante-esque poem of that title, yet it is also framed like an illuminated manuscript, part of the frame forming the "gold bar" between the Damozel in heaven and the lover on earth.

In the later years of the century, then, Pre-Raphaelitism in many respects merges the ideas of chivalry with those of Ruskin, one of their keenest defenders, to create a new vision of ideal labor relationships. Ironically, many of the buyers of their paintings were wealthy industrialists, such as the Levers of Liverpool. Yet they created an ideal of individual craftspeople who were not alienated from their labor but committed to works of art. Morris presents these ideas in *A Dream of John Ball*, a vision of an idealized socialist medieval past, but more particularly in *News From Nowhere*, a dream-vision of the future where people spend their time in making beautiful objects. Morris founded a company that produced many textile and wallpaper designs inspired by medieval art, while his Kelmscott Press sought to recreate the early years of printing. "The Haystack in the Floods," written in the 1850s, contains brutal images of medieval behavior; yet in his maturer years, Morris seems to have favored a decorous image of the past.[23]

The visionary quality of socialist and aesthetic Medievalism presents a contrast with the other emergent strain of Medievalism of the later nineteenth century, the scholarly quest for authenticity. From the 1830s, not just in Britain but also in France and other European states, scholars began to show a new interest in reproducing the past in the form of printed versions of medieval texts. The Camden Club was just one of many publishing societies from the 1840s onwards that were devoted to reprinting medieval literature and history. A larger range of early works had become available to the ordinary reader through series such as Bohn's Standard Texts. The Early English Text Society, which continues to produce scholarly editions to this day, was founded in 1864 by Frederick J. Furnivall; he was also a founder-member of the Chaucer Society (1868) and the Ballad Society (1869). Even the British government became involved in the preservation of early texts through the Rolls Series, begun about the same time.

Another important milestone was the founding of the Folk-Lore Society in 1878. The word "folk-lore" was coined in 1846 by William John Thoms, who was looking for a particularly English word. The collection of "provincial antiquities" had been common in the eighteenth century, yet less specific cultural claims were attached to it The Folk-Lore Society would probably have argued that some of the customs and beliefs that it uncovered in the memories of British rural communities pre-dated the medieval period; yet it helped to contribute to a sense of a national past in which not just the socially elite had ancient traditions, but also the uneducated poor. Immensely influential on the folk-lore revival was the prolific Andrew Lang, the author of *Custom and Myth* (1884) and editor of the very popular series of collected fairy-stories from many nations, each book named after a color; the first was *The Blue Fairy-Book* of 1889.[24] In the 1880s the American scholar F.J. Child and his friends collected and edited English and Scottish popular ballads. Such work received additional validation when Carl Jung argued that the collective unconscious gave power to stories such as folktales and Arthurian myth. Jessie Weston, following the researches of J.G. Frazer, argued for use of archetypal symbol in *From Ritual to Romance* (1919), which T.S. Eliot claimed as a source for *The Waste Land*.[25] In this collection, Susan Aronstein demonstrates in her article on the mythopoetic men's movement that such assumptions continue to be a cultural force. An indication of the urge for authenticity is the superior attitude that these folklorists adopted towards earlier ballad-collectors such as Percy and Scott.

Many of the societies dedicated to recovering medieval texts and traditions functioned very much as social clubs, and although the titular leaders were usually men, women played an active role, and some, such as Jessie Weston, were important scholars in their own right. I would suggest that an area of Medievalism that would repay more study is the gender implications of the shift in influence from these socially-based (and in the most part elitist) clubs to the equally elitist but more clearly male-dominated world of the University as medieval studies emerged as a professional discipline.

Meanwhile, historians found ways to combine a belief in progress with an interest in the medieval past. Leopold von Ranke seems to have been among the first to advance the idea of "scientific" history, a careful sifting of the documentary evidence to create an authentic account of the past and discover "how it really was" (*wie es eigentlich gewesen*). The introduction to his *History of the Popes*, for example, gives a detailed account of his archival sources, and announces that Ranke's personal "indifference" makes him a more appropriate historian than those with a commitment to the materials:

> An Italian, or Roman, a Catholic, would enter on the subject in a spirit very different from mine. By indulging in expressions of personal veneration, or, perhaps, in the present state of opinion, of personal hatred, he would give to his work a peculiar, and, no doubt, more brilliant colouring; on many points he would be more elaborate, more ecclesiastical, more local. In these respects, a Protestant, a North German, cannot be expected to compete with him. He regards the papal power with feelings of more indifference; and must, from the first, renounce that warmth of expression which arises from partiality or hostility; and which might, perhaps, produce a certain impression in Europe. ... Popery can now inspire us with no other interest than what results from the development of its history and its former influence.[26]

Yet as Hayden White has observed, Ranke too was working from a number of conceptual assumptions, including the hardly insignificant one that human existence has sense and purpose. For Ranke, White argues, nationhood is an ideal opposed to moral universality.[27] Thus even Ranke's quest to reconstruct an authentic past of which he himself is not a part is still part of a model of progressive history leading to the nineteenth-century state. Even in the early twentieth century, Ranke's historical writings still provided a model for studying the past, holding, for example, a key place in George Peabody Gooch's *History and Historians in the Nineteenth Century*.

Similarly, in Britain, Edward Augustus Freeman, who mocked the historical errors of *Ivanhoe*, wrote a huge history of the Norman Conquest in which the Norman invasion is interpreted as a necessary step towards the creation of the modern English; similar ideas are articulated in Charles Kingsley's essay series *The Roman and the Teuton* (1864). Matthew Arnold's immensely influential 1864 essay "The Function of Criticism at the Present Time" responded directly to those optimistic Britons who claimed that the "Anglo-Saxon race" was "the best breed in the world."[28] The sound and meaning of the phrase "Wragg is in custody," Arnold suggests, reflect "the touch of grossness in our race." Yet in addition to challenging his contemporaries' Medievalism, Arnold also advanced an anti-Medievalist theory that achieved the level of an orthodoxy in English criticism: namely, that criticism should, in its quest to "see the object in itself as it really is," be "disinterested." As Arnold's examples show, "disinterestedness" is clearly contrary to Medievalism, since criticism maintains it by "keeping aloof from practice; by resolutely following the law of its own nature, which is to be a free play of the mind on all subjects which it touches" (270). The "business" of criticism is "simply to know the best that is known and thought in the world, and by in its turn making this known, to create a current of fresh and true ideas." Perfectibility cannot be achieved simply through racial identity, but only through approaching the greatest ideas free of the prejudices of one's individualism. Hence Arnold and others advocated a model of education based on the pursuit of knowledge; in this model, knowledge functions almost as a moral absolute. In the Preface to the published edition of John Henry Newman's *The Idea of a University*, based on "Nine Discourses delivered to the Catholics of Dublin" in 1852, Newman emphasizes that the University is "a place of *teaching* universal *knowledge*," and that its morality comes through the pursuit of knowledge uninhibited by doctrine.[29]

In the decades that followed, opportunities for higher education in the United States and Britain grew dramatically with the establishment of the "red-brick" universities and land-grant institutions. Divergence between Medievalism and medieval studies could now be marked as a distinction between professional and amateur. For those within the profession, the achievement of objectivity in pursuit of the authentic Middle Ages remained a central critical question until the last quarter of the twentieth century. The difference between Medievalism and medieval studies might be summarized as oppositions:

> *Medieval Studies*: Professional; within the academy; research-based; objective; committed to discovering the authentic past.

> *Medievalism*: Amateur; outside the academy; based on cultural preconceptions; subjective; shaped by the individual's needs and desires.

Yet even the first two oppositions prove slippery. Were the founders of the Early English Text Series amateurs or professionals? Does a professional appointment in a research institution prove that a scholar's reading of the medieval past is not based on cultural preconceptions?[30] Since medieval studies cannot, at least in hindsight, be entirely free of Medievalism, one solution is to find a working definition of Medievalism that enhances, rather than proves the failure of, our understanding of the Middle Ages.

II

I have suggested that in the second half of the nineteenth century, and for most of the twentieth century, one generation's medieval studies was the next generation's Medievalism. I will now turn to recent theoretical developments in medieval studies and the implications for Medievalism, and by considering some newer books by medieval scholars, argue that Medievalism and medieval studies need no longer represent an opposition.

For most of the twentieth century, medieval scholars continued to pursue objectivity as the only credible critical approach to the Middle Ages. Johan Huizinga, for example, pronounced confidently in 1915:

> Even romanticism was never completely serious in its imitation of the Middle Ages. The copying of historical forms in nineteenth-century art, like the copying of medieval architectural styles, has no significance in this respect. The reality of history ... became too clearly conscious for modern humanity to continue to seek its salvation in the imitation of an imagined past.[31]

Ranke's ideal of researching the past "as it really was" proved a remarkably constant goal for historians and literary historians. Although Hans Robert Jauss had somewhat earlier raised the question of the effect of the critic's subject position in approaching the medieval text,[32] it was not until the 1980s that medieval scholars began openly to explore the assumptions that had formed their field, and to acknowledge that their discipline. In *Negotiating the Past: The Historical Understanding of Medieval Literature*, Lee Patterson effectively demonstrates that like most other areas of humanistic study, medieval literary studies had emerged in the nineteenth century with the professionalization of scholarship. Whereas Huizinga had contrasted true history's pursuit of truth with that of imaginative recreation of an individualized human past, Patterson points out that

> The appeal to "history" so commonly made in current critical discourses of all varieties is necessarily only a reconstruction fabricated according to processes of interpretation that are identical to those applied to the "not-history" of the literary text.[33]

Patterson is primarily discussing the historicist discourse that re-entered literary study in the 1980s, yet historicist literary criticism's appeal to "history" seems to assume that "history" is, as its nineteenth-century proponents had argued, a locus for interpretive stability. Although many later scholars had scoffed at figures such as Gaston Paris (who, after all, was a second-generation professional scholar) for a lack of objectivity, ironically, the goal of critical objectivity proved itself to be the imposition of the nineteenth-century notions of "scientific" study that were especially problematic for literary studies, and yet in some respects were being re-inscribed as literary critics turned back to "history." In medieval studies, the interplay between history and literature is especially complex. Before and during the nineteenth century, the recovery of a work of medieval literature could be a goal in itself, and was very often a political act. Yet if medieval studies does more than recover and place a value on texts, the question arises as to whether they are only valued as historical documents – that is, for what they reveal about the society that produced them, as opposed to as aesthetic objects in themselves.

Hence the re-examination of medieval studies emerged at the same time as, and partly as a response to, New Historicism. Yet whereas New Historicism called into question critical responses to "texts in themselves" (the goal of New Criticism), and posited instead a return to considering the text as a production of its historical and political context, the division between "literature" and "history" was not so clear in the case of medieval studies. Self-evidently, in the traditional university structure, even if that tradition is little more than a century old, history departments teach medieval history, and language and literature departments teach medieval languages and literatures. History departments can describe their goal as "finding out" about the Middle Ages, but literature departments, even during the reign of New Criticism, seem rarely to have taught medieval literature ahistorically as productions of language that could be appreciated in isolation from the material conditions of their production. Moreover, as I have suggested, simply to claim that medieval literature is "good" is enmeshed in political significance. Conversely, to place medieval literature as an origin point for where modern literature came from in a kind of whig-historical progress is in many respects an anti-medievalist endeavor. In many instances, medieval literature becomes very like medieval history, its goal being "finding out" about the Middle Ages with an implicit pursuit of authenticity, the further understanding of the "real" Middle Ages.

Perhaps one reason why the *Studies in Medievalism* series has prevailed since its founding in 1979 (the other being the knightly determination of its founder Leslie Workman, to whom all studies of Medievalism must be heavily indebted) is that by focusing on recreations of the Middle Ages, the journal has both avoided this problem of authenticity and has crossed disciplinary boundaries. For Workman, following the Ruskinian model, Medievalism defines itself against classicism: some volumes quote Lord Acton's restatement of Ruskin as an epigraph:

> Two great principles divide the world, and contend for the mastery, antiquity and the middle ages. These are the two civilizations that have precded us, the two elements of which ours is composed. All political as well as religious questions reduce themselves practically to this. This is the great dualism that runs through our society.

At least until the 1980s, Workman also saw Medievalism as distinct from "scientific" medieval studies because it involves reading the past with a marked consciousness of one's own present. *Studies in Medievalism* describes its focus as "any aspect of the post-medieval idea and study of the MiddleAges and the influence, both scholarly and popular, of this study on Western society after 1500,"[34] and for 20 years it has continued to publish articles covering many disciplines.[35]

This did not, however, resolve the critical difficulties for those identifying themselves as scholars of literature written before 1500. In 1986, Paul Zumthor hence characterized the study of medieval literature as a discipline in crisis:

> How many works devoted to medieval literature give the reassuring impression that their author believes what he says? Very few. The reader often receives the opposite impression, that a bit of bad conscience is lurking somewhere: that the learned author whose prose he is reading is incessantly seeking alibis, because, even in his own eyes, to be a medievalist is not a self-evident achievement.[36]

Zumthor draws attention to the self-consciousness of discourse, noting that,

> beginning several years ago, we have returned, not without problems

or arguments, to the perception of what was for a long time (especially in the Middle Ages) a commonplace truth: one does not speak *about* writing; one writes.

Whence, among our contemporaries, or colleagues, even our circles of medievalists, a sort of awareness has arisen shamefaced, veiled, sometimes disguised as aggressiveness, but nonetheless increasingly evident. There is a self-questioning of language, compelled to recognize itself for what it is: the repository of something unknown that creates us, and yet the dissimulator of this same unknown; but a repository that continually betrays itself, and an inept dissimulator. Thus, it constitutes the locus of our ambiguities, our denials, and at the same time makes up the stuff of our fantasies, the utopia of our dreams. (15–16) ... [W]e know today that texts do not lend themselves to being grasped, and that no critical activity can, or should, attempt this "objectivity" from the outset. Far from it. Criticism will achieve some degree of coherence only by questioning those very conditions that make its practice possible, those modalities of interference between the text and the subjectivity of the critic. (17)

Zumthor's recognition that unprejudiced reading is an impossibility is a start of breaking the barrier between Medievalism and medieval studies forged in the second half of the nineteenth century. About the same time, the methodology of poststructuralism allowed for the categorization of the nationalism that had shaped so much of medieval studies as itself a form of discourse.

With this new theoretical impetus, the 1990s proved a significant decade for medieval studies. The essays edited by Marina S. Brownlee, Kevin Brownlee, and Stephen G. Nichols as *The New Medievalism* define their title as differing

from a cognate rubric like the New Historicism in not predicating a specific methodology, designating instead a predisposition to interrogate and reformulate assumptions about the discipline of medieval studies as broadly conceived.[37]

Nichols's phrasing seems remarkably close to Ruskin's when he describes the New Medievalism as "arising initially from the need to interrogate the nature of medieval representations in its differences and continuities with classical and Renaissance mimesis." Yet Nichols credits poststructuralism with finally freeing medieval studies "from the generic and linguistic taxonomies imposed by the invention of the discipline in the nineteenth century."[38] The majority of the essays are concerned with raising consciousness that many assumptions about medieval literature have been shaped by their reception in the past, thus opening up many new possibilities for interpretation. The collection ends on a strongly Medievalist note with Hans Ulrich Gumbrecht's essay "Intertextuality and Autumn/ Autumn and the Modern Reception of the Middle Ages," where Gumbrecht presents the concept of the "typically medieval" as ever-changing:

> In one respect it certainly makes sense now to consider the presence of "typically medieval" motifs and text structures in the *cancioneros* of the early fifteenth century as a *form of reception* of "medieval literature": the function that they assume here depends on the quality of their distance from the everyday life of the fifteenth century. ... Only if the printed *cancioneros* of the late fifteenth and early sixteenth centuries had appropriated subject matters and forms typical of the Middle Ages (which, however, does not seem to have been the case) could one speak of a "modern reception of medieval literature" in the full sense of the concept. This statement implies the proposal to pick up a transference – at any given time configured differently, but yet not to be ignored any more – between texts and reception tendencies as the red thread of a pragmatics of modern reception of medieval literature.[39]

A very different work published the same year is Norman F. Cantor's *Inventing the Middle Ages*. Cantor's book has already been expertly critiqued by medieval scholars,[40] so my main focus here will be on its assumptions about Medievalism. Cantor takes as his subject not the Middle Ages itself, but the twentieth-century scholars of the Middle Ages, demonstrating through brief biographies how the personalities of the scholars shaped their vision. *Inventing the Middle Ages* effectively shows how scholars like Schramm, Kantorowicz, Panofsky and Lewis injected their own personal circumstances into their reading of the Middle Ages; the book is thus a further nail in the coffin of the nineteenth-century model of scientific history. Yet whereas Lee Patterson, R. Howard Bloch and others have reminded us that medieval studies took shape as a discipline in the later nineteenth century, Cantor is simply dismissive of the Victorians. Cantor's overview of nineteenth-century medievalism is revealing in its lack of self-awareness:

> After the 1840s, Victorian culture superseded romantic idealism with nationalism, deterministic organicism, and racist social Darwinism and imposed these conditioning perceptions on further interpretation of the Middle Ages. This did not improve the understanding of the realities of medieval life and thought. Assertion of these dogmatic Victorian modes precipitated a decline from the naive but occasionally inspiring Gothic image embraced by the earlier romantic advocates of the Middle Ages.

Did the nineteenth-century historians misunderstand the Middle Ages because they were early pioneers who worked with a very narrow data base? Or was there something about the Victorian mind – its love of huge entities, vulgarly simple models, hastily generalized and overdetermined evolutionary schemes – that made it unsuitable for doing lasting work in interpreting the Middle Ages? We may say that both conditions were at work in fostering the Victorian misconstruction of the Middle Ages.[41]

At the same time that he is criticizing the Victorians[42] for asserting the "relative simplicity" of the medieval world, Cantor assumes that everyone in the later nineteenth century thought much alike. One suspects that Cantor indulges just as much as the Victorians that he condemns in what he calls "retromedievalism," the desire to return to a past that seems more attractive than the present, and perhaps he has a point. "Retromedievalism" may be a highly selective view of an age when life was cheap, but surely life was never so cheap as in the mid-twentieth century horrors that shaped the minds of so many of the scholars that he discusses, and nobody can be blamed for wishing to escape them. A more serious criticism of the work, in my thinking, is Cantor's lack of awareness of the nineteenth-century imposition of a narrative of progress upon past events. When he argues that modern scholars must know the Middle Ages better than their Victorian counterparts because more research has been done, Cantor seems just as enticed by the notion of the progress of knowledge and reason as the Victorians. Oddly, Cantor seems to pursue the ghost of a "real" Middle Ages at the same time that he lays that ghost to rest.

Cantor's model for twentieth-century medieval scholarship is diaspora, the dispersion of European scholars in the face of Nazism. In contrast, the essays in *Medievalism and the Modernist Temper*, edited by R. Howard Bloch and Stephen G. Nichols, revert to the more nineteenth-century model of a nationalist struggle between French and Germanic nations:

> by far the most common contributing factor is that of nationalistic rivalry between Germany and France. Indeed, throughout the nineteenth century, a pattern emerges according to which military defeat and wounded nationalistic pride give rise to the urge to recover the medieval past as a means, first, of compensating for loss and then, eventually, of refashioning territorial claims that potentially result in a renewed military clash."[43]

Noting that "study of medieval literature and culture has never been more alive or at a more interesting, innovative stage," Bloch and Nichols observe that "the institutional signs of a New Medievalism are everywhere."[44] This prompts a return to origins, as the essays trace the work and personalities of the founders of the discipline, particularly in Germany and France. Many of the essays are lively and informative: I was particularly impressed by John M. Graham's "National Identity and the Politics of Publishing the Troubadours," R. Howard Bloch's essay on the Abbé Migne, and Seth Lerer's discussion of Erich Auerbach, a figure strangely, or even perversely, neglected by Norman Cantor. I also admire Laura Kendrick for boldly admitting that

> If a twelfth-century troubadour could be resurrected and asked to criticize what had been written about him or attributed to him by subsequent scholars, he would be baffled by our distinctions between authentic and pseudo-medieval texts, between scholarly editions and amateur inventions, between history and fiction. The basic rule for becoming a professional medievalist has been that we must believe ourselves to be returning to, restoring and founding our criticism and literary history upon, authentic medieval texts that are as close as possible to authorial originals. Our erudition is fundamentally falsifying, our science a discipline of imposture – and this from the beginning, but increasingly so, and with less and less tolerance for such self-critical analysis, from the turn of the nineteenth century on.[45]

The collection nevertheless highlights a problem in the way that the discipline of literary studies has emerged, so that scholars never stray outside their periods of specialization. Many of the essayists write as though they are coming to the materials for the first time, experts on medieval studies straying into the nineteenth and twentieth centuries. For example, John Ganim's essay on "The Myth of Medieval Romance," the main discussion of English Medievalism in the collection, covers materials that will seem familiar to many scholars of later periods, and shows little awareness of earlier treatments of the same material. The reference to John Ruskin as "William Ruskin" is somewhat revealing; this is the only mention of Ruskin in the entire book. Similarly, the point that Gaston Paris's relationship with his father, also a medieval scholar, influenced his approach to the Middle Ages – an approach that in its turn was enormously influential on the popular imagination – is surely valid. Yet three writers (John M. Graham, David F. Hult and Michael Camille) present it almost as discovery.[46] The larger point, surely, is not that nobody knew that Gaston Paris asserted his scholarship in a different way from his father Paulin, but that formerly, those who believed that Gaston Paris's version of the Middle Ages was shaped by his relationship with his father would feel compelled to dismiss the younger Paris as a Medievalist rather than a "true scholar" – and many did.

An unmentioned ghost in this collection may be Lacan; yet another ghost may be Norman Cantor (I am inclined to give contributors the benefit of the doubt and assume that many of them simply do not know Leslie Workman's *Studies in Medievalism*). Essayists seem to have taken to heart the concluding sentence of Richard W. Pfaff's review of *Inventing the Middle Ages*, "The widespread circulation of this mean-spirited and tendentious work is a grievous blow to medieval studies." For example, Cantor is not mentioned even in Alain Boureau's essay on Kantorowicz, although admittedly, Cantor may have invited such a snub when he wrote "There is no published memoir or critical assessment of Kantorowicz that is of significant value."[47] Overall, however, *Medievalism and the Modernist Temper* shows a discipline coming to terms with its origins: for example, Bloch and Nichols write in their introduction,

> those who write about the millennium between the fall of Rome and the discovery of the New World have come more and more to see that their assumptions regarding the period are as historically determined by the framing perceptions of the last century as they are by the artifacts of the medievalist's study.[48]

Expanding on this self-recognition is a new book series sponsored by the Centre for Medieval Studies at the University of Sydney titled *Making the Middle Ages* – acknowledging that the Middle Ages are not simply waiting to be uncovered but need to be made. The first volume in the series, *Medievalism in the Modern World: Essays in Honour of Leslie Workman* brings together articles both by those who would traditionally describe themselves as medieval scholars (for example, Paul E. Szarmach); those who work more directly in matters of reception (Alice Chandler and Kathleen Verduin are two of many); and those who elegantly bridge the two (such as Tom Shippey). As Richard Utz notes in his introduction, Leslie Workman himself has moved from a conscious distinction between medieval studies and Medievalism towards the view that all readings of the Middle Ages are influenced by both, to use Carlyle's phrase, "past and present."[49]

This prompts the question of where Medievalism can go next. Two recent works have connected Medievalism with gender studies. In *The Shock of Medievalism*, Kathleen Biddick draws on gender and postcolonial theory to present medievalism as mourning. For Biddick, the recognition and implied rejection of nineteenth-century methodology may have been overstated, since "medieval studies is still intimately bound to the fathers."[50] She thus argues that "medievalism inhabits medieval studies as an abiding trauma." The model of trauma, which is, she writes, "a temporal process that is located, not in one moment alone, but in the relation between two moments. ... Trauma also resists representation since its traces recur fragmentarily in flashbacks, nightmares, and other repetitive phenomena"[51] proves a useful one – yet Biddick seems also intent on imposing a postcolonial model on her material. Although her argument that the medieval (English) peasant is an invention of the British Indian colonial era is somewhat more muted here than in earlier discussions, she does not seem to want to abandon the idea entirely, and in some parts of her argument the connection seems strained.[52]

I suspect that Biddick's problem is that she continues to think of Medievalism as a nineteenth-century construct. The chapter on "Gothic Ornament and Sartorial Peasants," for example, asserts that "the Gothic Architectural Revival is typically regarded as the outcome of the Anglican Counter-Reformation."[53] In fact, although Anglicans did speak of "the revival of church architecture," in many respects, they were legitimizing a movement that had decidedly "queer" origins in the works of earlier figures such as Walpole and Beckford, Beckford himself being both a Medievalist and an Orientalist.[54] By locating the Gothic Revival in the nineteenth century, Biddick loses some opportunities to explore her interesting connection between Gothic extravagance, Indian excess and "queerness." She also makes problematic assumptions concerning the 1991 film *Robin, Prince of Thieves*, a work that also unites Medievalism and Orientalism.[55] The trajectory of Robin Hood from aristocrat (as in Ritson) to yeoman (as in Scott) to peasant (as in Marxist readings of the 1950s and 1960s) is a useful illustration of how medieval scholarship can be later reread as Medievalism. Yet Biddick seems to think that the tradition of Maid Marian dressing as a man – which she correctly notes most likely reverses the origin of Marian as played by a man in mummers' plays – is a twentieth-century innovation, whereas the idea appears in earlier sources such as Thomas Love Peacock's 1822 novel *Maid Marian*.

Biddick pointedly presents her work as a series of essays, rather than as a monograph, and at points, the linking structure is declaredly her own memory. Sometimes, this works well, but although Biddick has forewarned her readers about "shock," the juxtapositions of William Gibson's *Neuromancer* trilogy and "colonial images of cannibalism" from Biddick's Catholic childhood may work better for some readers than they did for me. Biddick is asking important questions about the nature of cultural memory, but the ultimate conflation of Medievalism with patriarchy may perhaps be making Medievalism more important than I myself would wish to claim: Medievalism may in some instances be an emanation of patriarchal-traditionalist thinking, rather than its cause.

Whereas Kathleen Biddick's work declaredly takes Medievalism as its subject, Allen J. Frantzen's *Before the Closet: Same-Sex Love from Beowulf to Angels in America* (1998) primarily focuses on what is known of same-sex love in Anglo-Saxon writings, and later interpretations of the significance of this knowledge. Questioning the arguments of John Boswell in *Christianity, Social Tolerance, and Homosexuality* (1980), Frantzen reexamines the evidence in the Anglo-Saxon Penitentials and other writings (nearly all of which from this period are by members of the clergy), and finds that the Anglo-Saxons firmly denounced the sins of Sodom. The thorough investigation of the evidence might initially suggest that Frantzen's goal is much like that of nineteenth-century scholars, to discover the "real" Anglo-Saxon era, or at least the shadowy part of it relating to the forms of sexuality forbidden by the Church. Yet the book is Medievalist in some important respects. First, Frantzen reviews the evidence as presented by earlier scholars with a clear awareness of the assumptions (about their own identities and about the materials they examine) from which they begin. Second, he concludes that many assumptions about the behavior of the Anglo-Saxons were based on the Victorian desire to remake the people they claimed as their ancestors in their own self-image, one with a very rigid definition of appropriate sexuality. Finally, Frantzen recognizes that although much recent culturally-based criticism has been influenced by Michel Foucault, Foucault's tendency to generalize the character of historical epochs is particularly problematic when discussing the medieval period. Although Frantzen adopts a Cantor-esque tone when he asserts that Foucault's "medievalism was remarkable only for its superficiality, lack of detail, and indifference to documents and their nuances,"[56] he immediately explains the difficulties when Foucault's reading of "the discourse of sodomy" is applied to the earlier Middle Ages.

The book's most provocative implications for Medievalism, however, come through its use of the discourse of queer theory. Frantzen is cautious in aligning himself with queer readings of medieval texts and traditions because in his opinion, many such readings ignore intertextual evidence and hence

> do little more than use concepts derived from Foucault, elaborated by [Eve Kosovsky] Sedgwick or [Judith] Butler, to launch closely textual examinations that make glancing references to history but otherwise, in their detailed and ingenious analysis, resemble nothing so much as the version of formalism traditionally known in the academy as New Criticism.[57]

Nevertheless, even though Frantzen critiques "the lack of critical rigor that obscures many queer readings," he acknowledges that "queer theory has helped to close the gap between personal and professional styles in academic writing."[58] Although feminist criticism helped point the way, queer criticism is liberated from the burden of "disinterestedness" and "scientific history" of the nineteenth century since the queer critic pointedly declares his or her own subject interest. Frantzen declares that his "own shadows" are part of this book, and hence he can be both medieval scholar and Medievalist – the reading of *Angels in America*, for example, would not be out of place in *Studies in Medievalism*. The insertion of the personal as the organizing structure for at least the beginning and ending of this book may have the result that some of the connexions and analogies drawn seem close to free association: the reading of operatic "trouser-roles" in Chapter One, for example, is neither well-integrated into the rest of the study, nor particularly insightful. On the other hand, by declaredly inserting himself into his critical study at the same time that he bases his argument on well-researched evidence, Frantzen has found one possible solution to the problem of how to approach the medieval past. Medievalism has taught the field of medieval studies that since even the most careful and sincere use of archival evidence will be influenced by the circumstances of the user, we may as well acknowledge that we always cast our own shadows on the past that we recreate.

III

Leslie Workman has described Medievalism as "the continuing process of creating the Middle Ages." I would further suggest that this process of creation involves cultural adaptation. These adaptations occur in a number of disciplines (literature, the visual arts, music, etc.), and may be loosely divided into the use of medieval narrative, form, and perceived codes of values, although these uses overlap in significant ways. In the first category, writers or artists rework myths such as those of King Arthur and Robin Hood, or specific historical figures and events, such as the life of Joan of Arc and the Hundred Years' War. Use of form includes adaptations of Gothic architecture and poetic structures such as the ballade. I would suggest, though, that the use of narrative and/or form without reference to a value-system believed to derive from the Middle Ages is not Medievalism, but either antiquarianism (which explores the past *as* the past), or parody. In many cases, Medievalism selects form or narrative to reinforce what are seen as positive medieval values in danger of being lost in the contemporary world – although sometimes, as in the case of European imperial expansion in the nineteenth century, medieval example can serve as a justification for the way that the world already is.

The following articles, presented chronologically, show the very selective ways in which medieval themes, forms and characters have been used by later writers, spanning aesthetics, culture, politics, law and sexuality. The first two articles center on discussions of poetics that contradict the still-common notion that following the English Reformation and well into the eighteenth century, English suspicion of the Roman Catholic church, coupled with an admiration for the classical tradition, left no place for Medievalism. In "Samuel Daniel's Defense of Medievalism," Kelly Quinn demonstrates how Thomas Campion's *Observations on the Art of English Poetry* (1602) reflects the standard view of the period between the fall of the Roman Empire and the advent of fifteenth-century humanism as one of artistic barbarism. Samuel Daniel's *Defence of Ryme* does not merely defend rhyme and metre against Campion's advocacy of quantitative verse, but also uses the techniques of Renaissance humanism to defend the medieval period itself. As Quinn notes, Daniel chooses not to identify the medieval period with Roman Catholicism, but rather with the development of a tradition truly English.

A similar preoccupation with English tradition and its debt to the Middle Ages can be seen in Richard Hurd's *Letters on Chivalry and Romance*, the subject of Kristine Louise Haugen's "Chivalry and Romance in the Eighteenth Century: Richard Hurd and the Disenchantment of *The Faerie Queene*." As Haugen notes, Hurd's treatise, published at a time of new interest in the "gothic," has long been considered a seminal work in the history of British Medievalism. Haugen's essay, however, takes the discussion in a new direction by examining the relationship between the *Letters* and the eighteenth-century preoccupation with "verisimilitude," and by suggesting that for Hurd, the truth about the medieval past can only be rediscovered through text – notably, Edmund Spenser's *Faerie Queene*. Whereas other critics of the time praised Spenser for his imagination, "for Hurd, by contrast, the *Faerie Queene* was no fantasy at all, but utterly real and historical" (p.50), since a work of literature can faithfully portray the realities of medieval life and culture.

Although Daniel and Hurd's Medievalist defenses focus on discussions of literature, they also open up interdisciplinary possibilities, since both writers insist that literature is the most accurate reflection we have of the realities of medieval society. The other articles in this issue represent some of the other interdisciplinary applications of Medievalism. Mark Schoenfield's "Waging Battle: *Ashford v. Thornton, Ivanhoe*, and Legal Violence" explores the uses made of a historicized sense of law both in early nineteenth-century legal cases and in another seminal text that influenced Medievalism not only in Britain but also in the United States and Europe, Sir Walter Scott's *Ivanhoe*. The already sensational case of the murder of Mary Ashford in 1817 gained even more notoriety because the defendant Abraham Thornton offered to prove his innocence through the medieval ritual of Wager of Battle. Schoenfield traces the connections between this case and the plot of *Ivanhoe*, which, perhaps embodying Scott's own ambivalence about the Middle Ages, seems simultaneously to question and confirm the validity of a mode of trial where divine rather than human justice functions as judge. If *Ivanhoe*, like many other Medievalist texts, embodies a quest for origins, it represents not merely a key moment in the development of what it means to be English, but also a key moment in the history of English law as the relative merits of Wager of Battle and trial by jury (which was also claimed by legal theorists as a medieval institution) are debated in novelistic terms.

The search for both origins and continuity was a central issue in British Medievalism, yet these were even more imperative in nineteenth-century France, a nation that underwent so many disjunctures. The two articles on France in this issue, Sarah Hibberd's "Marianne: Mystic or Madwoman? Representations of Jeanne D'Arc on the Parisian Stage in the 1820s" and Elizabeth Emery's "The 'Truth' About the Middle Ages: *La Revue des Deux Mondes* and Late Nineteenth-Century French Medievalism," explore the role of Medievalism in restoring a sense of national identity. Sarah Hibberd shows how closely the representation of Joan of Arc on the Parisian stage during the Bourbon restoration of the 1820s was interlinked with other forms of discourse. Making the significant point that even in the Napoleonic era, not especially known for its Medievalism, Jeanne D'Arc was employed as an icon of resistance against England, Hibberd then shows how the image changed in the 1820s, when the political implications of the monarchy and church's complicity in Jeanne's fate became uncomfortable. As the figure of Jeanne D'Arc becomes associated with new discourses on female madness, at first sight, Medievalism might appear to be depoliticized – yet this depoliticization serves a specifically political goal for the restored Bourbon monarchy.

A different act of restoration was necessary after France's humiliating defeat by Prussia in 1870–71, which ended the rule of Napoleon III. Elizabeth Emery has discovered that between 1871 and 1876, almost one quarter of the art and history articles in France's leading periodical *La Revue des Deux Mondes* were on medieval themes. Although France had undergone another political disjuncture through the establishment of a republic, unlike the first Republic, the appeal was primarily not to classical models, but rather to France's strength in its medieval traditions. Emery's unravelling of the pointedly "interested" use of the medieval past in *Las Revue des Deux Mondes* has a special irony, since Matthew Arnold cited it in "The Function of Criticism at the Present Time" as existing "as just an organ for a free play of the mind, as we [the British] have not."[59] In fact, just as in Britain, French Medievalism becomes a search for continuities and national characteristics.

Britain in the later nineteenth century is represented in this collection by Frederick S. Rosen and Chene Heady's articles, yet both complicate the standard concept of Victorian longing for the decorous order of the medieval past. In "Medieval Religion, Victorian Homosexualities," Rosen explores not the envisioning of a chivalric past, but rather of a monastic past, in the works of late Victorian sexologists. Desire thus more openly manifests itself as a longing for the kind of sexual community that these writers imagined was possible in medieval society, but not in their own. Intriguingly, the Middle Ages thus becomes not a place of order serving as a refuge from the chaos of modern life, but instead, a place of freedom.

Chene Heady makes the important observation that Ruskinian Medievalism did not entirely die with the coming of the First World War. Whereas the sexual theorists that Rosen examines tend to detach the social aspects of medieval Catholicism from religious belief, for G.K. Chesterton, the subject of Heady's article, the Roman Catholic faith was an essential part of his envisioning of the Middle Ages. Chesterton's vision of order, Heady argues, is located in the symbolism of the Middle Ages, a culturally stable relation between sign and signification no longer possible in the age of Modernism.

The final article in the collection, Susan Aronstein's "The Return of the King: Medievalism and the Politics of Nostalgia in the Mythopoetic Men's Movement," explores one of the ways that Medievalism continues to manifest itself in the contemporary world, particularly in the United States. Medievalism has always been especially problematic for the United States, a nation created through the disavowal of the Old World. At the same time, however, that Thomas Jefferson was appealing to human universalities in the creation of the United States Constitution, he was also interested in the concept of a common Saxon heritage. While some Americans believed that their identity was partly shaped by racial characteristics emerging in the early Middle Ages, a perhaps more common, although often unstated, American response towards Medievalism is envy: European nations have a sense of history, whereas Americans are "new" and rootless. Americans have found a variety of methods to overcome their lack of Medievalism: Mark Twain tried not entirely convincing scorn, but more common responses include touring; the establishment of art collections such as the Cloisters of New York; and American Gothic architecture. Another manifestation of American Medievalism is the number of (usually male) societies that practice their Medievalism behind closed doors, such as the Freemasons. Aronstein draws attention to the Jungian roots of the men's movement, demonstrating how the use of medieval myth is open to everyone, a means of overcoming the nationalism of nineteenth-century Medievalism. Yet at the same time Aronstein notes a different kind of desire: not for a national past as such, but for a model of human relations that they detect in medieval narrative, with strong men at the center of culture and women relegated to a subsidiary role. At the end of the twentieth century, Medievalism was still showing itself as continuing to be a locus for desire, an attempt to find satisfaction in a world of unstable values. Followers of Medievalism can only wait and see how it will be adapted to the needs and desires of the new millennium.[60]

NOTES

1. To avoid confusion, "Medievalism" is capitalized when it refers to the later reception of the Middle Ages, or the study of this reception.
2. As the essays in this issue suggest, Medievalism is by no means an exclusively English concern; as a nation filled with the relics of deliberate disjunction from the Medieval, however, England's relationship with its Medieval past represents particularly complex possibilities.
3. See, for example, A. Dwight Culler's discussion of Ruskin and Victorian Medievalism in *The Victorian Mirror of History* (New Haven: Yale University Press, 1985), 152–84.
4. Alice Chandler, *A Dream of Order: The Medieval Ideal in Nineteenth-Century English Literature* (Lincoln: University of Nebraska Press, 1970). Although Chandler's title suggests a focus on English literature, her final chapter is devoted to Henry Adams.
5. Donna B. Hamilton sets out these arguments in "Richard Verstegan's *A Restitution of Decayed Intelligence*: A Catholic Antiquarian Replies to John Foxe, Thomas Copper, and Jean Bodin," *Prose Studies* 22/1 (April 1999), 1–39. On Saxonism as selective Medievalism, see J.G.A. Pocock, *The Ancient Constitution and the Feudal Law: A Study of English Historical Thought* (Cambridge: Cambridge University Press, 1957); and Christopher Hill, "The Norman Yoke," in *Puritanism and Revolution* (London: Secker and Warburg, 1958), 50–122.
6. Andrew Bradstock (ed.), *Winstanley and the Diggers, 1649–1999* (London: Frank Cass, 2000).
7. For British self-construction in opposition to Catholic France, see Linda Colley, *Britons: Forging the Nation 1707–1837* (New Haven: Yale University Press, 1992), particularly the opening chapter, "Protestants."
8. On antiquarian book and manuscript collectors, see Nicholas A. Basbanes, *A Gentle Madness: Bibliophiles, Bibliomanes, and the Eternal Passion for Books* (New York: Henry Holt, 1995), esp. 89–110; Seymour de Ricci, *English Collectors of Books and Manuscripts (1530–1930) and Their Marks of Ownership* (Cambridge: Cambridge University Press, 1930).
9. Batty Langley, *Gothic Architecture, Improved by Rules and Proportions* (1742). See Samuel Kliger, *The Goths In England: A Study in Seventeenth and Eighteenth Century Thought* (Cambridge, MA: Harvard University Press, 1952).
10. Sir William Blackstone, *Commentaries on the Laws of England*, 4 vols. (London, 1765–69), 3:268.
11. E.J. Clery quotes the February 1765 *Monthly Review*, which had initially accepted the "preposterous phenomena" of *The Castle of Otranto* as "sacrifices to a gross and unenlightened age," but withdrew "that indulgence we offered to the foibles of a supposed antiquity" on discovering that Walpole had written it. See Clery, *The Rise of Supernatural Fiction 1762–1800* (Cambridge: Cambridge University Press, 1995), 53–4.
12. For example, see Lynn Hunt, *Politics, Culture, and Class in the French Revolution* (Berkeley: University of California Press, 1984).
13. Fred Botting, *Gothic* (London: Routledge, 1996), 5.
14. See Reginald Horsman, *Race and Manifest Destiny: The Origins of American Racial Anglo-Saxonism* (Cambridge, MA: Harvard University Press, 1981).
15. See Clare A. Simmons, *Reversing the Conquest: History and Myth in Nineteenth-Century British Literature* (New Brunswick: Rutgers University Press, 1990), 34–5.
16. Thomas Carlyle, *Past and Present* (1843; London: Chapman and Hall, 1890); Kenelm Henry Digby, *The Broad Stone of Honor* (1822), revised ed., 4 vols. (London: Lumley, 1844–46).
17. See Felix Barker and Ralph Hyde, *London As It Might Have Been* (London: John Murray, 1982, rpt. 1995), 95–105. This book contains many other examples of real and proposed Gothic buildings.
18. For an overview of Pugin's influence, see Paul Atterbury and Clive Wainwright (eds.), *Pugin,*

A Gothic Passion (New Haven: Yale University Press, 1994). Alexandra Wedgewood's chapter on the Palace of Westminster contains many striking pictures of the medieval themes.

19. Sir Charles Eastlake's account of the Gothic Revival, first published in 1872, is still a useful overview of the subject, with many illustrations of nineteenth-century Gothic buildings. A recent account giving particular attention to American Gothic design is Susan B. Matheson and Derek D. Churchill, *Modern Gothic: The Revival of Medieval Art* (New Haven: Yale University Art Gallery, 2000).

20. Mark Girouard, *The Return to Camelot: Chivalry and the English Gentleman* (New Haven: Yale University Press, 1981), 88–110.

21. Michael Glencross has a useful bibliography of sources on French Medievalism in his *Reconstructing Camelot: French Romantic Medievalism and the Arthurian Tradition* (Cambridge: D.S. Brewer, 1995).

22. See Julian Treuherz, "The Pre-Raphaelites and Medieval Illuminated Manuscripts," in *Pre-Raphaelite Papers*, ed. Leslie Harris (London: Tate Gallery, 1984), 153–69. The most extensive visual study of Rossetti is that of Alicia Craig Faxon, *Rossetti* (New York: Abbeville Press, 1989); see also the studies of Jan Marsh.

23. The Kelmscott Chaucer, for instance, is illustrated by Burne-Jones, but none of the racier stories of the *Canterbury Tales* are illustrated at all, and Chaucer the Narrator seems to retain his dignity even when carried in an eagle's beak. On Morris's visionary socialism, see E.P. Thompson, *William Morris, Romantic to Revolutionary* (London: Lawrence and Wishart, 1959). Aymer Vallance's *The Art of William Morris* (1897; rpt. New York: Dover Books, 1988), remains a useful overview of Morris's ideals and art.

24. Andrew Lang, *Custom and Myth* (London: Longman, 1884); *The Fairy Book Series* (London: Longman, 1889–).

25. J.G. Frazer, *The Golden Bough: A Study in Magic and Religion*, 11 vols. (London: Macmillan, 1890–1915); Jessie Weston, *From Ritual to Romance* (1919; rpt. Gloucester, MA: Peter Smith, 1983).

26. Leopold von Ranke, *The History of the Popes*, trans. E. Foster, 3 vols. (London: Bohn, 1847) 1:xvii–xviii. Interestingly, in his introduction, Foster seems worried by Ranke's scientific indifference towards Catholicism.

27 Hayden White, *Metahistory: The Historical Imagination in Nineteenth-Century Fiction* (Baltimore: Johns Hopkins, 1973, rpt. 1987), 172–5.

28. Matthew Arnold, "The Function of Criticism at the Present Time," in *The Complete Prose Works of Matthew Arnold*, ed. R.H. Super, 11 vols. (Ann Arbor: University of Michigan Press, 1960–78) 3:272. Subsequent references follow this edition.

29. John Henry Newman, *The Idea of a University Defined and Illustrated* (1852), ed. Charles Frederick Harrold (New York: Longmans, 1947), xxvii.

30. A familiar example here is C.S. Lewis, who, although a lifelong Oxford scholar and an important contributor to the interpretation of medieval literature, is now more popular for his fantasy fiction than for his scholarship, where the fact that Lewis's world-view was clearly influenced by his cultural context is presented as more of a problem. A.N. Wilson, for example, opens *C.S. Lewis, A Biography* by noting that "More than most men, he was the product of his upbringing and ancestry" (New York: Norton, 1990), 1.

31. Johan Huizinga, "Historical Ideals of Life," in *Men and Ideas: History, the Middle Ages, the Renaissance*, trans. James S. Holmes and Hags van Marle (New York: Meridian Books, 1959), 91.

32. Hans Robert Jauss, "The Alterity and Modernity of Medieval Literature," trans. Timothy Bahti, *New Literary History* 10 (1979), 181–229; first published in German in 1977.

33. Lee Patterson, *Negotiating the Past: The Historical Understanding of Medieval Literature* (Madison: University of Wisconsin Press, 1987), 42.

34. Leslie Workman, Editorial statement, *Studies in Medievalism* (1979–).

35. Tom Shippey now edits *Studies in Medievalism*. The journal's publisher, D.S. Brewer, has been a major sponsor of Medievalism, notably through its "Arthurian Studies" series.

36. Paul Zumthor, *Speaking of the Middle Ages (Parler du moyen âge)*, trans. Sarah White (Lincoln: University of Nebraska Press, 1986), 14.

37. Stephen G. Nichols, "The New Medievalism: Tradition and Discontinuity in Medieval

Culture," in *The New Medievalism*, ed. Marina S. Brownlee, Kevin Brownlee and Stephen G. Nichols (Baltimore: Johns Hopkins University Press, 1991), 1.
38. Ibid., 1–2.
39. Ibid., 328–9.
40. Major criticisms included Cantor's choices as to which scholars were significant, and his use of gossip in reconstructing their personalities. See, for example, the reviews by Richard W. Pfaff in *Speculum* 68 (Jan. 1993), 122–5; and by Nicholas Howe in *Studies in the Age of Chaucer* 15 (1993), 180–85.
41. Norman F. Cantor, *Inventing the Middle Ages* (New York: William Morrow, 1991), 29.
42. Unlike the admitted Anglocentricity of this overview, Cantor's subject is not primarily English Medieval studies; by "Victorians," he appears to refer to those living in the later nineteenth century in all Western nations.
43. R. Howard Bloch and Stephen G. Nichols (eds.), *Medievalism and the Modernist Temper* (Baltimore: Johns Hopkins University Press. 1996), 13–14.
44. Ibid., 1.
45. Ibid., 95.
46. For an earlier treatment of the subject, see Deborah Nelson, "Gaston Paris in Context: His Predecessors and his Legacy," *Studies in Medievalism* 2/2 (Spring 1983), 53–66.
47. Cantor, *Inventing the Middle Ages*, 423.
48. Bloch and Nichols (eds.), *Medievalism and the Modernist Temper*, 2.
49. Richard Utz and Tom Shippey (eds.), *Medievalism in the Modern World* (Turnhout: Brepols, 1998), 5. Since I myself was a contributor to this volume, I shall not analyze its contents in detail.
50. Kathleen Biddick, *The Shock of Medievalism* (Durham: Duke University Press, 1998), 1.
51. Ibid., 10–11.
52. In "The Historiographic Unconscious and the Idea of Robin Hood," published in *The Salt of Common Life: Individuality and Choice in the Medieval Town Countryside and Church*, ed. Edwin Brezette DeWindt (Kalamazoo: Medieval Institute, 1995), she writes "It is perhaps not too much to claim that the medieval English peasant village was invented in imperial India" (455). In *The Shock of Medievalism*, this becomes "In a paradoxical way, the medieval English village community was invented by the India service" (65–66). Biddick nevertheless seems reluctant to abandon the implied claim that the "peasant" was an imperial invention. Although the word "invented" certainly is "too much," I do not wish to be dismissive of Biddick's observation that an idealized conception of the English rural past was useful to the Victorian imperialist consciousness.
53. Ibid., 30.
54. Similarly, Edgar Allan Poe called his stories "Tales of the Grotesque and Arabesque," connecting the literary Gothic with Oriental architecture.
55. My own reading of national identity within the film is somewhat different, and starts from the premise that in this film Kevin Costner is Kevin Costner playing Robin Hood (as opposed to the role of Robin Hood being played by Kevin Costner). The "Anglo-Saxon" American Kevin Costner treats the material with uneasy reverence, whereas the British Alan Rickman is comfortable with making fun of the medieval past, and the African-American Morgan Freeman at times looks as though he wonders how he came to be part of this story at all.
56. Allen J. Frantzen, *Before the Closet: Same-Sex Love from Beowulf to Angels in America* (Chicago: University of Chicago Press, 1998), 7. In this context, I take "medievalism" to imply "medieval scholarship."
57. Ibid., 16.
58. Ibid., 25.
59. Arnold, "The Function of Criticism at the Present Time," 270.
60. I am grateful for research assistance from John McCombe, and for advice and suggestions on parts of this introduction from Nicholas Howe, Karen Winstead, and the Ohio State University Department of English's First Draft Group.

Samuel Daniel's Defense of Medievalism

KELLY A. QUINN

In 1603, at the dawn of the Stuart reign, Samuel Daniel published his *Defence of Ryme*,[1] explicitly written in response to a treatise published a year earlier by Thomas Campion: *Observations in the Art of English Poesie*. Campion had argued in favor of quantitative verse – that is, poetry based on Greek and Latin metrics – and in so doing, he resurrected a part of the humanist agenda which had largely lain dormant since the 1580s. Although pockets of support for the quantitative movement would continue into the seventeenth century, Daniel's powerful essay is generally considered to have settled the argument definitively.[2]

My article takes as its starting point some questions about the purpose of Daniel's impassioned response to Campion. Daniel handily points out internal contradictions within Campion's *Observations* and inconsistencies between Campion's poetic theory and his respected body of poetic work. The clumsiness of Campion's treatise makes Daniel's task an easy one. Daniel tells us that he himself is naturally self-doubting and reluctant to engage in debate: "though irresolution and a selfe distrust be the most apparent faults of my nature, and that the least checke of reprehension, if it sauour of reason, will as easily shake my resolution as any man's liuing, yet in this case I know not how I am growne more resolued."[3] The prevailing narrative voice throughout his body of work suggests this attitude is no mere literary convention. Why does Daniel, normally deferential, respond with such vehemence to a debate already considered settled and an argument so easily defeated in Campion's own terms? Why is he so eager to publish what was originally, so we are told, a private letter?

Campion's treatise presents a real threat. This threat surely does not lie, however, in its cumbersome metrical argument, which shows scant promise of persuading English poets to reform their practices. Rather, the surface concern with metrics conceals a deeper, broader, and more profound set of interests. The quantitative verse movement arises out of humanism, and relies in large part on the anti-medievalism so prevalent in humanist thinking. Daniel is himself a part and product of the humanist movement, but his riled response to Campion stems, I argue, from a rejection of anti-medievalism. Campion's argument in support of quantitative verse is tangential to Daniel's central concerns, but becomes a convenient vehicle for his attack on the traditional humanist disparagement of the medieval period. The so-called *Defence of Ryme* is an expedient excuse for Daniel's defense of medievalism.

Three terms require introductory explanation. The first two are somewhat anachronistic: "medievalism" and "humanism" are nineteenth-century introductions to the language, and were unavailable to Campion and Daniel. Though they lack the term "medieval," Elizabethan writers do have a sense of the period. They define it, however, slightly differently from the way modern historians do. Campion refers disparagingly to the period between the fall of the Roman Empire and the advent of Reuchlin (1455–1522), Erasmus (1466?–1536), and More (1478–1535). Thus, the achievements of fourteenth- and fifteenth-century Italy, which later ages have tended to label post-medieval, or the flowering of the Italian Renaissance, are included in his middle period of intellectual wasteland. For his part, Daniel defends the likes of the fifteenth-century Italian Pico della Mirandola along with twelfth- and thirteenth-century Englishmen in his *Defence*. Whereas we tend to see the transitions between cultural epochs occurring at different times in different places, Campion and Daniel do not, it seems, share a sense of this distinction. For them, the medieval period ends in southern and northern Europe at the same time.

Humanism is likewise a retrospective term. Definitions of Renaissance humanism are notoriously varied, but a general definition is essential since I present Daniel in the context of humanism. A recent useful definition catalogues approval of classical antiquity, hostility toward the Middle Ages, and opposition to scholasticism, which humanists considered overly technical and abstract. In particular, humanism emphasizes the liberalizing influence of classical philosophy, literature, and political thought, the narrow dogmatism of scholastic thought, the importance of education as a means of reforming society, and the superiority of rhetoric, philosophy, history, and poetry to logic and theological disputation.[4]

The third term requiring explanation is quantitative verse. Although this article is not focused on metrics, the essays of Campion and Daniel are, and so the background of the quantitative verse movement will be useful. Simply put, quantitative verse is based on the time value of syllables, which is, as Campion puts it, "contained in the length or shortnes of their sound."[5] Quantitative verse is contrasted to rhyme or rhythm, overlapping terms which traditionally denote accentual verse.[6] Definitions and distinctions, however, were considerably confused during the Elizabethan period. While classical quantity was based on oral properties of language, Derek Attridge's remarkably lucid discussion of the Elizabethan movement shows that the education system, unawareness of the proper pronunciation of Latin, and an abstract, complex system of rules combined to produce a system of quantitative verse curiously divorced, in fact, from the spoken language. The Elizabethans defined length according to, for the most part, position (for instance, the distribution of vowels and consonants), without regard to the actual time value of the syllable.[7] The audible basis of classical meter, then, becomes a wholly intellectual and visual matter in sixteenth-century England.

The artistic intellectualism of quantitative verse, in contrast to the supposedly instinctive, natural practice of rhyme, helps to explain its appeal to humanists. Quirky as it may now appear, the English quantitative verse movement was hardly isolated: Italian and French predecessors provided models for English disputants.[8] The movement appears to reach England in the 1540s, when Thomas Watson experiments with quantitative verse, Roger Ascham quotes it in his 1545 *Toxophilus*, and, as Ascham's later work attests, he debates the topic with friends at Cambridge.[9] The matter is taken up in more detail in Ascham's 1570 *The Scolemaster*, published posthumously, in which he laments England's propensity for "our rude and beggerly ryming, [which was] brought first into Italie by *Gothes* and *Hunnes*, whan all good verses and good learning to, were destroyed by them ... and at last receyued into England by men of excellent wit in deede, but of small learning, and lesse iudgement in that behalfe."[10] The sentiment echoes and reverberates. Blenerhasset's fervent wish in the 1578 *Second Part of the Mirror for Magistrates*, for instance, uses markedly similar language: "It is great marvaile that these ripewitted Gentlemen of *England* have not left of their Gotish kinde of ryming, (for the rude *Gothes* brought that kind of writing fyrst), & imitated the learned Latines & greekes."[11] The association of rhyme with the "rude" Middle Ages, then, is clearly an element of the quantitative verse movement from its earliest inception in England.

Around 1580, the movement reaches its full strength. Such figures as Spenser, Harvey, and Sidney participate enthusiastically.[12] The Spenser-Harvey correspondence of 1579 and 1580 details efforts to define, modify, and popularize quantitative verse. Spenser happily notes that Sidney and Dyer "haue proclaimed in their ἀρείῳ πάγῳ a generall surceasing and silence of balde Rymers ... [and] they haue ... prescribed certaine Lawes and rules of Quantities of English sillables for English Verse."[13] The details of the Areopagus group have never been firmly established, but here, at least, part of its agenda is made clear. Following shortly after, in 1586, William Webbe quotes Ascham approvingly on the matter of "this tynkerly verse which we call ryme,"[14] and argues that if framers of alehouse songs and the like "might be accounted Poets (as it is sayde some of them make meanes to be promoted to the Lawrell) surely we shall shortly haue whole swarmes of Poets."[15] Webbe concedes that "Learning was not generally decayde" during the medieval period, but insists that, nevertheless, "Poetry was in small price among them, it is very manifest."[16] The early- to mid-1580s, then, witness pronounced support for the quantitative verse movement.

The later years of the decade, however, and especially the 1590s, yielded if not, in Webbe's apocalyptic words, "whole swarmes of Poets," a plentiful body of respected accentual verse. At the same time, Puttenham's influential 1589 *Arte of English Poesie* dismisses attempts at classical meter as "but vaine & superstitious obseruations nothing at all furthering the pleasant melody of our English meeter."[17] Practice and theory combine to mark the triumph of the longstanding accentual tradition over recent experimentation in quantitative verse. Gregory Smith's assessment that the anonymous 1599 *First Booke of the Preservation of King Henry the VII*, written in quantitative verse, is the work of "a monomaniac out of touch with the times,"[18] may be, as Attridge argues, an overstatement, but even Attridge concedes that "the author failed to appreciate that the quantitative movement had, by comparison with the native tradition, proved to be unsuccessful."[19] By the turn of the century, quantitative verse is no longer relevant.

This was the climate into which Campion introduced his *Observations in the Art of English Poesie* in 1602. If *The First Booke of the Preservation of King Henry the VII* seems at best eccentrically anachronistic, Campion's argument for quantitative verse appears distinctly belated.[20] Campion is well aware of changed sensibilities: in 1601, one year before the publication of *Observations*, his preface to the *Book of Ayres* announced that he included but one song in quantitative verse. The rest, he writes, "are after the fascion of the time, eare-pleasing rimes without Arte."[21] That a former practitioner of rhyme should now attack it worries Daniel, since it makes Campion's argument more insidious. The discrepancy between Campion's practice and theory, however, provides Daniel with fodder for rebuttal. Campion's reputation heretofore depended largely on his rhyming. Now, Daniel argues, it is as if Campion "were become vnfaithfull to himselfe, and, seeking to leade vs out of the way of reputation, hath aduentured to intricate and confound him in his owne courses" (2:375). While Campion's conversion to quantity could strengthen his argument, Daniel chooses instead to construe it as a weakness.

Campion's ten-chapter treatise divides into two parts. The second of these parts is the less interesting: eight chapters discussing the rules and applications of quantitative verse. Incomprehension of the quantitative verse movement has led many to dismiss Campion's system outright. In fact, as Daniel will show, his recommendations for quantity are cleverly, but self-defeatingly, made. Following Sidney, who welded quantity and accent,[22] Campion proposes an anglicized version of quantitative verse which does not violate accent. In supporting quantity, Campion only reinforces accent.

The more substantial part of Campion's proposal lies not, however, in the practical rules of quantity it sets forth, but in the reasons given for them in the first two chapters of his essay. Campion approves of quantity because it offers a musical appeal to the ear and admirable symmetry. Most emphatically, he recommends it because it redresses the decline of learning and of Latin. Learning, Campion argues, "after the declining of the *Romaine* Empire and the pollution of their language through the conquest of the *Barbarians*, lay most pitifully deformed till the time of *Erasmus, Rewcline,* Sir *Thomas More,* and other learned men of that age, who brought the Latine toong again to light." He goes on: "In those lack-learning times, and in barbarized Italy, began that vulgar and easie kind of Poesie which is now in vse throughout most parts of Christendome, which we abusively call Rime and Meeter" (2:329). Even before he reaches the chapter which purports to treat deficiencies of rhyme, then, Campion's support of quantity seems to rest largely upon his dislike of rhyme – a dislike which, thus far, is based less on aesthetic grounds than on historical and intellectual principles.

Campion's second chapter details "the vnaptnesse of Rime in Poesie" (2:329). Here, he lists his objections to rhyme. Rhyme is merely, he argues, overuse of a single rhetorical figure, *similer desinentia,* and lacks proportion. It forces writers to distort their matter, and has no precedent in religious writing. Custom, which supports rhyme, ought not to dissuade from the pursuit of perfection. Rhyme is easy, and appeals to the lazy. Finally, England ought to surpass the other vernaculars and be the first to "second the perfection of the industrious *Greekes* and *Romaines*" (2:332), "whose skilfull monuments outliue barbarisme, [and who] tyed themselues to the strict obseruation of poeticall numbers, so abandoning the childish titillation of riming" (2:331). Rhyme is disparaged, then, because it uses little art and requires little learning.

There is not much, if anything, unique to Campion's treatise: rather, he anthologizes arguments familiar to readers of Ascham, Harvey, Spenser, Sidney, Webbe, and others. Apparently it is as clear to Campion as it is to his readers that he fights a losing battle in his support for quantitative verse, which by his own suggestion survives best when it accommodates itself to the native accentual tradition. Campion's attempt to ground his argument in xenophobia and distrust of the Middle Ages, however, suggests a potent currency to these attitudes. If his argument is unconvincing in its own terms, its strength must lie in its associations: in his attitudes, then, rests the persuasive power of his treatise.

Campion bears the mantle of typical nationalist humanism. The mantle, however, no longer fits properly, and it falls to Daniel to show its failings generally, and not just on prosodic principles. He presents two counterarguments to Campion's system. His first attack against Campion's self-contradiction is subtly disguised. Daniel suggests that Campion's achievements as a rhyming poet give his argument weight and credibility, observing that "this detractor (whose commendable Rymes, albeit now himselfe an enemy to ryme, haue giuen heretofore to the world the best notice of his worth) is a man of faire parts and good reputation; and therefore the reproach forcibly cast from such a hand may throw downe more at once then the labours of many shall in long time build vp againe" (2:358). Campion's resuscitation of an old movement, Daniel hints, is newfangledness: Campion is "desirous of credite by his new-old arte" (2:359). By referring in admiring tones to Campion's accomplishments in rhyme, Daniel criticizes his opponent's newfound and inconsistent position. Supposedly anxious that Campion's rhyming past strengthens his argument, Daniel demonstrates implicitly that Campion's former achievements weaken his present project.

Daniel's attack on the contradictions within the *Observations* is more direct. The extent to which Campion is successful in his proposed schemes for quantitative verse, as we have seen, lies in his adaptation of classical quantity to English accent. Daniel systematically examines each meter of this anglicized system and finds "Onely what was our owne before, and the same but apparelled in forraine Title" (2:377). Campion's metrical experiments, then, succeed in redefining quantity to make it palatable to the English, but effect no change in accentual verse, and only label it differently. Whereas Campion had attempted to profit from nationalist sentiment, Daniel portrays the quantitative movement as an attack on English traditions and an importation of foreign labels. In choosing rhyme, he argues, one is truly patriotic. Daniel gainsays Campion's nationalism, and shows that in this sense too Campion practices a "new-old arte."

Daniel might have persuasively and effectively ended his argument here. Instead, he precedes his dismissal of the surface concern of Campion's argument with a discussion of the central concerns of his own counterargument, which addresses the cultural forces informing Campion's work. The quantitative movement was deeply implicated in and fostered by humanism: it is humanism, rather than its manifestation in an unlikely metrical argument, that attracts the full force of Daniel's attention. This attention takes several attitudes: arguments such as "Custome ... is before all Law[;] Nature ... is aboue all Arte" (2:359) and "Perfection is not the portion of man" (2:374) directly challenge humanist precepts. Daniel's most sustained attack, however, is on the humanist anti-medievalism propelling Campion's work.

Derek Attridge reports emphatically that Daniel is "plainly" not a Renaissance humanist, but for all his astuteness on matters metrical, he misjudges here.[23] Daniel's rhetorical adeptness is evident not only in his tactic of attacking anti-medievalism through the metrical arguments which are an offshoot of it. He also uses humanism as a tool in the attack. Daniel is himself a humanist. As he frets that Campion's rhyming made his criticism more damaging, Daniel's own participation in humanism gives his *Defence* its particular force. By involving humanism in his attack on one of its precepts, he makes his argument appealing to humanist thinkers.

Part of Daniel's technique in making his critique of anti-medievalism humanist is to use humanist values and criteria in his evaluation of Campion's treatise. The Renaissance prided itself on the recovery of classical texts, which afforded new potential for scholarship, and humanism's impact was greatly manifested in the education system. On the grounds of learning, as we have seen, Campion judges and finds the medieval period lacking. Typical of his age, Campion extols the virtues of the classical world: "Learning first flourished in *Greece*; from thence it was deriued vnto the *Romaines*" (2:329). Then tragedy struck, according to Campion's account of Europe's intellectual history: learning "lay most pitifully deformed" until Erasmus, More and their ilk "brought the Latine toong again to light, redeeming it with much labour out of the hands of the illiterate Monks and Friers" (2:329). In those "lack-learning times," rhyme arose. Rhyme is objectionable, then, because it is a product of ignorance.

Daniel accepts the humanist criterion of learning as a paramount value and a useful measure of judgment. His dispute against Campion here requires not that he challenge Campion's terms, since they both agree on the importance of learning, but rather his generalizations. He does so first by challenging the alleged supremacy of the ancients, whom, he says, we admire "not for their smooth-gliding words, nor their measures, but for their inuentions ... [f]or to say truth, their Verse is many times but a confused deliuerer of their excellent conceits" (2:364). Daniel's comments here are doubly striking. Not only does he disparage classical writers, he also suggests the divisibility of matter and form, foreseeing the possibility of incongruence between matter and form in a way that the standard line of humanist thought, with its contentions about the links between rhetoric and philosophy, did not.[24] According to the humanist criterion of learning the ancients are found flawed, and not worthy of slavish admiration and relentless imitation.

The medievals, on the other hand, fare better in Daniel's assessment than they do in Campion's. First Daniel defends the so-called barbarians:

> The *Gothes*, *Vandales*, and *Longobards*, whose comming downe like an inundation ouerwhelmed, as they say, al the glory of learning in *Europe*, haue yet left vs stil their lawes and customes as the originalls

of most of the prouinciall constitutions of Christendome, which well considered with their other courses of gouernement may serue to cleare them from this imputatation of ignorance. (2:367)

Daniel places Campion in a paradoxical position. If the barbarians are ignorant, as Campion claims, he is party and heir to that ignorance, as a member of the society they established. If he concedes that they are not ignorant, then he himself is, for not having known so. He cannot escape the imputation of ignorance.

Daniel has only just started, however. He moves from implicit to explicit labeling of Campion's argument as ignorant:

And is it not a most apparent ignorance, both of the succession of learning in *Europe* and the generall course of things, to say "that all lay pittifully deformed in those lacke-learning times from the declining of the Romane Empire till the light of the Latine tongue was reuiued by Rewcline, Erasmus, and Moore"? (2:368)

We should recognize here the paraphrase of Campion as cited above. This is one of only two sentences Daniel incorporates directly from Campion's essay: that it so lodged in his mind testifies to the inflammatory nature, to him, of Campion's anti-medievalism.

The achievements of fourteenth- and fifteenth-century Italy begin Daniel's refutation of Campion's accusation. Daniel lauds Italian humanists for their learning. There was, he argues, a "mightie confluence of Learning in these parts," which, aided by "the new inuented stampe of Printing, spread it selfe indeed in a more vniuersall sorte then the world euer heeretofore had it" (2:369).[25] The likes of Petrarch, Boccaccio, Pico della Mirandola and a host of others "adorned *Italie*, and wakened other Nations likewise with this desire of glory, long before it brought foorth *Rewclen*, *Erasmus* and *Moore*" (2:369). We are less inclined than Daniel to consider these Italian luminaries medieval, and instead tend to place them, as we do him, in the Renaissance. He follows Campion's designations, however, and it appears that to Daniel, the exoneration of the Italian humanists here is an exoneration also of the idea of the Middle Ages.

Daniel also defends the period which we unquestionably agree with him in considering medieval. He appeals to nationalist sympathies, tapping into the "esoteric" brand of humanism most English humanists embraced, rejecting the more international, universal outlook of, say, Erasmus.[26] Before the Italian achievements, he says, "our Nation [was not] behinde in her portion of spirite and worthinesse, but concurrent with the best of all this lettered world" (2:369). He lists, among others, the venerable Bede, Walter Map, Roger Bacon, and William of Ockam as part of "an infinite Catalogue of excellent men, most of them liuing about foure hundred yeares since,

[who] haue left behinde them monuments of most profound iudgement and learning in all sciences" (2:370). In the category of learning, Daniel finds the medievals exemplary. The Middle Ages, then, are more true to the spirit of Renaissance humanism than Campion himself.

Daniel may admonish Campion for his unmitigated praise of the Greeks and Romans, but he is not himself averse to the humanist practice of bolstering an argument with appeals to classical authority. He adapts and quotes from classical authors, including Horace, Juvenal, Seneca, Cicero, and Tacitus, frequently through the *Defence*, though without explicit mention of names.[27] Aristotle, however, merits full recognition: "And these *Rhythmi*, as *Aristotle* saith, are familiar amongst all Nations, and *e naturali et sponte fusa compositione*: and they fall as naturally already in our language as euer Art can make them" (2:360). This choice of authority may show a clever bridging of the medieval past and Renaissance present: although Aristotle's authority generally waned, or at least became less central, at the close of the Middle Ages, his influence in literary criticism in fact began in the Renaissance.[28]

While Daniel establishes his own humanist credentials, he also manages to impute to Campion some of the qualities that made the medieval period unpopular. Seeing in the classical poets "verie painefull" attempts to fit "the quiet streame of their words" to quantitative verse, Daniel laments that

> such affliction doth laboursome curiositie still lay vpon our best delights (which euer must be made strange and variable), as if Art were ordained to afflict Nature, and that we could not goe but in fetters. Euery science, euery profession, must be so wrapt vp in vnnecessary intrications, as if it were not to fashion but to confound the vnderstanding. (2:365)

Daniel's description is reminiscent of the more pejorative definitions of medieval scholasticism, which focus on its obscure convolutions and dogmatism. Daniel suggests that, in contrast, "Ryme is no impediment to [man's] conceit, but rather giues him wings to mount, and carries him, not out of his course, but as it were beyond his power to a farre happier flight" (2:365). Though "[p]erfection is not the portion of man" (2:374), Daniel's rhyme, he suggests, can get one closer to this humanist ideal than Campion's quantity. The characterization of quantity as a set of rigorous, baffling rules makes Campion's proposals objectionable to humanist sympathies. By making these rules seem medieval, or at least scholastic, Daniel manipulates humanist biases to his own ends.

Daniel's defense of medievalism is informed, of course, by his perspective on history generally; it also provides a springboard to the expression of that perspective. Arthur B. Ferguson and, building upon his work, D.R. Woolf, have covered well, and in greater depth than I can do here, Daniel's historical perspective in the context of Renaissance historical thinking.[29] Ferguson and Woolf both characterize Daniel according to his ambivalence and Woolf follows Ferguson in his discussion of the tension – or as he argues, balance – between Daniel's relativism and uniformity. Daniel's humanist belief in the uniformity of human nature is amply demonstrated through the *Defence*. He chastises Campion's valorization of the ancients by saying: "We are the children of nature as well as they; we are not so placed out of the way of iudgement but that the same Sunne of Discretion shineth vppon vs; we haue our portion of the same virtues as well as of the same vices" (2:366–7). Shortly afterwards, he emphasizes that "this manifold creature man ... hath always some disposition of worth, intertaines the order of societie, affects that which is most in vse, and is eminent in some one thing or other that fits his humour and the times" (2:367). Like other humanists, Daniel believes in the existence of universal, essential characteristics.

Parity with the ancients does not mean, however, that the peoples of the past, recent or distant, are knowable. Daniel's relativist view of history pronounces instead that "it is but the clowds gathered about our owne iudgement that makes vs thinke all other ages wrapt vp in mists, and the great distance betwixt vs that causes vs to imagine men so farre off to be so little in respect of our selues" (2:370). His explanation of history profits further from the notion of perspective. He goes on to instruct that one must not think that

> reading an Historie (which is but a Mappe of Men, and dooth no otherwise acquaint vs with the true Substance of Circumstances then a superficiall Card dooth the Seaman with a Coast neuer seene, which alwayes prooues other to the eye than the imagination forecast it), that presently wee know all the world, .and can distinctly iudge of times, men, and manners, iust as they were. (2:370)

History, then, provides only a general notion of the conditions of the past. Daniel's relativism is less central, perhaps, to humanism than uniformity is, but it is, nevertheless, part of the acknowledged set of humanist beliefs.[30] His historical reasons for an argument against judgment of the past, then, are carefully grounded in widely accepted attitudes. Again, Daniel attempts to make his conclusions persuasive by basing them upon uncontroversial premises. His argumentation, like his history, is marked by a certain subtlety.

Daniel thus engages with a wide range of humanist ideas. Most of the ideas we associate with humanism make some appearance in the *Defence*, implicitly or explicitly, as support for or target of his arguments. One important feature of late sixteenth-century humanism, however, is glaringly, perplexingly absent: anti-Catholicism. Anti-medievalism was strongly associated with anti-Catholicism. Witness Ascham in 1570: "In our forefathers tyme, when Papistrie, as a standyng poole, couered and ouerflowed all England, fewe bookes were read in our tong, sauyng certaine bookes of Cheualrie, as they sayd, for pastime and pleasure, which, as some say, were made in Monasteries, by idle Monkes or wanton Chanons."[31] Likewise Thomas Nashe refers in the 1589 *Anatomie of Absurditie* to "these bable bookemungers" who seek "to restore to the worlde that forgotten Legendary licence of lying, to imitate a fresh the fantasticall dreames of those exiled Abbie-lubbers, from whose idle pens proceeded those worne out impressions of the feyned no where acts of [assorted characters in medieval romances]."[32] Even Puttenham, also in 1589, refers to rhyme as the "idle inventions" of simple, unlearned clerks in "orders *Monastical*."[33] Campion adds nothing new, then, when he praises those who redeem Latin "out of the hands of the illiterate Monks and Friers" (2:329).[34]

Daniel's only reference to religious matters in the *Defence* is a reproof of humanism, in a suggestion that human learning may be overvalued: "It is not bookes, but onely that great booke of the world and the all-ouerspreading grace of heauen that makes men truly iudiciall" (2:367). He does not attempt, as we might expect, to play upon anti-Catholic sympathies. Nor, of course, does he embark on the risky business of defending Catholicism.[35] By omitting Catholicism from his discussion, Daniel implicitly suggests that it is irrelevant to the argument at hand, and that medievalism is extricable from it. Absence, however, is not the only way Daniel divorces medievalism and Catholicism. The association between rhyme and Catholicism lies not in theology, but in the idleness supposedly characteristic of monks and conducive to rhyme.[36] Daniel explicitly refutes charges of idleness against rhyme, which is, he writes, "farre more laborious than loose measures (whatsoeuer is obiected)" (2:365). Daniel does not dispute the idleness of monks. By showing rhyme to be the product of labor, however, he excludes it from the province of Catholicism, as it was popularly construed. In excising Catholicism, he neutralizes his pro-medievalist stance. Though it was formerly invested with contemporary, controversial religious and political significance, Daniel places the idea of the Middle Ages into the safer arenas of intellectual and aesthetic judgment. He successfully demonstrates that it is possible to discuss the medieval period without discussing the medieval church.

As we have seen, Daniel appeals to Renaissance humanist sympathies by using humanist attitudes and techniques. One final tactic ingratiates him with those he would persuade: his formulation of his audience. His citation of authorities tends less toward the classical than the contemporary. By drawing a carefully chosen group of political and cultural authorities into his argument, he gives weight to his appeal. He defines his audience variously in the dedicatory letter, establishing a respectful foundation to his treatise. The letter is addressed generally to "all the worthie Louers and learned Professors of Ryme within His Maiesties Dominions" (2:356). The body of the dedicatory letter proceeds to tell us that the *Defence* originated with a private letter to "a learned Gentleman, a great friend of [Daniel's], then in Court" (2:356). This learned friend is generally assumed to be Fulke Greville,[37] Sidney's friend and biographer, and a distinguished literary figure himself. This present version of the argument is patronized by "a noble Earle, who in bloud and nature is interessed to take our parte in this cause" (2:357). This allusiveness is quickly and fully remedied, for the *Defence* itself is addressed to William Herbert, the Earl of Pembroke. Pembroke's interest by blood was probably greater than his interest by nature: he was the son of Mary Sidney Herbert, Countess of Pembroke, and the nephew of Sir Philip Sidney. Daniel explicitly invokes the memory of Pembroke's mother when recalling his own training in rhyming: he says he was

> first incourag'd or fram'd thereunto by your most Worthy and Honorable Mother, and receiuing the first notion for the formall ordering of those compositions at *Wilton*, which I must euer acknowledge to haue beene my best Schoole, and thereof alwayes am to hold a feeling and gratefull Memory. (2:358)

This is not inflated flattery, since the evidence suggests a cordial, collegial, mutually beneficial working relationship between Daniel and the Countess of Pembroke.[38] The sincere gratitude, nevertheless, is craftily deployed here: to disagree with Daniel, he implies, is to tarnish the memories and legacies of the Sidneys.[39]

Daniel claims one more powerful potential ally, the King himself. The coincidence of the publication of the *Defence* and the Scottish king's accession as James I of England is no accident, Daniel claims. Rather, Daniel publishes in 1603 because the times "promise a more regarde to the present condition of our writings, in respect of our Soueraignes happy inclination should checke vs with a shew of what it would do in an other kinde" (2:357). He refers here to James I's poetic output, and also to a treatise he had published in 1584, when he was already King of Scotland: *Ane schort Treatise, conteining some reulis and cautelis to be obseruit and eschewit in Scottis Poesie.* Any prospective opponent to Daniel's as-yet-unpresented argument must counter, he suggests, the force not just of the Sidney legend and the Herbert family, but the King of England too.[40]

By drawing political and cultural authorities into his *Defence*, along with the broader base of poets generally, Daniel cleverly appropriates their authority and invites their support. Assured that they will concur with his arguments against quantitative verse, he implicates them in his more particular agenda. In my introduction, I asked why Daniel responds to Campion's eccentric, self-defeating argument with such urgency. Daniel's formulation of his audience – like his use of humanist principles – suggests that Campion's essay was an easy target, and that his rebuttal of Campion's proposals for a wholesale conversion to quantitative verse would find near-universal support. This support assured, he could then feed his more controversial argument to an audience predisposed to concur with him.

In his dedication letter, Daniel says that he wrote the letter which subsequently became the *Defence* "to hold [his friend] from being wonne from vs" (2:356). The body of the *Defence*, however, suggests that quite a contrary agenda is at work: Daniel seeks to win people to his unpopular cause of medievalism, not to sustain them in the popular practice of rhyme. His rhetorical strategies confirm his participation in humanism even while he seeks to dismantle one of its pillars. Like so many English humanists, Daniel seeks to establish for England a status comparable to that of ancient Greece and Rome. He proposes that they do so, however, by embracing, rather than rejecting, the medieval heritage. For Daniel, the defense of things medieval is the defense of things English.

NOTES

1. This date is most commonly given for the *Defence*, though G. Gregory Smith suggests it may have appeared in late 1602 (G. Gregory Smith [ed.], *Elizabethan Critical Essays*, 2 vols. [Oxford: Oxford University Press, 1904], 2:457 [hereafter cited in the notes as *ECE*]). The dedicatory letter, however, is addressed to lovers and practitioners of rhyme "within *His* Maiesties Dominions," (emphasis mine) and publication, therefore, must surely have followed Elizabeth's death and James's succession in 1603 (though Daniel indicates that he wrote a shorter version of its argument some time earlier).

2. One important seventeenth-century supporter of quantitative verse was Alexander Gil in his 1619 *Logonomia Anglica*. Ben Jonson, himself a proficient practitioner of rhyme, was also not persuaded by Daniel's argument. He told Drummond that he "had written a discourse of Poesie both against Campion & Daniel, especially this Last" (*Ben Jonson*, ed. C.H. Herford and Percy Simpson, 11 vols. [Oxford: Clarendon Press, 1925], 1:132). If this essay was written, it did not survive, and so Jonson's grounds for disagreement with Daniel are unknown.

3. Samuel Daniel, *A Defence of Ryme*, *ECE* 2:358. Subsequent references to Daniel's essay will be indicated by volume and page number in parentheses.

4. Paraphrased from O.B. Hardison, Jr., "Humanism," *The Spenser Encyclopedia*, ed. A.C. Hamilton (Toronto: University of Toronto Press, 1990), 379.

5. Thomas Campion, *Observations in the Art of English Poesie*, *ECE* 2:328. Subsequent references to Campion's essay will be indicated by volume and page number in parentheses.

6. Because accentual verse tended, through the medieval period, to feature end-rhyme, the etymologically related terms "rhythm" and "rhyme" became somewhat interchangeable. In the sixteenth century, rhyme can refer to rhyming verse, or it can refer more generally to non-quantitative verse. For sixteenth-century definitions of rhyme and rhythm, see Derek Attridge, *Well-Weighed Syllables: Elizabethan Verse in Classical Metres* (Cambridge:

Cambridge University Press, 1974), 94–6. For a concise overview of prosodic terminology in the period, see also Susanne Woods, *Natural Emphasis: English Versification from Chaucer to Dryden* (San Marino: Huntingdon Library, 1984), 1–20.

7. Attridge develops this argument throughout *Well-Weighed Syllables*. William A. Ringler, Jr., makes a similar point in reference to Sidney's experiments with quantitative verse in the *Old Arcadia* (*The Poems of Sir Philip Sidney*, ed. William A. Ringler, Jr. [Oxford: Clarendon Press, 1962], 390–92).

8. For the continental background to the English quantitative movement, see O.B. Hardison, Jr., *Prosody and Purpose in the English Renaissance* (Baltimore and London: Johns Hopkins University Press, 1989), 63–91. While the impact of the French movement was considerable, Hardison sees little influence of the Italian prosodists on any English writers of the sixteenth and seventeenth centuries other than Milton (91).

9. For quotations of Watson's and Ascham's own quantitative verse in *Toxophilus* (ostensibly a treatise on archery), see Ascham, *English Works*, ed. William Aldis Wright (Cambridge: Cambridge University Press, 1904), 4, 12, 14, 16, 24, 38, 64, 72, 75, 89, 92, 93, 104. For Ascham's recollections of discussions with Watson and Cheke in 1540s Cambridge, see *The Scolemaster* (1570) in *English Works*, 289.

10. Ascham, *Scolemaster*, *Works*, 289.

11. Thomas Blenerhasset, "Induction" following "The Complaint of Cadwallader," *The Second Part of the Mirror for Magistrates*, in *Parts Added to 'The Mirror for Magistrates'*, ed. L.B. Campbell (Cambridge: Cambridge University Press, 1946), 450. Campbell has the closing parenthesis following "greekes," but it clearly ought to follow "fyrst," and I have amended it accordingly. "The Complaint of Cadwallader" is in quantitative metre rather than rhyme because, Cadwallader tells us, its somber tones are more fitting to his tale.

12. Apparently resistant to Attridge's defense of the quantitative movement, O.B. Hardison, Jr., says that the most important fact about Spenser and Sidney's participation in it is that "when forced to choose between quantitative and romance versification, they both chose the romance tradition. Sir Philip Sidney wrote a pastoral novel adorned with quantitative poems, but his most famous poem is *Astrophil and Stella*" (Hardison, *Prosody and Purpose*, 112). There are problems with this assessment. Not only does the latterday neglect of Sidney's *Arcadia* speak more to latterday tastes than those of the sixteenth century (the *Arcadia* was enormously popular in its own day and in the centuries to follow), but the reasons for which the *Arcadia* is read or overlooked surely cannot have to do with its quantitative verse, which is but a minor part of the work. Furthermore, there is nothing to suggest that Sidney felt he must necessarily *choose* between quantity and rhyme. Similarly, while engaged in the writing of the *Faerie Queene*, Spenser writes to Harvey: "I am, of late, more in loue wyth my Englishe Versifying than with Ryming; whyche I should haue done long since, if I would then haue followed your councell," suggesting a less linear movement from quantity to rhyme than Hardison proposes (*Spenser-Harvey Correspondence*, ECE 1:89).

13. *Spenser-Harvey Correspondence*, ECE 1:89.

14. William Webbe, *A Discourse of English Poetrie*, ECE 1:240.

15. Ibid., 1:246.

16. Ibid., 1:239.

17. George Puttenham, *The Arte of English Poesie*, ECE 2:134.

18. *ECE* 1:xlvii.

19. Attridge, *Well-Weighed Syllables*, 133.

20. It has been suggested that Campion wrote the treatise as much as a decade before it was published, at which time it may have been somewhat (but not wholly) more timely. For the possible earlier dating of *Observations*, see G.B. Harrison, "Books and Readers, 1591–94," *The Library*, Fourth Series, VIII (1927), 279–80. My discussion of the *Observations* as a 1602 essay is not affected by these speculations, however, since my interest is in Campion's decision to *publish* in 1602, when the quantitative verse movement had lost much of its topical relevance.

21. *The Works of Thomas Campion*, ed. Walter R. Davis (Garden City, NY: Doubleday & Company, 1967), 15.

22. Ringler discusses Sidney's success in two of his poems in the *Old Arcadia* at combining

artificial and natural quantity and accent (*The Poems of Sir Philip Sidney*, 393). See also Attridge on these experiments (*Well-Weighed Syllables*, 185–6).

23. Attridge, *Well-Weighed Syllables*, 233. Other commentators tend to classify Daniel as a humanist but do not examine the applicability of the term. See, however, Albert J. Geritz's article "Samuel Daniel: Poet, Humanist, Wordling," a study of Daniel's verse dialogue *Musophilus* (1599 and 1611 editions), which argues for a qualified humanism. Geritz reads *Musophilus* as a psychomachian exploration of Daniel's ambivalence about the worth of poetry and learning, and anxiety about negotiation of the *triplex vita* (*Res Publica Litterarum* 2 (1979), 57–67).

24. For a brief discussion of the links between rhetoric and philosophy in humanist thought, see Paul Oskar Kristeller, "Humanism," *The Cambridge History of Renaissance Philosophy*, ed. Charles B. Schmitt and Quentin Skinner (Cambridge: Cambridge University Press, 1988), 113–37. Daniel is not unique, however, in his suggestion that matter and form are separable. Sidney, for instance, works from the same position in his *Apology for Poetry*.

25. Daniel's appraisal of the influence of printing is not always so positive. See, for instance, *The Civil Wars*, VI.37, which suggests that artillery and printing are the chief weapons of Nemesis (*The Complete Works in Verse and Prose of Samuel Daniel*, ed. Alexander B. Grosart, 4 vols. [London: Hazell, Watson and Viney, 1885], Volume II).

26. I follow Hardison's terminology here: he identifies two kinds of sixteenth-century humanism, one centered on Latin and international in outlook (exoteric) and the other centered on the vernacular and looking inward to the national culture (esoteric) (*Prosody and Purpose*, 93).

27. For identification of Daniel's sources, see *Samuel Daniel: Selected Poetry and a Defence of Rhyme*, ed. Geoffrey G. Hiller and Peter L. Groves (Asheville, NC: Pegasus Press, 1998), 198–226.

28. The *Poetics* became available in Latin translation in 1498 and in the Greek original in 1508. For a useful overview of the impact of Aristotle on late sixteenth-century England, see the entry on Aristotle in *The Spenser Encyclopedia*.

29. See Arthur B. Ferguson, *Clio Unbound: Perception of the social and cultural past in Renaissance England* (Durham, NC: Duke University Press, 1979), esp. 64–8 and 340–43, and D.R. Woolf's chapter "Samuel Daniel and the Emergence of the English State," in his book *The Idea of History in Early Stuart England* (Toronto: University of Toronto Press, 1990).

30. Ferguson takes Daniel as a representative, though not the most profound, "model of the ambivalence" of Renaissance thinking (*Clio Unbound*, 60). Woolf's estimation of Daniel is higher – he praises Daniel's analysis of historical development as much more subtle than that of his contemporaries – but he agrees that Daniel shares "certain of his beliefs with the majority of his contemporaries," (Woolf, *The Idea of History*, 104).

31. Ascham, *Scolemaster, Works*, 230–31.

32. Thomas Nash, *The Anatomie of Absurditie, ECE* 1:323.

33. Puttenham, *The Arte of English Poesie, ECE* 2:12–13.

34. The connection, if any exists, between Thomas Campion and the martyred Jesuit Edmund Campion (1540–81) or the Witham Campions believed to have harbored him, is unknown.

35. Nothing in Daniel's life or writings suggests Roman Catholic sympathies. His home county, Somerset, was not known for recusancy. As a student at Oxford, Daniel would have subscribed to the Thirty-nine Articles. He was closely associated with the staunchly Protestant Sidneys. There is a consistently conservative strain to his writing, but his objections to change appear to stem not from fervently held beliefs, political or religious, but rather the conviction that change itself is detrimental to society. In *Musophilus*, a perhaps deliberately obscure passage stakes out the middle ground. Daniel seems to suggest here that it is a mistake to assume that the early church was, because primitive, purer. He also suggests that to effect any more changes on the church would be a mistake, "[s]ince eu'ry change the reverence doth decay" (*Works*, 1:248). This practical attitude suggests an incompatibility with religious extremes of any kind.

36. For an extended treatment of the idleness of monks in contrast to every other segment of society, see Blenerhasset's "Complaint of Cadwallader" (*Parts Added to 'The Mirror for*

Magistrates', 448).

37. *ECE*, 2:457. Daniel's *Musophilus* is dedicated to Greville.

38. Mary Sidney Herbert's most recent editors write: "Of the poets in her household, Samuel Daniel was by far the most accomplished; perhaps because her achievement did not threaten his own, he seems to have considered her not just as a patron, but as a fellow poet" (*The Collected Works of Mary Sidney Herbert*, ed. Margaret P. Hannay, Noel J. Kinnamon, Michael G. Brennan, 2 vols. [Oxford: Clarendon Press, 1998], 1:41).

39. Daniel conveniently overlooks the quantitative verse of the *Arcadia* here. Richard Helgerson rightly points out that Daniel and Campion "divide the Sidneian legacy" (*Forms of Nationhood: The Elizabethan Writing of England* [Chicago and London: University of Chicago Press, 1992], 39).

40. Helgerson reads the inclusion of James I in the *Defence* somewhat differently, in accordance with the argument that political concerns lie at the heart of the *Defence*. He argues that Daniel's opposition to the "vniust authoritie of the Law-giuer," who is in this case Campion (2.376), "responds directly to concerns aroused by the accession of a king who claimed ancestral conquest as the ultimate sanction of his authority, a king who thought his will should be law" (*Forms of Nationhood*, 38). Helgerson further suggests that the publication of the *Defence* with the second and third editions of Daniel's "A Panegyrike Congratvlatorie to the Kings most excellent *Maiestie*" confirms a political agenda: the "Panegyrike," he argues, is meant to placate James should he take offense to the *Defence*. Perhaps Woolf would agree: surveying the scope of Daniel's historical thought, he concludes that "If any history deserved to be censored by a tyrannical monarch, nervous of the past, Daniel's Janus-faced [1618 *Collection of the Historie of England*] was a good candidate" (Woolf, *The Idea of History*, 103). By the time the *Collection* appeared, Daniel was used to political controversy: his 1607 play *Philotas* had been censured for resemblances to contemporary political imbroglios. My primary interest is not in the political but the cultural implications (so far as these can be separated) of the *Defence*: Helgerson's interpretation need not be mutually exclusive of mine, however.

Chivalry and Romance in the Eighteenth Century: Richard Hurd and the Disenchantment of The Faerie Queene

KRISTINE LOUISE HAUGEN

In the middle years of the eighteenth century, Richard Hurd decided that the whole previous history of literary criticism was a chronicle of obsessions with non-problems. It was in his search for an actual problem that Hurd hit upon the Middle Ages. The result, Hurd's *Letters on Chivalry and Romance* of 1762, has long been a primary exhibit in the story of how the eighteenth century rediscovered medieval literature and culture.[1] In this set of essays, Hurd canvasses what he takes to be the central characteristics of medieval courtly life, then discusses several postmedieval epic poems and their relationship to this medieval ("gothic") world. In his remarks on Ariosto, Tasso, Milton, and above all Spenser – whose *Faerie Queene* stands at the theoretical core of the argument – Hurd elaborates a new, "gothic" poetics supposed to be based in the conditions of medieval culture itself, and which Hurd contends is better suited to these poems than Aristotelian ("classical") poetics with its demand for a particular kind of narrative unity. Hurd is also diffuse on the virtues of the "gothic idea of poetry" in its own right, particularly on the pleasing effects of fairies and other elements of "superstition," which he considers aesthetically superior, *qua* superstition, to the anthropomorphic gods in Homer (48–55). In short, says Hurd, the gothic style affords an ideally wide scope to the poetic imagination and is "peculiarly suited to the views of a genius"; if Spenser and his fellow poets were "seduced" by the gothic "barbarities of their forefathers," theirs was a fortunate fall (4).

Hurd's treatise is significant in many ways, but not as a record of direct eighteenth-century encounters with medieval literature. As Hurd himself admitted, his information about chivalry came entirely from the voluminous essays of Jean-Baptiste de La Curne de Ste.-Palaye, and Hurd revealed almost proudly that he had never read any medieval romances himself – he knew they were by "bad writers" (24, 105).[2] The eighteenth century was indeed a time of rigorous scholarly engagements with medieval English texts, as the careers of Humphrey Wanley, George Hickes, Elizabeth Elstob,

Thomas Warton and Thomas Percy make clear.[3] But Hurd was at best an appreciative observer of philological and historical scholarship of this kind, and as a result the *Letters'* arguments about the Middle Ages tend to resemble – I borrow a phrase from Pierre Macherey – a planet revolving around an absent sun.[4]

I mean to show here that Hurd's engagement with the middle ages was driven by a methodological and theoretical polemic about the proper way of studying and discussing literary texts and those texts' relationship to the world outside themselves. A well-known account of eighteenth-century developments in this area provides a helpful context. Michael McKeon has convincingly argued that in the seventeenth and earlier eighteenth centuries, English approaches to "questions of truth" – essentially, questions about history, fiction, and texts – underwent a twofold dialectical development.[5] A "romance" view was succeeded by a "naive empiricism" marked by strong claims that historical truth was (or should be) transparently accessible through certain kinds of texts. This view in turn was challenged by an "extreme skepticism" that doubted whether it was possible to distinguish between historical and fictive texts after all. McKeon points out that the extreme skeptical position is thus in imminent danger of collapsing again into the "romance" view, a problem of which contemporaries were uncomfortably aware but were often unable satisfactorily to resolve.[6] For Defoe, Fielding, and Richardson, the answer to this impasse lay in different forms of realism centering on the notion of the probable or verisimilar. No longer was a given text either true or false, simply and literally; a gradually defined middle ground was opening, the ground of what is "like truth," and it was this epistemological space that the eighteenth-century English novel came to inhabit.

Hurd's *Letters* stand both inside and outside this narrative, because although Hurd too was preoccupied with what it meant for a text to be true, he never once called on the notion of the verisimilar that his contemporaries had found so useful. This was certainly due to the nature of the texts Hurd set out to discuss, and indeed, Hurd's inability to adapt his contemporaries' realism to his own project confirms the highly localized (although still, of course, important) status of eighteenth-century realism. The criterion of the verisimilar was inaccessible to Hurd, he apparently thought, as a practical consequence of the historical distance that separated Hurd and his contemporaries both from the Renaissance epics that Hurd discussed and from the "gothic" age that he claimed that those epics represented. The truth that Defoe's, Fielding's and Richardson's novels were "like" had been conceived as an empirically present truth, most of whose components any reader could independently observe in the world outside texts. The corresponding restrictions on the novels' subject matter made them doubly "domestic," as Margaret Doody points out: they were not only private in scope but also geographically and chronologically bound to present-day England.[7] Hurd, by contrast, was interested in claiming that *The Faerie Queene* and other texts bore a close resemblance to the Middle Ages, a world of which few eighteenth-century readers had any knowledge and to which, moreover, the only possible access lay through texts. But to demonstrate that *The Faerie Queene* was "like" texts from or about the middle ages would hardly have been to place it in contact with the concretely conceived real to which the eighteenth-century novel was supposed by realists to correspond. Hurd energetically rejected the skeptical conclusion that might seem to follow, and his insistence on the truth (not the verisimilitude) of *The Faerie Queene* sometimes seems to repeat the impossibly optimistic and by now outdated claims of naive empiricism. At the same time, certain aspects of Hurd's writing – above all, his fatal attraction to insoluble paradoxes, of which I will explore several here – serve to distinguish his claims about truth from these earlier ones. Hurd's deep and general suspicion of texts, including at some points the same texts he had set out to explicate, reveals that his argument is powerfully inhabited by the specter of skepticism, just as the *Letters* are haunted by a medieval that always remains slightly outside Hurd's grasp. The resulting argument might be thought of as a variety of historically realistic reading, so as to recognize that Hurd attempted to surmount the competing claims of empiricism and skepticism that also faced the theorists of the verisimilar. Thinking of Hurd as a realist also avoids the vexed and often contradictory connotations of the term "historicist" as applied to Hurd by David Carlson and Donald Marshall. Equally clearly, Hurd's realism ran on a kind of parallel track to that of the novelists, leaving him with few sources of aid and comfort on the multiple occasions when his argument threatened to succumb to the paradoxes he had built into it.

I propose to explore both the theoretical and methodological parts of Hurd's project by holding up the *Letters* at a relatively new angle. The majority of recent discussions have treated Hurd's account of the Middle Ages as the primary *explanandum*, and have been generally unimpressed with his knowledge of and sympathy with the medieval.[8] This is a salutary reaction to Arthur Johnston's classic portrait of Hurd as an ardent friend of the medieval, which obliged Johnston to overlook Hurd's avowed dislike for medieval texts themselves.[9] However, I propose to read the *Letters* primarily as an account of postmedieval epic poems – for purposes of clarity, I will discuss only Hurd's remarks on *The Faerie Queene* – so as to treat his account of the Middle Ages as a component in a larger and stranger argument rather than an end in itself. Conversely, the important status of the medieval in Hurd's text has generally not been discussed by students of Spenser reception; perhaps as a result, these writers have sometimes treated Hurd as an odd man out who must be discussed for reasons of completeness but always remains under a certain pall of suspicion.[10] I will suggest that Hurd's oddness, if such it is, is not simply a case of fortuitous eccentricity, and that the difficulty in inserting Hurd in a linear tradition of Spenser reception results from the difficulties of Hurd's own critical project, in which Spenser and *The Faerie Queene,* like the Middle Ages, were means to a markedly ambitious end.

The most immediately striking aspect of Hurd's *Letters* is, as I have suggested, his insistence that poems with a "gothic" subject matter are indissolubly connected with the concrete conditions of medieval courtly life. There is not much nuance in Hurd's account of this connection – certainly he seems to envisage a relationship of direct reflection and mimetic representation as he recites a list of social and political customs that appear both in medieval life and in the narratives of "gothic" poems (11–23). Yet when Hurd's realism is considered in the context of eighteenth-century commentary on Spenser, his apparently simple view takes on a polemical edge. Hurd's eighteenth-century predecessors in studying Spenser had exerted themselves heroically in hunting out all possible intertexts that might be considered models for passages in Spenser. This is the kind of enterprise to which Terry Eagleton apparently refers when he writes that literary criticism was based on rhetoric until the eighteenth century, and it was an enterprise for which Hurd entertained the greatest suspicions.[11] For example, in 1734 John Jortin, whose name appears regularly in the modern Spenser Variorum, had identified hundreds of passages in the most recondite Greek and Latin poets (and occasionally the bible) which he suggested that Spenser had imitated.[12] This procedure tended to place Spenser on a level with literally "classical" writers, constructing Spenser as a "classic" English writer simply by virtue of his copious citations of Greeks and Romans. In 1754, Hurd's friend Thomas Warton had undertaken an essentially similar project, but with a significantly broadened scope. Warton considered not only classical texts as potential sources for *The Faerie Queene,* but also Ariosto and Tasso and, even more significantly, English romances such as Malory's *Morte D'Arthur, The Lady of the Lake, Sir Bevis of Southampton,* and even Chaucer's *Rime of Sir Thopas.*[13] Warton was not shy in pointing out the merit in his own use of the previously neglected romances. Aside from serving the general ideal of constructing an exhaustive textual genealogy for Spenser's poem, he claimed to have shed new light on key parts of the text. In the most notable case, Warton identified a romance source for Spenser's narrative framework of twelve knights setting off from a feast to pursue twelve adventures, which is, of course, the most basic premise of the poem's plot. According to Warton, this was lightly adapted from the seven adventures in the romance called *The Seven Champions of Christendom*, which had been "highly fashionable" in the time of Elizabeth.[14] In this case, we might well notice not only Warton's industry, but also the somewhat subversive use to which he put the method of searching for intertextual parallels. Where Jortin's parallels had tended to identify *The Faerie Queene* with the classical texts with which it displayed such great similarities, Warton now suggested that the fundamental structure of Spenser's poem had come from a popular, native, nonclassical, and indeed medieval text.

We might think of Warton's work as a step forward in the construction of a distinctly British literary history.[15] Hurd, however, would have been inclined on principle to be unimpressed. In the "Discourse Concerning Poetical Imitation" that Hurd first published with his commentary on Horace's *Epistola ad Augustum* in 1751, Hurd had launched a major assault on the critical search for intertexts in general.[16] His argument was, in effect, a skeptical exposure of the assumption that *post hoc, ergo propter hoc* (after, therefore because of) which undergirded genealogical projects like Jortin's and Warton's. How can we really know, asked Hurd, that because two passages are similar one must necessarily be an imitation of the other? If two poets compare a running warrior to a lion, couldn't this be just a coincidence, a "natural" thought that might independently occur to both? Hurd advocated a liberal use of Occam's razor, proposing to accept no textual parallel as an imitation unless the putative source-text was utterly peculiar to the "genius of the age" in which it was written. The later parallel was not an imitation unless, in effect, it could not have been independently thought at the time it was written. On its face, this argument might seem to carve out a rather wide autonomous space for authorship: no longer are authors imitators until proven original, they are now original until proven imitators. Yet writers are also considerably constrained, for Hurd, by the changing and finite mentalities he calls the "genius of the age."[17] Historical boundaries affect what it is possible to think, and if an author writes "thoughts" impossible to think in his own age, they are indubitably the products of imitation. It seems to follow that an author can only be considered original if he writes what the genius of his own age permits or obliges him to think; if he ventures to write anything else he must be an imitator – a citer of texts like the Spenser of Jortin and Warton.

Hurd elaborated his assault on the method of intertextual parallels in 1757 in his *Letter to Mr. Mason; on the Marks of Imitation*, and in the *Letters on Chivalry* of 1762, he evidently sought to put his views into practice in an extended account of Spenser and others.[18] Hurd willingly accepted Warton's claim that *The Faerie Queene* had close affinities with the medieval era; the challenge, for Hurd, lay in demonstrating this without any appeal whatsoever to parallels between Spenser's poem and medieval texts. The medieval era, conceived as concrete, historical, and as far as possible unaffected by textual mediation, was thus the long lever with which Hurd undertook to move the critical world. It is not simple indolence, then, that causes Hurd to rely somewhat ostentatiously on Ste.-Palaye's *Mémoires* for his information about the middle ages. Although Hurd of course knew that Ste.-Palaye's treatise was based on the study of romances (the "proper Source" of information about the medieval [24]), the suspicion is great that in practical terms, Hurd felt Ste.-Palaye's text to be ontologically different from romances – that for Hurd, Ste.-Palaye's remarks ascended to the status of history by virtue of being written in the eighteenth century and cast in the form of a learned treatise. As Lionel Gossman has noted, Ste.-Palaye himself tended to read his relatively late and idealizing sources on chivalry not necessarily as guarantees that real medieval life had always been just as they said, but certainly as keys to what was truly important about the medieval world.[19] In other words, Ste.-Palaye too was inclined to treat texts as more or less transparent, to be used almost impatiently as a conduit to the real world behind them.

Again, Hurd's views stated in this way are unlikely to seem remarkable until we recall the context in which they were enunciated. The greatest critical truisms about Spenser in the seventeenth and eighteenth centuries involved his amazingly unbounded fancy and imagination, a characterization common to those who defended him and those who attacked him.[20] For Hurd, by contrast, *The Faerie Queene* was no fantasy at all, but utterly real and historical. This was a remarkable discovery by any standard. Hurd's relentless realism effects a kind of ludic deflation of Spenser's fantastic poem, precisely by denying that it involved any fancy at all. Like Don Quixote, another reader determined to extract every grain of truth from apparently intractable texts, Hurd performs what we might call a historical reduction, entirely bracketing or suspending the fantastic as a category. Neither fairies nor Arthur nor the Bower of Bliss can seem gripping in quite the same way once we have learned from Hurd that they merely reflect the medieval social world. The paradoxical consequence is that the literature of apparent fantasy can suddenly offer no escape from the real at all.

Hurd did not, of course, claim that the individual incidents in Spenser's narrative had actually happened – that a person named Una had been rescued by the Red Crosse Knight, that a person named Acrasia had imprisoned knights in a Bower of Bliss, and so on. His realism operates on a level that is both more abstract and more pervasive, and that bears a notable resemblance to Gyorgy Lukács's famous account of the way in which historical novels can be truthful.[21] For Hurd, *The Faerie Queene* faithfully reflected medieval social life and culture on the level of both its episodes and its narrative shape. Following Ste.-Palaye, whose *Mémoires* he treated as direct and raw records of medieval reality, Hurd observed that in the medieval world, knights really did perform chivalric adventures at the behest of ladies, great courtly entertainments really happened as in *The Faerie Queene,* and popular supernatural beliefs involved just the kinds of sorcerers and fairies we find in the text. Hurd even gave a gloriously structuralist description of the way in which politics, society, and culture were interlinked in the medieval society Spenser depicted. Feudal government was what we might call the base of the system; social forms, under the collective label of chivalry, were determined by this feudal form of government; and finally cultural forms, that is pageants and romance narratives, were determined by the social forms of chivalry (3–4, 6–10). So important to Hurd's reading of Spenser was the putative representation of this medieval world that it even drove Hurd's generic definition of the "gothic idea of poetry": Spenser's poem was gothic precisely because Spenser "chose the times of chivalry for his theme" (56).

Let me give a striking example of Hurd's efforts to read *The Faerie Queene* realistically rather than intertextually or authorially. It is an example that both shows Hurd at his most nearly profound and suggests some of the complications that beset his apparently straightforward system. Where Thomas Warton had found the source for Spenser's twelve knights (and thus Spenser's entire poem) in the romance called *The Seven Champions of Christendom,* Hurd's borrowed erudition supplied a precedent that, for Hurd's purposes, was incalculably better. In 1453, at the court of Philip the Good, duke of Burgundy, there had actually occurred a twelve-day feast involving twelve knights who undertook tasks for twelve ladies (63) – so Hurd learned from his ever-helpful source Ste.-Palaye.[22] As usual, Hurd offered no thoughts on how Spenser was likely to have learned of this feast; he merely reproduced Ste.-Palaye's references to the three French chroniclers who reported it. Treating the Burgundian feast itself as Spenser's source, Hurd proceeded to discover that the twelve-fold ritual of the feast was perfectly reproduced in the projected formal division of Spenser's poem into twelve discrete adventures. The multifurcate form of Spenser's text, even if it violated Aristotelian ("classic") unity, thus embodied a different, "gothic" unity, since Spenser's twelve adventures all proceeded from the same cause – the fictive feast of the Faerie Queene – and that feast had a medieval historical model (60–75). So under the pressure of Aristotelian poetics and its demand for unity, Hurd arrived at the claim that the very form of Spenser's poem was determined by the special conditions of medieval social life, a theoretical development that goes significantly beyond Hurd's initial claims about Spenser's merely accurate representation of the medieval social world itself. Hurd argues, in fact, that the poem's medieval contents constrained Spenser with absolute necessity to produce the kind of form he did:

> [T]he general plan of a work ... is and must be governed by the subject-matter itself. It was as requisite for the Faery Queen to consist of the adventures of twelve knights, as for the Odyssey to be confined to the adventures of one Hero. ... So that if you will say any thing against the poet's method, you must say that he should not have chosen this subject. (65; cf. 62, 75–6)

I shall now trace some of the fault lines in Hurd's argument, difficulties which reveal that Hurd's apparently simplistic methodological claims are maintained against the most extreme pressures from within the argument itself. I suggest that Hurd's reduction of *The Faerie Queene* to the historical is connected in the closest way with Hurd's notorious disinclination to engage with actual medieval texts, and further, that the way in which Hurd carried out his reduction amounts to a general assault on texts of several kinds. First and most obviously, Hurd's account of *The Faerie Queene*'s historicity leaves it somewhat unclear what *The Faerie Queene* itself could be for in the end: if the poem's meaning turns entirely on the historical realities it reflects, aren't those realities conveyed to the reader much more efficiently in nonpoetic texts like Ste.-Palaye's? Isn't Spenser's poem, for all the close relationship between its "subject" and its "method," a singularly circuitous device for reporting on the medieval world? Again, given that Spenser wrote in the late sixteenth century, when the medieval era was definitively past (*Letters* 109–12), exactly how did so many concrete medieval realities find their way into *The Faerie Queene*? Presumably Spenser's information came from reading the very romances and chronicles for which Hurd felt such distaste. Yet Hurd nowhere acknowledges this and certainly never discusses medieval texts as a part of *The Faerie Queene*'s genealogy. The closest Hurd comes to a concession on this subject is his remark that Spenser and his fellow poets were "seduced by [the] barbarities of their forefathers," a seduction that must actually have been textual but which Hurd's logic suggests should have taken place instead in flesh and blood (4). The problem, translated into the terminology of Hurd's "Discourse Concerning Poetical

Imitation," is that according to Hurd's account in the *Letters,* the genius of Spenser's age was radically different from the genius of the medieval era. This is to say that everything medieval in Spenser's poem is borrowed from elsewhere. Yet given Hurd's refusal to consider medieval texts as sources for Spenser, it also looks as if nothing in Spenser's poem is an intertextual parallel – a conclusion that precisely contradicts Hurd's own theory of imitation as stated in the "Discourse." It is Hurd's general suspicion of texts, I am suggesting, that causes him (for example) to regard Philip the Good's feast as the direct source of *The Faerie Queene*'s twelve-part structure, and in general to insist on a direct and extremely immediate relationship between the poem and the medieval world. On a practical level, of course, one might well argue that Hurd's improbable picture of a Spenser who does not necessarily read medieval texts is really the direct consequence of the critical method Hurd himself chose to pursue. Hurd's refusal to read or discuss medieval texts himself leads him to conceive of a Spenser who does not do those unpleasant things either.

Perhaps the most remarkable installment in what I am calling Hurd's assault on texts comes when Hurd has to address the delicate question of why all previous readers of *The Faerie Queene* had been so obtuse as to consider it a work of fiction. To meet this difficulty, Hurd importantly qualifies his argument about the poem's essentially gothic nature, which, as we have seen, he based on its gothic "subject" and its gothic "method." Hurd now went on to remark that *The Faerie Queene* was, in fact, gothic only in part (69–75). In one important respect the poem's method was also "classical," making it a text divided against itself, an unhappy hybrid. Hurd pointed the finger of blame at the figure of Arthur, a kind of *über*-knight who wanders through each of the books of *The Faerie Queene* that properly belong to other knights individually, and also at the moral allegory in which Arthur played a central part: Arthur possessed all of the twelve virtues that the other knights possessed individually, making him greater than the others and the perfect model of a knight.[23] According to Hurd, both Arthur and the allegory were clearly meant to create a mendacious kind of classical unity. They resulted from a misguided attempt to supplement the poem's multivocalic "gothic plan" with the literal-minded kind of unity derived from Aristotle. Spenser himself, Hurd hastened to point out, would not have fractured his poem in this way had he not felt forced to it: Spenser had been making an injudicious concession to the humanist "classic" tastes of his Elizabethan audience (70–71, 77).

The readers of Spenser's poem, not Spenser, are thus to blame for the text's imperfections – and moreover, these readers stand in a long and dishonorable line of obtuse, allegorical readers throughout history. In Hurd's Adam-like innocence of actual medieval literature, he seems to have assumed that allegory was not properly a literary form at all, in Spenser's time or any other. Allegory was instead a form of commentary, such as ancient commentators on Homer (and, he might have added, the Bible) had appended to a difficult older text in an attempt to counteract its alienness. As Hurd explained it, ancient allegories on Homer had been "principally designed to cover the monstrous stories of the *pagan Gods*" in an age when Homer's poems had come to seem morally and theologically barbarous (115). Renaissance allegorical commentary on Tasso and Ariosto had "served the lovers of Romance to palliate the no less monstrous stories of *magic and enchantments*" (ibid.). And Spenser, by a kind of profound category mistake, had inserted what was essentially an allegorical commentary into *The Faerie Queene* itself: he "gave an air of mystery to his subject, and pretended that his stories of knights and giants were but the cover to abundance of profound wisdom" (114). To Hurd, of course, this was a gross error on Spenser's part, since the whole value of Spenser's poem consisted just in its alienness, its real and uncompromising medievality.[24] *The Faerie Queene*'s hybridity is thus not only chronological and aesthetic, but also generic and even authorial: *The Faerie Queene* is both a poetic text and a clumsy commentary on that text, Spenser himself is both a poet and a somewhat desperate pedagogue.

Ultimately, Hurd's explanation of the error of all previous readers of Spenser rests on an unforgiving conception of the historical distance between the medieval era and Spenser, and for that matter between the medieval era and the eighteenth century. Much though Hurd deplored the putative aesthetic effects of the allegory and of Arthur, he also conceded that Spenser could hardly have done otherwise – and here Hurd hearkens back to the argument of the "Discourse Concerning Poetical Imitation," with its preoccupation with what can and cannot be thought in a given time and place. For Hurd, times had changed between the medieval era Spenser's poem represents and the humanist era which had to read it, so much so that Spenser's readers could scarcely believe in the reality of the events he depicted. They saw as wild imaginings the episodes that Hurd had revealed to be faithful historical recreations of medieval life. To them the medieval was, as history, unthinkable (109–11). Accordingly, Spenser had had to allegorize history as if it really were fiction: "the age would no longer bear the naked letter of these amusing stories" (113). I suggest that the historical distance Hurd values in the medieval era, the gap produced by its uncompromising and awesome otherness, is really the cavernous space that is left when Hurd has done away with all texts yet remains convinced that it is necessary to have direct contact with the past. On this account, even the material embodiment of *The Faerie Queene* as a printed book is an obstacle to the poem's establishing an absolute and absolutely satisfying measure of historical distance from its Elizabethan present. The audience called into being by this book is an agent of aesthetic pollution, insofar as it is solely for the audience's benefit that Spenser introduced the despised moral allegory; publication is a kind of descent of the poem into readership, a descent so terrible as to deform the poem itself by anticipation. Spenser's text would have been perfect only if it had been utterly unreadable to his Elizabethan contemporaries.

It might still be possible to argue that Hurd stumbled fortuitously into this telescoping series of paradoxes, that the gaps in his argument stem purely from his scholarly amateurism and perhaps a lack of connection between the far-flung layers of his thought. But one detail shows that this cannot be so. Hurd's splitting of *The Faerie Queene* into a "gothic" text and a "classic" text rested, as we have seen, on the claim that the poem's moral allegory was not authentically gothic (that is, medieval). Given Hurd's unfamiliarity with medieval texts, we might assume that this was a simple, if large, oversight on his part – until we notice that Hurd's faithful companion Ste.-Palaye straightforwardly contradicted him, in a passage Hurd could not have helped but read. In his description of the Burgundian feast which Hurd triumphantly identified as the real model for Spenser's twelve-part narrative, Ste.-Palaye had clearly reported that the twelve knights in the pageant were each accompanied by a lady named for one of the twelve knightly virtues: faith, charity, justice, reason, prudence, temperance, strength, veracity, generosity, diligence, hope and excellency. These virtues together, said Ste.-Palaye, "constituted the true and perfect knight."[25] Hurd can hardly have missed the similarity of these virtues to the allegorical virtues of Spenser's own twelve knights and Spenser's perfect knight Arthur, although Hurd himself said not a word about the virtues in the Burgundian pageant.[26] Had he acknowledged that a moral allegory of twelve virtues was eminently thinkable for real medieval knights, or at least for real medieval chroniclers describing their activities, Hurd's stark divide between Spenser's humanist readers and Spenser's gothic text would have crumbled into a picturesque and melancholy ruin. For the sake of his argument, that is, Hurd suppressed the same medieval past which, according to him, he was the first to recuperate as the true content of Spenser's text.

I have argued that Hurd's chain of paradoxes exemplifies a mode of realist reading deeply marked by the vestiges of what Michael McKeon calls "extreme skepticism." On the one hand, Hurd insists that *The Faerie*

Queene is valuable insofar as it is a reflection of the medieval world; his account of the poem's gothic "method" in particular suggests that texts can be connected in a deep and indeed overdetermined way to the real world which is the ultimate source of meaning. On the other hand, this apparent privileging of the historical text turns out to be quite evanescent. The skepticism that initially led Hurd to reject the method of intertextual parallels becomes a near nihilism that leaves no text unaffected, as Hurd rejects any notion of Spenser as a reader and even rejects *The Faerie Queene* insofar as the poem was designed to be read. Without detracting from the perverse specificity of Hurd's argument, I think we can identify some important precedents for this repeated gesture of negation – precedents that come not from mid-eighteenth-century discourse about the novel or from what is generally thought of as literary criticism at all, but rather from the ecclesiastical and philological milieu in which Hurd had been trained as a clergyman. Hurd's intellectual mentor William Warburton comes to the fore most obviously. Like Hurd, Warburton was a clerical critic of sacred, classical and English texts, and he made it his life's work to undertake only the most difficult and paradoxical arguments about a dizzying range of subjects – A.W. Evans' biography remains the most comprehensive account of Warburton's writings as well as the fear and loathing they aroused in many of his contemporaries.[27] Particularly relevant to the *Letters on Chivalry* is Warburton's virtuosic account of the Egyptian hieroglyphs, which, following Isaac Newton, Warburton denuded of all the mystical and theological significance that the sixteenth and seventeenth centuries had eagerly ascribed to them: for Warburton, the hieroglyphs had been invented by scribes and merchants for the speedy documentation of commerce and court business.[28] This almost comic reduction of the mysterious to the pedestrian certainly anticipates Hurd's deflation of *The Faerie Queene*, and Warburton's text had its own precedents reaching back into the seventeenth century. An earlier generation of clerics, for the most part much more obscure now than Hurd and Warburton, had vigorously applied themselves to the debunking of ancient texts that had previously been taken, at least by some, as historical, authoritative, and therefore privileged. In 1679 Isaac Vossius systematically argued against the authenticity of the ancient Sibylline oracles, which were supposed to have prophesied the coming of Christ; in 1680, Henry Dodwell argued that the *Phoenician History* attributed to one Sanchuniathon and thought to corroborate the narrative of the Old Testament was not actually by Sanchuniathon; in 1685 Humphrey Hody argued that the Letter of Aristeas, which was widely taken to guarantee the reliability of the ancient Septuagint translation of the Old Testament, was not actually by Aristeas; and in 1697 Richard Bentley argued that the letters of Phalaris, once widely used as a school text and recently celebrated for their manly literary merits by William Temple, were not actually by Phalaris.[29] None of these writers, of course, was a consistent skeptic in epistemological terms – on the contrary, they assumed that the great majority of ancient texts constituted straightforward reports on the ancient world and could thus be used to exclude the few texts in question from any claim to legitimacy. By concentrating their negativity on isolated texts, the seventeenth-century revisionists managed to have their skeptical cake and eat it too, a kind of double act that I suggest recurs in Warburton and Hurd, who had both certainly read these predecessors' work.

At the same time, there are telling differences. Where Bentley and his seventeenth-century colleagues specialized in claiming that a supposedly very old text was only somewhat old, Hurd's temporal reinterpretation worked in the other direction, as he claimed that Spenser's poem was for the most part not Elizabethan but medieval. And where the seventeenth-century clerics unsettled their contemporaries by exposing apparently historical texts as fictions, Hurd sought to raise eyebrows by exposing an apparently fantastic text as historical. In these respects Hurd's negativity is the reversal of a reversal, an adaptation of the seventeenth-century polyhistors' methods to a vernacular sphere and a changed theoretical climate. The striking point remains that Hurd's assault on texts in general was made available to him by previous generations of English clerical philologists, writers it would probably be more conventional to think of as the guardians of received texts. Hurd's aggressive reinterpretation of Spenser and the medieval, like Spenser's own poem according to Hurd, therefore operates in at least two worlds, speaking in part to readers who no longer existed.[30]

NOTES

1. *Letters on Chivalry and Romance* (London, 1762), rpt. with an introduction by Hoyt Trowbridge as *Augustan Reprint Society Publications* (Los Angeles: Clark Memorial Library, 1963), 101–2; subsequent references to the *Letters* will be given in parentheses in the text. See John M. Ganim, "The Myth of Medieval Romance," in *Medievalism and the Modern Temper*, ed. R. Howard Bloch and Stephen G. Nichols (Baltimore: Johns Hopkins University Press, 1996), 148–66, esp. 149–51; David R. Carlson, "Historicism and the *In medium sordes* of Hurd's *Letters on Chivalry and Romance*," *Exemplaria* 3 (1991), 95–108; Stephan Kohl, "Ruinen und Textfragmente: Mittelalterrezeption im England des 18. Jahrhunderts," in *Mittelalter-Rezeption IV. Medien, Politik, Ideologie, Ökonomie*, ed. Irene von Burg *et al.* (Göppingen: Kümmerle, 1991), 295–310; and Donald G. Marshall, "The History of Eighteenth-century Criticism and Modern Hermeneutical Philosophy: The Example of Richard Hurd," *The Eighteenth Century: Theory and Interpretation* 21 (1980),

198–211; see also Arthur Johnston, *Enchanted Ground: The Study of Medieval Romance in the Eighteenth Century* (London: Athlone, 1964) and Kenneth Clark, *The Gothic Revival: An Essay in the History of Taste* (London: Constable, 1950).

After this article was accepted for publication, I learned of the valuable new discussion of Hurd in Jonathan Brody Kramnick's *Making the English Canon: Print-Capitalism and the Cultural Past, 1700–1770* (Cambridge: Cambridge University Press, 1998). I agree with Kramnick on several important points – for example, the centrality of *The Faerie Queene* in Hurd's *Letters* and the general relevance of Hurd's doctrines about imitation – although the general direction of my argument is different.

2. Discussion in Carlson, "Historicism," 99–101.

3. In addition to David C. Douglas, *English Scholars: 1660–1730* (London: Eyre & Spottiswoode, 1951), see Richard L. Harris's introduction to *A Chorus of Grammars: The Correspondence of George Hickes and His Collaborators on the 'Thesaurus linguarum septentrionalium'*, ed. Harris (Toronto: Pontifical Institute, 1992), 3–146; Richard Morton, "Elizabeth Elstob's *Rudiments of Grammar* (1715): Germanic Philology for Women," *Studies in Eighteenth Century Culture* 20 (1990), 267–87, David Fairer, "The Formation of Warton's *History*," in *Thomas Warton's History of English Poetry*, 4 vols. (1774; rpt., London: Routledge/Thoemmes, 1998), 1:1–70; and Bertram H. Davis, *Thomas Percy: A Scholar-Cleric in the Age of Johnson* (Philadelphia: University of Pennsylvania Press, 1989).

4. Pierre Macherey, *A Theory of Literary Production*, trans. Geoffrey Wall (London: Routledge & Kegan Paul, 1966), 132.

5. Michael McKeon, *The Origins of the English Novel 1600–1740* (Baltimore: Johns Hopkins University Press, 1987), esp. 1–128.

6. Ibid., 118–23.

7. Margaret Doody, *The True Story of the English Novel* (1996; London: Fontana-Harper Collins, 1998), 292–3.

8. Broadly speaking, this approach is common to Carlson, "Historicism," Marshall, "The History of Eighteenth-century Criticism," Ganim, "The Myth of Medieval Romance," and Kohl, "Ruinen und Textfragmente."

9. Johnston, *Enchanted Ground*, 60–74.

10. Richard C. Frushell, *Edmund Spenser in the Early Eighteenth Century: Education, Imitation, and the Making of a Literary Model* (Pittsburgh: Duquesne University Press, 1999) valuably discusses Hurd's theory of imitation (133–4) but does not draw out the implications I argue for here in his discussion of Hurd on Spenser (147–9); see also David Hall Radcliffe, *Spenser: A Reception History* (Columbia, SC: Camden House, 1996) and Jewel Wurtsbaugh, *Two Centuries of Spenserian Scholarship (1609–1805)* (Baltimore: Johns Hopkins University Press, 1936).

11. Terry Eagleton, *Literary Theory: An Introduction* (Oxford: Blackwell, 1983), 205.

12. John Jortin, *Remarks on Spenser's Poems* (London, 1734).

13. Thomas Warton, *Observations on the Faerie Queene of Spenser* (London, 1754); on English romances, 13–37.

14. Ibid., 14.

15. See, for example, Howard Weinbrot, *Britannia's Issue: The Rise of British Literature from Ossian to Dryden* (Cambridge: Cambridge University Press, 1993).

16. "Discourse Concerning Poetical Imitation," in *Q. Horatii Flacci Epistola ad Augustum*, ed. Hurd (London, 1751), 107–207.

17. Hurd was not the first to use the term; its earlier history is discussed by Erich Hassinger, *Empirisch-rationaler Historismus. Seine Ausbildung in der Literatur Westeuropas von Guicciardini bis Saint-Evremond* (Bern and Munich: Francke, 1978).

18. Hurd, *A Letter to Mr. Mason; on the Marks of Imitation* (London, 1757).

19. Lionel Gossman, *Medievalism and the Ideologies of the Enlightenment: The World and Work of La Curne de Sainte-Palaye* (Baltimore: Johns Hopkins University Press, 1968), 281–2, 285–6.

20. See Radcliffe, *Spenser*, and R.M. Cummings (ed.), *Spenser: The Critical Heritage* (London: Routledge & Kegan Paul, 1971).
21. Gyorgy Lukacs, *The Historical Novel*, trans. Hannah and Stanley Mitchell (London: Merlin, 1962).
22. Jean-Baptiste de la Curne de Sainte-Palaye, "Troisième Mémoire sur l'ancienne chevalerie, Considérée comme un établissement politique & militaire," *Mémoires de littérature, tirés des registres de l'Académie Royale des Inscriptions et Belles-lettres,* 20 (1753), 635–59 at 636–41. The "Troisième Mémoire" was the third of five which Ste.-Palaye published in this volume of the *Mémoires de littérature*; all five were reprinted with additional essays in Ste.-Palaye's *Mémoires sur l'ancienne chevalerie: Considerée comme un établissement politique & militaire,* 2 vols. (Paris, 1759), of which a third volume appeared in 1781. Hurd did not cite Ste.-Palaye for this particular point, although Hurd had already acknowledged a general indebtedness to him (24–5).
23. This was Spenser's own explanation of Arthur's place in the allegory, which Hurd accepted. See *Letters* 73–4 and *The Faerie Queene,* ed. Thomas P. Roche, Jr. (Harmondsworth: Penguin, 1978), "A Letter of the Authors," 15–16.
24. This point is eloquently underscored by Ganim, "The Myth of Medieval Romance," 149–51.
25. Ste.-Palaye, "Troisième Mémoire," 640: "La conclusion des voeux fut célébrée par un nouveau spectacle. Une Dame vêtue de blanc en habit de religieuse & portant sur son épaule un rouleau dans lequel étoit écrit en lettres d'or Grace-Dieu, vint remercier l'assemblée, & présenter douze Dames conduites par autant de Chevaliers. Ces Dames qui figuroient différentes vertus, dont chacune portoit son nom sur l'épaule dans un billet ou brevet, devoient être les compagnes du voyage pour en assurer le succès. Elles passèrent successivement en revûe, & présentèrent l'une après l'autre leur brevet à Grace-Dieu qui en faisoit lecture, & récitoit à chaque fois un couplet de huit vers. Il n'est point hors de propos de les nommer ici, pour faire encore mieux connoître *quelles vertus constituoient le véritable & parfait Chevalier: foi, charité, justice, raison, prudence, tempérance, force, vérité, largesse, diligence, espérance & vaillance étoient leurs noms*; & toutes enfin commencèrent à danser en guise de mommeries & à faire bonne chère, pour remplir & rachever plus joyeusement la fête." (Emphasis added.)
26. Spenser's stated plan was to write a book for each of "the twelue priuate morall vertues, as Aristotle hath deuised" ("A Letter of the Authors," 15). It is not clear what these were all meant to be; the six complete books and seventh unfinished book treat the virtues of holiness, temperance, chastity, friendship, justice, courtesy and constancy. Discussions are in *The Works of Edmund Spenser: A Variorum Edition,* ed. Edwin Greenlaw *et al.,* 10 vols. (Baltimore: Johns Hopkins University Press, 1932–57), 1:327–30, 341–3, 353–7, and 361–2, and a new source (Francesco Piccolomini's *Universa philosophia de moribus* of 1583) is suggested by John Erskine Hankins, *Source and Meaning in Spenser's Allegory* (Oxford: Clarendon, 1971), 2–5.
27. See Evans, *Warburton and the Warburtonians: A Study of Some Eighteenth-Century Controversies* (London: Oxford University Press, 1932).
28. William Warburton, *The Divine Legation of Moses Demonstrated,* 2 vols. (London, 1738–41), 2:17–357; discussion in Madeleine V.-David, *Le débat sur les écritures et l'hiéroglyphe aux XVIIe et XVIIIe siècles et l'application de la notion de dechiffrement aux écritures mortes* (Paris: SEVPEN, 1965), 93–103; Jacques Derrida, "Scribble (Writing/Power)," trans. Cary Plotkin, *Yale French Studies* 58 (1979), 116–47, and Erik Iversen, *The Myth of Egypt and Its Hieroglyphs in European Tradition* (Princeton: Princeton University Press, 1993), 103–105.
29. Vossius, *De Sibyllinis aliisque quae Christi natalem praecessere Oraculis* (Oxford, 1679); Dodwell, "A Discourse on Sanchuniathon," printed with Dodwell's *Two Letters of Advice* (London, 1680); Hody, *Contra historiam Aristeae de LXX interpretibus dissertatio* (Oxford, 1685); Bentley, *A Dissertation upon the Epistles of Phalaris,* 2nd edn. (London, 1699). Discussion of Bentley is in Joseph M. Levine, *The Battle of the Books: History and*

Literature in the Augustan Age (Ithaca: Cornell University Press, 1991) and Anthony Grafton, *Forgers and Critics: Creativity and Duplicity in Western Scholarship* (Princeton: Princeton University Press, 1990), 72–4.

30. I am very grateful to Thomas P. Roche, Jr., Hans Aarsleff, Anthony Grafton, Jonathan Lamb, and Richard Serjeantson for their comments on earlier versions of this article.

Waging Battle:
Ashford v. Thornton, Ivanhoe,
and Legal Violence

MARK SCHOENFIELD

In 1774, Parliament contemplated a response to the destruction of tea in Boston harbor. The "Bill for the Administration of Justice in Massachusetts's Bay" included a clause depriving the colonies of the civil Appeal of Murder, and its response, the Wager of Battle.[1] The debate proceeded on the assumption that to abolish these as American liberties, which permitted an individual to treat criminal acts as private wrongs, presaged their dissolution throughout Great Britain. Mr. Dunning rose "to support that great pillar of the constitution, the Appeal of Murder." Noting that the Appeal "has been called and treated as a remnant of barbarism and Gothicism," he continues, "The whole of our Constitution, for aught I know, is Gothic."[2] The arguments pitted objections to the Appeal – that it constituted double jeopardy, its methods were barbarous, it trumped a jury, and interfered with the Crown's prerogatives to administer justice and to regulate violence – against the desire to authorize modern criminal procedure through continuities with ancient customs and rights. The symbolic work of the Appeal and the virtually disused Wager was maintained despite their absurdity in light of contemporary standards of adjudication, and the measure was withdrawn.

The Appeal of Murder functions as part of a system that William Blackstone, characterizing English law, imagined as a "Gothic castle erected in the days of chivalry, but fitted up for the modern inhabitant"; Blackstone extends this metaphor with details of "moted ramparts" and "inferior apartments" that, though "cheerful and commodious," have "approaches" that "may be winding and difficult."[3] In this metaphor, Blackstone replaces a historical antagonism with an image of harmony, a rhetorical trope that anticipates a displacement Jerome McGann has identified as characteristic of conservative romantic ideology.[4] For the law of chivalry, truth (of guilt, of debt, of social status) emerged through such rituals of the body as trial by ordeal or battle and torture, and was confirmed by bodily punishments: death, evisceration, burning and branding. For the modernizing eighteenth-century legal system, by contrast, the production of truth relied on popular representations of criminal trials as linguistic scenes that highlighted verbal evidence, the rudiments of expert testimony, the proffering of alibis based on new forensic technologies, and the greatly expanded role of lawyers. The heteroglossic structure of the English legal system registered these diverse historical pressures that both signaled the desire of the law to function as a single integrated system and prevented such integration because it depended upon the historical differentiations it sought to eradicate. Thus, a criminal trial ending with the judge's ritualistic admonitions about reasonable doubt in his address to the jury began with the ancient claim in the indictment that the defendant was possessed by the devil.

The residual presence of chivalry within modern law reflected contradictory epistemologies which various legal theorists attempted to mediate. Having pointed out in the 1774 debate that the *law* of chivalry, encoded on the Appeal and Wager, was "superstitious and barbarous to the last degree" (quoted in Kendall, 298), Edmund Burke, in *Reflections on the Revolution in France*, transmuted chivalry into a mode of manners that stands guard against the encroachment of "sophisters, oeconomists, and calculators."[5] This symbolic rhetoric continued until 1817, when the death of Mary Ashford forced England to acknowledge that legal chivalry persisted as a vital portion of the contemporary law, and that the violence of its methods were inextricable from the symbolic work of social cohesion that the 1774 Parliament, Burke, and Blackstone had assigned it. After Ashford's drowned body was discovered, two distinct and contradictory legal actions – a trial by indictment and an Appeal of Murder – were lodged against Abraham Thornton, who, having been seen the previous night dancing with her at a country dance and then accompanying her home, was suspected of her murder. The legal incoherence of these events compelled a wide range of responses, including wide press coverage, several hastily-written dramas, and Walter Scott's *Ivanhoe*.[6] These responses, intervening in on-going debates about the role of the juror and the lawyer as figures and bearers of rationality, exposed the trace of chivalric, superstitious practices that depended upon the legibility of gendered bodies.

I

On 9 August 1817, the *London Times* reported the trial of Abraham Thornton for the murder and rape of Mary Ashford.[7] In the first paragraph, *The Times* notes the public curiosity to see the trial of the "builder and bricklayer" whose "excessive corpulency has swollen his whole figure into a size that rather approaches to deformity. His face is swoln and shining, his neck very short and very thick, but his limbs are well-proportioned." After recounting the testimony and summarizing the judge's instructions, *The Times* announces that after the twelve-hour trial, "The jury in 5 minutes returned a verdict of – *Not guilty*."[8] *The Times* adds that "it came out incidentally during the trial, that the human form was not capable of being molded into finer symmetry than distinguished the person of Mary Ashford," and that the "court, though the ladies were necessarily excluded, was crowded to excess throughout the day." In this supplement, the idealization of Mary Ashford is echoed through the idealization of the absent women as "ladies," while the excess of the male crowd finds its counterpart in Thornton's excess flesh. In part, the sensation of the trial stemmed from the gender politics that it absorbed from the controversies surrounding the corpulent Regent and the Princess of Wales, and the crisis of the stability of status law provoked by their conduct.[9] At the same time, issues of the reliability of testimony, the standards of evidence, and the concept of reasonable doubt drew the trial into the wider debate on legal modernization. The verdict measured circumstantial forensic evidence (especially footprints, possibly trampled by investigators and marred by rain, that indicated a struggle) against Thornton's alibi corroborated by reported sightings of him (that were complicated by the notorious inaccuracy of country clocks).[10] Of particular significance for Thornton's credibility was whether Thornton acknowledged (consensual) sexual relations with Ashford before or after her blood was discovered on him. Put another way, had he spoken before Ashford's blood "testified"? Although witnesses varied in their account, the judge, in his address to the jury, asserted it proven that his admission was prior. These two aspects of the public's interest – gender and evidence – are coordinated by the shift in criminal law from the body as the locus of truth to an evidentiary system of rational procedures to establish empirical truth. These new procedures, however, could not evade the historical entrenchment in the legal system of a complex matrix of signifiers, symbols and ritualistic procedures that emerged from assumptions about the legible body. The discourse of forensic autopsies produced a newly readable body that was comparable, but not identical, to the medievalist body of truth.

Disputes about the brief time of the jury deliberations and the timing of the murder (in relation to Thornton's alibi) combined to render the trial as a repetition, not resolution, of the crime; for at least one commentator, Thornton's acquittal impugned Ashford's honor just as Thornton himself had assailed it.[11] As suggested by the double sense of "honor" (and "innocence" elsewhere), referring to both an attitude and bodily condition, an alleged rape and murder proved salient in exposing the diachronic and incoherent structure of legal truth-seeking procedures. *The Times* asserted, "such is the unrelieved sense of horror and indignation of the crime which *has been committed by some one*; and which rests, like an oppressive cloud, on the unappeased sense of public justice." This claim of the certainty of a crime depended on blood as a clear signifier of criminality; the prosecutor stated, "from that spot [where a large quantity of coagulated blood was discovered], the blood was distinctly traced for a considerable space on the grass." Although in the prosecution's case, the blood is used to trace the movement of Ashford's body, in the newspaper accounts, its presence on the ground and on her dress were offered as unequivocal evidence of violence. This inference, however, required the suppression of the coroner's account which pointed out that Ashford was menstruating at the time of her death and that, as she was a virgin (a point averred as indubitable), "there might have been lacerations though the intercourse had taken place by consent...The exercise of dancing was likely to have accelerated the *menses*" (Hall, 98). Misrepresenting the account of Ashford's body in the process of idealizing her, *The Times* obscured the multiple signifying functions of blood, which pointed not only to criminality but also of womanhood. Such multiplicity, however, registers the complexity of transforming events into testimony and testimony into resolution in the presence of symbolic overtones.

In a subsequent edition, *The Times* reported (quoting the *Lichfield Paper*), that the acquittal "has excited the most undisguised feelings of disappointment in all classes of people, from one end of the country to another" ("Law Reports" 15 August 1817, 3 e). One theatrical intervention, George Ludlam's Birmingham play, *The Mysterious Murder, Or, What's the Clock, Founded on a Tale too True* (1817), challenged the alibi and introduces Maria (Ashford's representation in the play) as a model of virtue. In her opening remark, she notes "I've been as good as my promise" (5); her comment, reflecting the suspicion that Thornton's witnesses had perjured themselves, invokes the problem of validating oaths. Ultimately, in the play, only Maria's body and its resurrection in the ending guarantees the reliability (or falsehood) of testimony under oath. In the *Birmingham Commercial Herald*, "A Friend to Justice" asserted the accuracy of Thornton's alibi, and suggested that Mary Ashford, rather than being the angelic figure other representations had proposed, had consented to her own seduction (Thornton's position at his interrogation) and then committed suicide in despair.[12] The Reverend Luke Booker, in *A Moral Review*, challenged the claim of the "Friend to Justice" in order "to rescue the Name of the ill-fated Woman whose Memory he traduces, from calumny and reproach." Persisting in seeing this case as a measure of modern masculinity, Booker insists that "to depreciate Virtue, – that Virtue which preferred Martyrdom to pollution, is unmanly" (2–3).

Pressured by public opinion and perhaps convinced by his sense of honor (or desire for a monetary settlement), William Ashford, Mary's sibling and heir, availed himself of the right of an Appeal of Murder, a legal strategy to retry Thornton under a civil rubric and bring him before what Ashford's legal team hoped would be a more sympathetic jury. Instead, Abraham Thornton, in answering Ashford's formal accusation of his sister's murder, "pleaded as follows: 'Not guilty; and I am ready to defend the same by my body.' And thereupon taking his glove off, he threw it upon the floor of the Court."[13] This action initiated a Wager of Battle in the form proscribed by chivalric law, more familiar to the audience as a scene of medieval history or a fictional rendering. *Ashford v. Thornton*, tried before Lord Ellenborough in 1817 and in the presence of over 70 lawyers, disclosed in a moment of drama that rippled through the literary and legal worlds, the violent underpinnings of a legal system that prided itself on refinement and civilization and increasingly relied on a convincing representation in the public arena of the civility. Richard Rush, the Minister from America, recorded that, "It was a mode of trial for dark ages...In the highest tribunal of the most enlightened country in Europe, I was listening to a discussion whether or not this mode of trial was in force in the nineteenth century! It was difficult to persuade myself of the reality of the scene."[14] The discussion itself rendered the anachronism visible since it proceeded in the hyper-courtroom in which "space behind the bar was literally choked with Barristers"[15] and reinforced the surreal effect Rush noted.

The fallen glove becomes a tableau for contemporary journalism to mark the "universal surprise" of the moment – a surprise, however, plausibly regarded as a rhetorical commentary on the status of law, since in 1815, in a publicized case, "a murderer, named Clancy, had escaped similarly by an unexpected offer of battle."[16] Manchester and London newspaper reports as well as *The Gentleman's Magazine's* account focused on the glove:

> During this interlocution [a lengthy debate about a continuance], the appellee's glove was permitted to remain on the floor at the feet of the appellor, who did not take it up. Mr. Reader [Thornton's attorney] observed, that it ought to remain in the custody of the Court, and it was handed by the officer to the Master. (*Times* 18 November 1817, 3 e)[17]

The glove becomes an unassimilated signifier, a marker of an obsolete practice of violence which remained the invisible horizon for the common practices of criminal trials. Because of the topical organization of *The Times* and *Gentleman's Magazine*, reports of this case were framed by accounts of other murders and executions, by exclamations of repulsion and fascination with both violence and its violent punishment. As a vestige of private revenge law, the hurled gauntlet and accompanying spontaneous yet ritualistic words – "I am ready to defend the same by [or 'upon'] my body" – had literary representation as an honest expression of outrage in

Shakespeare, various eighteenth-century epics, and Scott's earlier poetry. Such a fiction, however, could not be sustained, since reports of the trial disclosed the challenge as a calculated legal maneuver developed in the eleven days between William Ashford's formal accusation and Thornton's response, a delay granted because Reader, only recently apprised of the proceeding, told the court he was not ready to advise his client on how to plead. Although technically performed without benefit of counsel, this Wager manifests the lawyers' constant orchestration, including Thornton's being handed gloves to put on just before removing one to throw down. His gauntlets had been designed for the occasion, unlike the gages of chivalric knights that presumably formed a part of their armor and dress.[18] Rather than speaking the prescribed words, Thornton reads them ("rather inaudibly," *The Times* reports) from a paper handed to him by Mr. Reader, and a discussion ensues about whether that constitutes the required oral challenge. The glove, rather than falling dramatically to the ground, as it seems to in the *Gentleman's Magazine* version, takes an ineptly comic route according to the *Times*: "In falling, it struck the head of the appellor, William Ashford." Further, the seamless ceremony of the Wager that signified and enacted the cohesive knowledge of an authorized chivalric class was here marked by continual interruption and confusion. With each act by either Appellor or Appellee, the other side must request a delay to choose the appropriate response, so that the case spills over into the next term, and is itself interrupted by other pressing court business. The naming of the parties gets confused:

> Mr. Clarke: You should say that you appear for the *appellee*, not for the *defendant*.
>
> Mr. Reader: I am informed, my Lord, that I ought to have called my client the appellee; – perhaps so, I might be mistaken; but I do not apprehend that it is a point of much importance to the issue. (*Times,* 24 November 1817, 3 e; the mistake was repeated by Justice Bailey on 20 April 1818 and by *The Times* in indirect quotation.)

The confusion between the terms, and Reader's emphasis on their similarity, reminds the court that the appeal is a second trial, and raises the specter of double jeopardy, a legality which could not be explicitly alleged but probably contributed to the court's construing discretionary matters in Thornton's favor. Throughout the trial, Thornton's lawyers maneuver to discuss the first trial, even peripherally, at many opportunities, and Ashford's lawyers insist upon its irrelevance. Thus, within the trial, the court's own uneasiness with judicial history becomes part of the legal strategies. Even Lord Ellenborough found it difficult to remember what kind of trial this was; on 29 January 1818, "Lord Ellenborough was about to consult with Mr. Barlow, on the Crown side, when his Lordship corrected himself, and observed that this case was on the civil side of the Court."[19]

Mr. Clarke, appearing for Ashford, argued that the Wager of Battle was "an obsolete practice, and it may be considered a very extra-ordinary and astonishing circumstance, that a person charged with the crime of murder should be permitted to repel the charge by committing another murder"; Lord Ellenborough interposed here, wishing "to correct an expression you have used; you say, 'by committing another murder'; if it be the law, what the law authorizes is not murder" (*Times*, 18 November 1817, 3 e). Clarke's initial statement implies that "murder" exists as a category of natural law, definable with reference to the act alone; Ellenborough, whose efforts in criminal sedition and libel suits exert the court's definitional powers throughout his career, insists that "murder" is a legal category that cannot be adjudicated outside the constraints of the legal system. Further, Ellenborough's comment reminds the crowded court of the law's right to authorize violence.

Two specific debates indicate the delicate balance between medievalist sensibilities and modernist reforms that *Ashford v. Thornton* disrupted. In 1815, a bill was introduced into Commons to abolish the pillory as a punishment. In ancient law, the pillory served as a communal locus by which state authority could be confirmed by the populace; Blackstone had suggested that the actual punishment was not the pillory itself, but the shame associated with it, although such shame was materialized through brutal practices which included nailing ears to the pillory. The primary rationale for its abolition was the uncertainty of the severity of punishment that depended on crowds that might fatally stone criminals or might offer them umbrellas and refreshments; this confirmation of law was too unreliable as a ritual. The repeal was passed unanimously in Commons, and was greeted favorably in the Lords until Lord Eldon addressed the issue.[20] He insisted that the punishment was necessary for fraud and perjury, those crimes which, in themselves, amounted to a derailment of the legal system. In asserting the peculiar suitability of this punishment for perjury (and the violation of social oath that fraud implied), the Lord Chancellor acknowledged that the procedures of evidence required not only violence, but a violence in which the populous was engaged as a regulated simulacrum of the "mob" feared by him.[21] Lord Ellenborough, among others, concurred, and the result was that the bill was redesigned to consider a whole series of laws, and that, in its final form, the pillory remained for the crimes of fraud and perjury. As another example, dueling, the simulacrum of the Wager of Battle, held a curious liminal position; although dueling was clearly illegal, even juries regarded it as justified by the often improvable nature of a slander, for which the courts could not offer a proper remedy. Despite patent examples of its irrationality, dueling was offered as a necessary legal supplement that needed to be at once permissible and illegal. Not surprisingly, this contradiction found its harmonizing image in the honor of women and self, for which, in chivalric terms, dueling was defended.[22] Legal theorists viewed the shadow presence of both pillory and dueling not as medieval residuals that impeded modernization, but as necessary symbolic presences for achieving it.

II

Representations of Abraham Thornton's two trials and the role of rationality in jury trials are nestled within assumptions about the common law, primarily the supposition that the common law had developed as a discursive strategy for organizing disparate political power under a single rubric that, in all its variations, rehearses the same two signifying gestures of constructing the state as the regulator for violence and of the individual body as the site of that regulation. In particular, the revisions to which *Ashford v. Thornton* contributed enabled a shift from understanding the body as the locus of knowledge to a system of rationality by which truth was a discursive and professional product that could be applied to the body or other forms of property.

A key legal fiction for the revisionary practices in which Trial by Jury was consolidated as the core of English criminal law was the invention of the "reasonable man" as a standard for interpretation; he was at once the ideal reader of a contract, the ideal subject who made political representation possible through his collective similarity, the ideal husband into whom a wife – as *femme couverte* – could be gathered; in short, the ideal citizen. For the common criminal law, the task was to insert the figure of the reasonable man as a unifying strategy into a law that was disparate, contradictory, and riveted on the distinction between private and public wrongs. As a juror, this figure would – by the disciplining procedure of the court, the scrutiny of the press, and the peer pressure of his eleven comrades – act without reference to his own allegiances, even as vested interests, whether defendant, plaintiff or judge, would plead their position as the unbiased reasonable one. In the presentation of their cases, the lawyers, bolstered by the polite customs of the court, sought to model reasonability as an extension of civility; this civility, however, was rooted in the medieval forms of address that functioned to encode ritualistic power[23] and so threatened to expose the rationality as rhetorical convention.[24]

In public debate, the reliability of the jury method was linked to the consolidation of state power as well as to the freedom of the press and to various reform movements; it served to focus national pride and identity, as well as to extend the sense of individual autonomy and economic agency. Against the corruptions of government, radicals put their faith – rhetorically and actually, and with varying degrees of success – in jurors as embodying the true spirit of English liberty.[25] The signifying work of the jury trial was itself pressured in the public rejection of Thornton's acquittal and the public support of William Ashford's appeal, demonstrated by the hisses that *The Times* reported met Thornton's entrance and exit from the court. The *Gentleman's Magazine* had proclaimed in 1792 that often the "slender capacities" of juries "scarcely enable them to discriminate plaintiff from defendant" and proposed to limit the role to "gentlemen" who possessed "education, rank, and property" (December, 1792; 1194); although this argument explicitly concerned only education, its immediate correspondence with rank and property, following Burke's example in *Reflections*, indicates the more ideological concerns of the magazine. Meanwhile, Blackstone's truism of this "glory of English law," that liberty must survive "so long as this palladium remains sacred and inviolate" (4:343) was cited persistently in treatises and periodicals. Jeremy Bentham, believing juries largely incompetent, proposed a new institution of "quasi-jury," while Henry Brougham worked to increase the authority of the jury, in particular by giving them control over written evidence.[26] What unites the panegyrics and attacks on the jury system is that they were virtually unfounded.[27] Claims of illiteracy were rampant, yet unsubstantiated; charges of corruption circulated largely through fictional media; and claims for the accuracy of verdicts were incoherent, since no standard outside the verdict could adjudicate it except by rewriting the narratives of the crime. Therefore, the commotion about jury trials – in journals, novels, legal tracts, even poems – were expressions of, and interventions in, ideology.[28] The public perception of the hastiness of the verdict in Thornton's favor was likewise a result of the disapprobation about the jury's result, rather than the duration of the deliberation; their huddling in court for five or six minutes to reach their decision was typical: "Always, or nearly so, they gather round their foreman, and in about two or three minutes, return their verdict," Cottu reported in 1820.[29]

Consistent with his praise on the English jury, Blackstone asserted that English common law rejected torture as an appropriate form of truth-production; confession could not be extorted through pain. John Langbein points out that the "self-congratulatory writing" echoed by Blackstone was not only false but was produced by jurists such as Thomas Smith and Edward Coke who were themselves "designated in commissions to examine particular suspects under torture."[30] As with the fictional reconstruction of Saxon trial-by-jury, distinguishing English jurisprudence from French torture trumpeted English rationality. Langbein suggests that the relatively short history of English torture made such representations plausible. The erasure of this history, however, also underscores the extent to which proof remained a matter of the body, as torture or ordeal remained the horizon of criminal procedure, and abuses of prisoners could secure confessions or amount to punishment in advance of a sentence. While decrying torture, Blackstone recognizes Trial by Ordeal as a common-law process (4:336–40). Ordeal differs from torture in that no verbal confession is sought; rather, the body is charged to speak its truth. In this sense, Ordeal and Wager of Battle were similar practices that rendered confession unnecessary, and the distinction between them and torture concerned less how the body was physically manipulated than how it could be made to verify accusations.[31]

The emergence of the figure of the reasonable man from these layers of legal violence required two key postulates. The first was that, by the introduction of trial by jury and its accompanying rules of evidence, the law had replaced, not internalized, a system of violence. The second was that the law was an arbiter of the marketplace, not invested in any particular outcome. Such claims were asserted by scholars like Blackstone and Chambers and by such judges as Lord Mansfield and Lord Ellenborough, and opposed by a range of social critics. Bentham argued that a rhetoric of disinterest was used to mask the violent means by which the firm of "Judges & Co." acted as agents for aristocratic and mercantile class interests.[32] William Godwin, similarly, represented the economic and class interests of the courts as shaping judicial decisions through his characterization of the biasing effect of kinship between Forester and Falkland in *Caleb Williams*. *Ashford v. Thornton* became an occasion for the legal system to assert its "disinterest" even as it marked its horizon of violence.

Ludlam's play *What's the Clock* framed the trial by a subplot of the lawyers' corruption and a larger argument about the class bias. Rather than a bricklayer, Thornton becomes Abram Thorntree, the son of a wealthy property-owner. This shift allows the playwright to position the crime in terms of class dynamics, and at the moment when the rape is occurring, an otherwise irrelevant character is brought onto stage, a milkman. He declaims against those "born with silver spoons in their mouths! Or they would not have had ingenuity enough to have got iron ones to eat with, and must have been contented with wooden spoons like myself" (18–19); the off-stage action of private violation is presented through the critique of class. The play then replays Thornton's arrest, interweaving snippets from newspaper accounts with moments disparaging his character and reinforcing his wealth.

As the jury was popularly seen as a defender of liberties, especially those of the radical press, Ludlam would not suggest that the jury had erred. Instead, he invents Quibble, a lawyer desperate for fees, who pays perjurers to support his client's alibi. His financial straits comment on upper-class behavior, because his business is Criminal Conversation and with the current morality (as reflected in the regency), nobody bothers to sue over infidelity.[33] The lawyers, not the jury, are marked as the problem as the play blames the acquittal on the convergence of greedy lawyers and impoverished workers. The play then adds a scene in which *The Times*'s idealization of Mary is given dramatic shape. In a churchyard, five men and five women kneel before a monument inscribed to Maria Ashfield, whose "Prudence and Virtues, rendered her universally belov'd; yet by a monster in human form, fell a victim to Cruelty and Lust." The monument was erected "to perpetuate the fatal Effects of Inordinate Passions"; as the mourners sing two verses, Maria descends "in radiant clouds, a crown of gold on her head." This supplemental gesture offers the victim, Mary Ashford, as a stabilizing, transcendent signifier, pointing literally to heaven and to the divine justice invoked both by the play's preface and, just before the trial, by Thorntree's father. As a monument, she serves to admonish against passions and to discipline towards rationality as the converse of passion. The image of justice is, like the battered corpse of Ashford, resurrected in the name of the social. Luke Booker likewise proposed a monument for Ashford's actual grave, not to her prudence but as a warning against the imprudence of attending dances in an age when chivalry was dead and individual masculine desire was rampant and undisciplined; in his treatise, he invokes Ashford's aged grandfather as a relic of disciplined masculinity. For both the play and treatise, a memorialized Mary Ashford could contribute to – but also warn about the limits of – a more reasonable man.[34]

III

In 1819, Scott published *Ivanhoe* with, as Gary Dyer notes, the dedicatory epistle back-dated to 17 November 1817, the "date on which Thornton challenged his accuser" (Dyer, 389). Its Wager of Battle was cited by reviewers and Walter Scott's private correspondents as its dramatic high point, its most preposterous contrivance, and the extension of the other famous violent scenes, the tournament and the siege. Lady Louisa Stuart wrote Scott, in the midst of praise, that "the sudden death of Bois-Guilbert" is "too much a *make-shift*." Stuart proposes a broken blood vessel as an elegant solution, but it is precisely such straight-forward signifiers that Scott wishes to problematize.[35] Rebecca's trial for sorcery in *Ivanhoe* responds to the legal disruption caused by the resurrection of legally-authorized private combat in *Ashford*, Scott being fully aware of the controversy.[36] He writes to Lord Montagu: "Are you not delighted with the whim of Mr. Reader the lawyer who wrote so much about the trial by battle in the case of Thornton being to appear in the capacity of Royal Champion?" (*Letters,* VI 202).[37] This joke depends upon the representative functions of both champion and lawyer (both appear on behalf of another) and on the continuities between battle and argument as well as between legal and public representation (for which the jury served as master ideological emblem). Scott extends the jest by pointing to the double-jeopardy implicit in the Appeal of Murder, and the collision indicated by that doubleness between ancient and modern forms of criminal law: "It is but a hard case for any impugner of the title since should Reader fail to slay him in the lists he might try him afterwards for high treason." This witticism, reversing the order of challenges in *Ashford,* acknowledges the circular logic of legal status, since the accusation of high treason would depend on the confirmed status of Royal Champion in order to ensure a legitimate monarch against whom to offer treason. The office of Royal Champion persisted beyond the abolition of the Wager of Battle, which technically rendered it null. As such, however, the champion figures the interconnectedness of chivalric and modern law, since as early as Henry IV – who insisted he would fight in his own person – the Champion was only a "simulacrum" (Neilson, 332), and one Scott could admire; when he witnessed George IV's coronation, although generally disappointed, he thought that the Champion "looked and behaved extremely well" (quoted by Neilson, 332). Such anachronism in the political arena corresponded to Scott's commentary on chivalric law in terms of modern conceptions not just in the letter to Montagu, but in his representation of Wager of Battle in *Ivanhoe.*

In the chivalry that provides a mythic position from which romantic writers constructed both continuity and difference, violence was a central state action, undisguised and characteristic of legal proceedings. *Ashford v. Thornton* posed a threat to legal self-representation as having transcended its violent origins, and pressured legal apologists to defend the historically insupportable contention that Trial by Jury was a Saxon invention that had been temporarily replaced by the Norman wager of battle, but that its obvious superiority (a metonymy for Saxon cultural superiority) led inevitably to its resurrection. The court in *Ashford,* echoing both Hume and Blackstone, point out that the Wager of Battle was introduced by the French, while, in Blackstone's words, "the trial by jury [which 'seems to have been co-eval with the first civil government' of 'the earliest Saxon colonies'] ever has been, and I trust ever will be, looked upon as the glory of the English law" (III:379). Sharon Turner, however, attributing the jury trial to the Anglo-Saxons in his 1805 *History of the Anglo-Saxons,* acknowledges that "no record marks the date of its commencement," while Francis Palgrave reluctantly admits in his *Rise and Progress of English*

Commonwealth, that "the jury appears unknown until enacted by the Conqueror."[38] Although Blackstone and his proponents willfully elide earlier forms of oath-taking, compurgation, and trial by ordeal with the jury system that, developed under Norman rule, became formalized under Henry II, for the Court of *Ashford*, the relation between Trial by Jury and Wager of Battle was constructed from conflicting evidence as a distinction between the civilized, eternal and English and the barbaric, temporal and foreign.[39]

In a compromise between historical precision and ideal law, Walter Scott's representation of the Wager of Battle in *Ivanhoe* responded to the contemporary debate surrounding *Ashford* by suggesting that, although the law had not eliminated its violent horizon, it had sufficiently displaced it – and its various terms of heroism and chivalry – to allow for the law's disinterested contribution to bourgeois economic development. Nonetheless, for Scott, the transformation from Wager of Battle to Trial by Jury was a partial solution that could not expel prejudices nor regulate the haphazard signification of bodies, especially in the midst of contemporary physiognomy to which the narrator alludes throughout *Ivanhoe* to confirm his assessments of character. Scott asserts the outmodedness of the Wager, and signals its replacement by a system of evidence and rationality that produces commercial stability. The key weakness of the Wager, as Scott represents it, is viewing murder as a private wrong to be arbitrated by codes of revenge rather than as a public disturbance regulated by a law indifferent to particular individuals. Scott offers this shift as consonant with the rise of economic values that depends upon both the expulsion of Isaac and Rebecca and the death of Richard as threats to a new order figured by the quiet domesticity of Rowena and Ivanhoe. For Adam Smith, the imperfection of the Saxon compurgatory system (the procedure transmogrified in the public imagination to the jury trial) "is said to have given occasion to the practice of judicial combat" on the grounds that "nobles would be very highly displeased to be ousted of their rights by the oaths of mean persons, and at a time when perjury was the most common of all crimes."[40] Operating on assumptions about the economic necessity of class stability, Scott further argues that the sanctity of the King's law derives not from the body of the king, but from the necessities of the nation. Similarly, and by analogy, the rights of the individual are maintained not for his personal good, but for their contribution to the national good.

In a sequence that follows the structure of Thornton's trials, Rebecca endures two judicial inquisitions, the first advancing through the presentation of testimony and the second a Wager. Scott emphasizes the continuities of these moments, and particularly interweaves into the testimony, assumptions about the truth of the body on which the Wager ideologically depended. In the evidentiary trial before the Grand Master,

Rebecca's body is central to the interpretation of the evidence:

> Less than half of his weighty evidence would have been sufficient to convict any old woman, poor and ugly, even though she had not been a Jewess. United with that fatal circumstance, the body of proof was too weighty for Rebecca's youth, though combined with the most exquisite beauty. (422)[41]

The image of "weight" is literalized when a soldier, testifying that she "made certain signs upon the wound," draws from his pouch (in parody of Rebecca's extraction) the "very bolt-head which, according to his story, had been miraculously extracted from the wound; and as the iron weighed a full ounce, it completely confirmed the tale, no matter how marvelous" (421). Scott's complex blending of pseudo-forensic and verbal testimony emphasizes that the evidence is interpreted through pre-conceptions, not only of the Grand Master who has "determined the sentence before-hand" (407) but of the arrayed audience caught under the spell of the ceremony and operating within the terms of chivalry. When Rebecca unveils her face, in a scene that echoes the series of near-rapes that structure her experience of England, "The younger knights told each other with their eyes that Brian's best apology was in the power of her real charms, rather than of her imaginary witchcraft" (420). The status of the feminine within the chivalric code operates to make "beauty" compelling, thereby at once validating passions and providing a jurisprudence of their regulation; crucially, however, for the homosocial knighthood, Bois-Guilbert's harassment of Rebecca finds its excuse in the same body which the Grand Master proposes to purify through burning.[42]

Describing the court, *Ivanhoe*'s narrator moves down the hierarchy from the "Grand Master" to "inferior persons" connected with the order, to "peasants from the neighboring country" who were admitted because "the pride of Beaumanoir" was "to render the edifying spectacle of the justice he administered as public as possible" (411). He focuses the spectacle on himself, as he joins in the opening psalm "with a deep mellow voice, which age had not deprived of its power." The Templars recognize the signifying work that the display accomplishes, and the repetitions of the Grand Master's name allows Scott to conjure, with irony, another Beaumanoir. As A.N. Wilson indicates, the name is "fictitious" and Scott would have known that the historical Grand Master was either Robert de Sable or Guilbert Horal (*Ivanhoe*, 579). Yet as Henry Lea points out, Philippe de Beaumanoir's legal treatise, written in 1283, encapsulates French jurisprudence and "is peculiarly interesting as a landmark in the struggle between the waning power of feudalism and the Roman theories which gave intensity of purpose to the enlightened centralization."[43] Beaumanoir had championed St. Louis's efforts to abolish the Wager of Battle, and to substitute alternative legal processes. Further, his name puns on *"maner,"* [also spelled *mainour* in *Ashford*] a term on which the right to wage battle turned. At issue is whether proofs of Thornton's guilt were adequate to oust his right of battle; Mr. Chitty, for the appellor, argues that to be "taken with the *maner,*" that is, caught in the act, is sufficient, and that the strong circumstantial evidence amounted to equivalent proof. The court rejects this argument as reflecting popular prejudice and not good pleading,[44] just as the narrative of *Ivanhoe* insists on its readers' rejection of Beaumanoir's "ascetic bigot[ry]," readable in both his habits and "physiognomy" (391). This bigotry secures his certainty about the guilt of Rebecca and is also generalized into a pervasive attitude about medieval customs by Bois-Guilbert's comment on first hearing the charge against Rebecca: "Will future ages believe that such stupid bigotry ever existed?" (405). As *Ashford* showed, the answer is yes, and by their own experience.

The narrator recognizes that "in modern days" the evidence against Rebecca "divided into two classes – those which were immaterial and those which were actually and physically impossible" (420) – and depend upon the Grand Master's charismatic bigotry for their plausibility. Rebecca, whose modern medicinal and economic understanding is matched by her legal sense,[45] implicitly concurs in her speech just prior to Waging Battle as her last alternative for justice. Thornton's lawyer, similarly, had addressed "your Lordship and the public" to explain the recommendation of the Wager as a response to "the extraordinary, and I may add, unprecedented prejudice disseminated against him throughout the country." Yet in the initial trial against Thornton, the competing theories of defense and prosecution disputed the determination of what was immaterial and impossible, and, in the Appeal, Lord Ellenborough's court had to sift legal history using the same criteria.[46] The question of whether jury or judge should adjudicate the materiality or possibility of evidence was an on-going concern for legal reformers from Pitt to Romilly to Peel, so Scott's presentation of evidence as distinctive categories is rhetorical, and also moderate; in usual legal practice and the popular representations of trials, narrative (in)coherence and (im)plausibility are the substitutes for the ideal categories of (im)material and (im)possible. Scott's point was not that the modern had overcome prejudices, but that they were inevitable, could only be moderated by checks, and only appeared in clear form once incorporated into historical narrative.[47]

Near the end of the trumped up evidentiary proceeding, Rebecca demands of Bois-Guilbert, "to thyself I appeal whether these accusations [of witch craft] are not false?" (422). His (non)answer, "the scroll, ! the scroll!" is taken by Beaumanoir as "testimony" that under Rebecca's bewitchment he can only name "the fatal scroll, the spell inscribed on which is, doubtless, the cause of his silence." Rebecca recognizes another interpretation, and, like Thornton reading his challenge from "a paper [Mr. Reader put] into the appellee's hand," Rebecca reads from "the scroll" that Bois-Guilbert has slipped into her hand, and following its advice, demands a champion. Although Rebecca's quick destruction of the scroll is needed to secure her oral pleading, *Ashford* achieved an oral pleading by simulacrum. In part, Scott's strategy of anachronism suggest that the past becomes imaginable only through its continuities to the present.

Trying to dissuade Rebecca from waging battle and compel her confession, Beaumanoir offers her an image of two disparate gloves: "Seest thou, Rebecca, as this thin and light glove of thine is to one of our heavy steel gauntlets, so is thy cause to that of the Temple." Rebecca retorts that adding her "innocence into the scale" and a "glove of silk shall outweigh a glove of iron" (426). Such confidence is romance, since, historically, weakness was an excuse to avoid a Wager and force the accused into an evidentiary proceeding. As Mr. Clarke puts it, "The court will no doubt look to the person of the appellant, and seeing that he is weak in body, few in years, and in other qualities by no means capable of combating in battle with the appellee, they will, perhaps, not permit the issue to be put upon personal contest" (*Gentleman's*, 464). Reason, not faith, equals the scales in court, and as *The Times* emphasizes, Mr. Clarke insists that the "allowance of the plea [of Wager] is in a great measure discretionary." The evidentiary proceeding ends with the decision of Beaumanoir to accept Rebecca's challenge, though refusing it was within his jurisdiction (the trial had begun with the Grand Master's refusal to accept Bois-Guilbert's challenge offered in equally good form, but treated as a symptom of his bewitchment). As with *Ashford*, the convenience of the court determines the time schedule, but in the reverse manner. Rather than delays, Rebecca is given three days only to secure a champion. Her appeal for a postponement is rejected as "diverse weighty causes call us on the fourth day from hence" (427). This appears as a modern legal maneuver since the Grand Master had previously indicated he would be staying to correct the deficiencies of the order.

The novel draws attention to these modern echoes at the opening of the penultimate chapter in which the Wager of Battle occurs:

> But the earnest desire to look on blood and death is not particular to those dark ages; though, in the gladiatorial exercise of single combat and general tourney, they were habituated to the bloody spectacle ... Even in our own days, when morals are better understood, an execution, a bruising match, a riot, or a meeting of radical reformers, collects, at considerable hazard to themselves, immense crowds of

spectators, otherwise little interested, except to see how matters are to be conducted, and whether the heroes of the day are, in the heroic language of insurgent tailors, 'flints' or 'dunghills'. (494)

From the one sentence to the next, Scott shifts not only time, but the implied society, in which combat over honor is transformed into combat over wages (flints and dunghills), and the subjects of spectacle shift from the ordered architecture of the Chivalric court and code to social riots and radical reformers. This shift, for a contemporary reader, would have pointed to one of the dissonant aspects of *Ashford v. Thornton*, namely that the proposed battle was between a "bricklayer" and, in the *Quarterly*'s phrases, the son "of a Peasant" and "eldest brother and heir of the deceased," who was heir only to the right of this appeal, and his very assertion of that inheritance propels its abolition. The ceremonial consonance of the Wager of Battle, offered in *Ivanhoe* through the detailed description of the preparations, depends upon a certain homogeneous society in which both Rebecca and the "black slaves" who stoke the fire that will burn her must be demonized (the slaves are assumed by the audience to be conversing with the devil, and Rebecca, even acquitted of witchcraft, continues to bewitch). In contrast to this "spectacle," the *Quarterly Review* imagines the scene of a Wager in the present day as "a singular sight to behold [as] the present learned and venerable judges of the court of King's Bench, clothed in their full costume, sitting all day long in the open air of Tothill Fields, as the umpires of a match at single stick" (178). In an effort to make the "many absurdities of this ceremonial" so evident that they "do not require to be particularly pointed out," the *Quarterly* joins to this description a story from France, in which a dog successfully brings his master's murderer to justice by doing battle. These two descriptions rely for their humor on the incongruity of the participants with their situations (dogs are not human; judges rule indoors on laws, not outdoors as umpires) and also direct attention towards the class incongruity of the contemporary battle by linking it to the species-incongruity in the French report. In *Ivanhoe*, by contrast, Gurth's adherence to his class position is solidified by his loyalty to his superiors through his challenge of one of Locksley's underlings. In this structure, Scott makes use of one of his typical devices for mediating class conflict, by having the servant plot provide a comic echo of the aristocratic plot.

Rebecca's commitment to chastity is her indirect mode of faithfulness to Ivanhoe, her chivalric rescuer, about whose own chastity of mind the narrator chooses not to "inquir[e] too curiously" (519). Rebecca's fidelity, which for a Christian would mark chivalric goodness, becomes, like her healing, a measure of her witchery and a threat to domestic tranquillity. In his *Essay on Chivalry*, Scott develops a torturous explanation for the coexistence of chivalric adultery and chastity that reflects modern tensions and presumptions about feminine charm (18–22). The initial intercepted letter that plants the idea of bewitchment in Beaumanoir's mind is using the term only figuratively; similarly, Bois-Guilbert, just before he learns of the charge of witchcraft exclaims, "The devil, that possessed her race with obstinacy, has concentrated its full force in her single person" (404). The repetitions of this figurative use renders the literal charge plausible. If our age, Scott's irony suggests, can recognize the bigotry of previous ages, it is not through historical distance, but similarity. What figurative repetitions constitute reality is itself the frame of adjudication, not a subject to be adjudicated. As Scott knew, the law had not purged itself of witchcraft, for although a person could not be tried for being a witch, she might be convicted of impersonating one, because the force of popular superstition rendered such impersonation socially effective.

Scott sets the stage of the battle, however, in a way that subtly challenges the legal and social coherence of the ritual that has been visually emphasized. Ivanhoe demands, "Does the Grand Master allow me the combat?" Like Ellenborough in *Ashford* who reluctantly grants battle despite William Ashford's physical unsuitability for combat, Beaumanoir agrees, although grudgingly because of Ivanhoe's obviously weakened state and his desire to have "thee honourably met with." But, like Ellenborough, he maintains he acts through legal necessity, although he adds a caveat: "provided the maiden accepts thee as her champion" (505). Whether this condition has been met is dubious; like Reader, who expresses astonishment that Thornton will be allowed to "repel the charge [of murder] by committing another murder," Rebecca, retracting her initial permission, asks "why shouldst thou perish also?" (505). The question goes unnoticed, and the dual begins when the Grand Master "pronounced the fatal words *Laissez aller.*" This emphasis on the linguistic provides another transition between chivalric judicial combat and modern judicial sentence, but also underscores how the selective hearing of the court, ancient and modern, is consonant with preconceptions.

On the first pass, Bois-Guilbert falls anticlimactically dead. With this odd occurrence, Ivanhoe and Bois-Guilbert resemble the lawyers in *Ashford,* who never fight out the actual case, but have the decision resolved at the level of legal maneuver. The original for Bois-Guilbert's death was, according to Mrs. Skene, "the sudden death of an advocate of [Scott's] acquaintance,"[48] reinforcing Scott's link between lawyer and champion. In this scene, Bois-Guilbert can be viewed as both Champion for the Templars, and, with his threats of violence against Rebecca, as Thornton's double receiving justice through divine intervention or guilty conscious, the latter being consistent with *The Murdered Maid: or, The Clock Struck Four!!!*

(produced in 1818) which "show[s] a guilty Thornton escaping punishment through bribery" and in which "he ultimately goes mad and kills himself" (Dyer, 403). By contrast, *The Times*, though almost certainly accepting Thornton's guilt, commented that the guilt in no way registered on Thornton:

> In the countenance of the prisoner was visible the same easy confidence which we formerly noticed; he waited and looked around him with perfect indifference. An ordinary spectator, if called upon to point out the man whom it was supposed had committed an atrocious offense, would perhaps have selected the prisoner last. (*Times*, 24 November 1817, 3 e).

In *Ivanhoe*, countenances are more reliable, registering emotions in accordance with a legibility that Brougham and others used to argue the effectiveness of the jury trial, in which the jurors can observe the defendant's reaction to testimony. As a parodic example, Bois-Gilbert's eyes, in death, "were fixed and glazed" (506); they open, not to see but to be inspected and to confirm Ivanhoe's conflation of Bois-Gilbert as the Templars' champion, chosen by Beaumanoir, and as the accused. In answering the Templars' challenge on Rebecca's behalf (in a confusion of roles reminiscent of *Ashford*), he attaints Bois-Gilbert as "a traitor, murderer and liar" (504).

Two interpretations of Bois-Guilbert's death are offered. The modern narrator explains that he "had died a victim to the violence of his own contending passions." Immediately following, the Grand Master, the example of ancient legalism turned fanatical, declares, "This is indeed the judgment of God." Ivanhoe, declining his claim on Bois-Guilbert's armor (a claim Scott probably knew to be anachronistic for the Wager of Battle in the time of Richard), moderates between these two interpretations; his action having been confirmed as "manfully and rightly done" (the phrase appears twice in the opening sentences of the final chapter), Ivanhoe declares:

> I will not despoil him of his weapons ... God's arm, no human hand, hath this day struck him down. But let his obsequies be private, as becomes those of a man who died in an unjust quarrel. (507)[49]

A reader, like the internal audience, might applaud these words, but they are spoken at the whim of Ivanhoe; he might have done otherwise. Moreover, by denominating the quarrel – and not Bois-Guilbert's position within the quarrel – as unjust, Ivanhoe impugns the system of battle; at stake is the problem of a procedure of justice. The alternative to battle, the jury, is not explicitly invoked, and the superstitions of the audience, from whom jurors would have been selected, suggests that a jury by itself would be inadequate. The jury requires a jurisprudence and culture of rationality.

Ivanhoe's moderation prepares the way for the entrance of the king, and a series of legal (and quasi-legal) dispositions ranging from the "judicial investigations" detailing the fate of the conspirators against Richard to the marriage and settlement of Rowena and her offer to "wean" Rebecca from her "erring law." In each case, the narrative emphasizes the arbitrary nature of the decisions – Richard's whim, or Cedric's. Immediately after Ivanhoe's declaration, Richard enters, has Malvoisin arrested, and chides Ivanhoe for his participation in the Wager. With the expulsion of the Knights Templar, the Saxon-identified, Norman-born King seems to expel the wager of battle, and reintroduces the Anglo-Saxon forms of arrest. The head of the Knights Templar resolves to sue to Rome, and Richard dismisses this threat as irrelevant on English soil. English law has arrived, yet, in the midst of cheers to the long life of the king, Ivanhoe points out to Essex that "it was well the King took the precaution to bring thee with him, noble Lord, and so many of thy trusted followers." This precaution was the Constable's idea, not Richard's, who, disappointed at not fighting in single combat, taunts the Templars about their "sun-burn'd" ladies to coax one to "splinter a spear" with him. Just as Ivanhoe regarded his battle with Bois-Guilbert as private, the king regards treason as a personal affront to be challenged in the person of the king, and arbitrated as he pleases. Beaumanoir answers Richard that Templars do "not fight on such idle and profane quarrel" and asserts that the proper tribunal of the "Pope and Princes of Europe shall judge our quarrel" (508–9) The claim of jurisdiction again sets evidentiary proceeding against Wager, but moves its final resolution to beyond the narrative and into the slow workings of history which whittles superstition into rationality, but continues to depend upon force.

The tenuousness of the chivalric code, in which disputes are private, reaches its prosaic conclusion in Richard's early death and Ivanhoe's banishment to obscurity. Recognizing that the Wager of Battle scene in *Ivanhoe* has a contemporary referent contextualizes Scott's refusal to validate Richard as more than "generous, but rash and romantic." From a legal perspective, all three traits are faults that inject the personal and unpredictable into legal decisions; hence, Ivanhoe's annoyance at Richard's choice to meet his brother John, a traitor, on friendly terms as if, in Essex's words, "they had met after a hunting party" (511). Ivanhoe asks Essex whether no one dared point out to Richard that he "invites men to treason by his clemency." The Earl's retort explicitly links the behavior of Richard and Ivanhoe as generous, rash and romantic and denies the reliability of providential intercession: "Just … as a man may be said to invite death who undertakes to fight a combat, having a dangerous wound unhealed." Although Ivanhoe tries to distinguish the cases, in that he risks only his life, and Richard the welfare of the kingdom, this distinction ignores the way they both view their own lives as private, insular property rather than as nodes of a complex economic social order.

Whereas Ivanhoe, Richard and Rebecca (when Ivanhoe appears) are motivated by passions akin to those fatal to Bois-Guilbert (in the narrator's interpretation), a jury trial functions, according to the *Quarterly*, to keep "down the influences of mere passion or sentiment ... and severely impels [jurors] along the path of duty"; this effect, however, is contingent on the jury seeing itself as the final arbitrator, and the availability of an "appeal of murder" compromises this position, and unleashes passions "so fatal" to "public good and justice."[50] Ellenborough's final words on *Ashford v. Thornton* repudiate private or personal desires: "Whatever prejudices therefore may justly exist against this mode of trial, still as it is the law of the land, the Court must pronounce judgment for it" (*Times*, 21 April 1818, 4 b). His language stresses that the judgment is for the "mode of trial," and not for Thornton, although this distinction is largely strategic. He echoes Reader's explicit rationale of electing battle to evade the "unprecedented prejudice" against his client. Ellenborough deliberately overstates the certainty of Thornton's right to a Wager of Battle in order to more forcefully assert the court's objective stance; both on the face of the law presented in court and in the legal history of the Wager of Battle available to the court, the decision to oust the Wager fell within the court's discretionary power. Further, as Rush noted, despite reluctantly agreeing with the judgment, "in a case like this, long disuse added to obvious absurdity, would have worked the silent repeal of the law; according to the doctrine of desuetude under the Roman law" (183). Acting in support of violence, the court eschews its own passions as the root of a more dangerous violence, one that could return the court system to an earlier stage still present as a palimpsest. If champions have become lawyers, for Scott, it is in part because lawyers can imagine themselves champions. If the body has yielded to rationality as the locus of truth, rationality remains an incomplete epistemology, depending for its supplementation on the mythology of the body. Scott concludes *Ivanhoe* with a paraphrase of lines from Samuel Johnson's "Vanity of Human Wishes": Richard has "left the name at which the world grows pale,/ To point a moral, or adorn a TALE" (519). Though the tale adorned is primarily *Ivanhoe* (and perhaps the Waverley novels), the moral, pointed toward a modern judiciary recovering from the exposure of its own incoherence, reclaims the Wager of Battle for the fictional and historical realms that, for Scott, rendered modernity intelligible.

NOTES

1. These terms refer to an ancient legal right of the heirs of a dead person to "appeal" a suspected murderer, that is, to "call" him into court, independent of any public action against him. This could result in either a jury trial or a Wager of Battle, in which the heir and the accused (or, in some cases, their champions), fought. In most assessments of the procedure, the accused, if defeated, was immediately hanged; if he held his own until the stars appeared, he was acquitted (although in some interpretations, he could still be tried in the name of the King by an indictment).

2. Mr. Stanley objected that, in its practice as a "civil suit," the "trial by Appeal" was always "for the sake of obtaining money," but "taking it in its utmost sense, it is nothing but barbarism and cruelty." An abridgement of the debate appears in E.A. Kendall, *An Argument for Construing Largely the Right of An Appellee of Murder to Insist On Trial by Battle; and Also for Abolishing Appeals*, 3rd edn. (London, 1818), 206–304. All works will be cited in the text after the initial reference.

3. William Blackstone, *Commentaries on the Laws of England: A Facsimile of the First Edition of 1765–1769*, 4 vols. (Chicago: University of Chicago Press, 1979), 3:268.

4. Jerome McGann, *The Romantic Ideology: A Critical Investigation* (Chicago: University of Chicago Press, 1983), 86.

5. Edmund Burke, *Reflections on the Revolution in France*, 1790, ed. C.C. O'Brien. (New York: Penguin, 1969), 170. Walter Scott, in his "Essay on Chivalry" for the *Encyclopedia Britannica*, offers a similar argument (rpt. in Walter Scott, *Essays on Chivalry, Romance, and the Drama* [London, 1887], 1–65). For both Scott and Burke, however, the permeability between manners and law was evident in libel trials, divorce actions, and other legal regulations of social interactions.

6. The best account of the relationship of the trial to literature, and one to which my own is indebted, is Gary Dyer's "Ivanhoe, Chivalry, and the Murder of Mary Ashford," *Criticism* 39/3 (Summer 1997), 388–408. Dyer's use of *Ashford v. Thornton* allows him to position *Ivanhoe* in the contest in which "conservatives and radicals had been battling over who owned chivalry"; hence "Bois–Guilbert's political coloring suggests that *Ivanhoe* attempts to reclaim chivalry not only from brutes like Thornton but also from the British radicals, apparently influenced by French thinking, who had been so vocal and active since Waterloo" (400–401). I thank Gary Dyer for both his published work and generous advice and discussion for this paper.

7. *The London Times*, "Criminal Trials," 2 c. The event of the previous day was actually two proceedings, the first a trial for murder in which the prosecution sought a conviction and a second *pro forma* motion on which Judge Holroyd directed the jury to acquit on the charge of rape. This structure was reversed in the popular debate which "gave her rape the priority over her murder" (Dyer, "Ivanhoe, Chivalry, and the Murder of Mary Ashford," 388) because, as Hall (paraphrasing the judge's instructions to the jury) put it, "if she were a consenting party, there was no intelligible reason why he should murder her" (*Trial of Abraham Thornton*, 30). Of the nearly 50 reports on murder trials in 1817 in *The Times*, only this one included a rape charge. The trial was reported widely in newspapers, and subsequent accounts were published over the next several years, including two editions of *Thornton's trial!! : The trial of Abraham Thornton, at the Warwick Summer Assize, on Friday, the 8th day of August, 1817, for the murder of Mary Ashford, in the Lordship of Sutton Coldfield, before the Hon. George Sowley Holroyd, Knight*.

8. A more complete, though not entirely trustworthy record of the trial edited by John Hall, reports: "The jury consulted together about six minutes without retiring and returned a verdict of 'not guilty'." Sir John Hall, ed., *Trial of Abraham Thornton* (New York: John Day Co, 1927). Hall argues in his introduction for the correctness of this judgment based on Thornton's alibi and the shoddiness of the way in which the evidence against him was gathered. Hall's materials also includes a bibliography of many of the contemporary references and a listing of many of the relevant newspapers.

9. The social turbulence of Regency England penetrates *Ashford v. Thornton*, which was delayed by The Home Secretary Lord Sidmouth's filing of "articles of peace" against Arthur

Thistlewood, who had challenged him to a duel in response to anti-radical stances in Parliament (*Times*, 7 Feb. 1818, 3 c) and which abutted a case, also overseen by Ellenborough, regarding the suspension of *habeas corpus* (*Times*, 26 Jan., 3 b). Robert Gifford, who pursued the case against Thistlewood, would also open against Queen Caroline in the Lords; see William Holdsworth, *A History of English Law* (London: Methuen, 1952), 13:664.

10. So complex were these matters that *The Times* inserted a description of the relevant land and distances, and many subsequent accounts included charts or maps. J.M. Beattie points out that the rules of evidence arose from the construction of exclusionary rules in the eighteenth and early nineteenth century which filtered what was admissible to put before a jury and corresponded to "a market having formed among lawyers practicing at the criminal bar." See *Crime and the Courts in England, 1660–1800* (Oxford: Clarendon, 1986), 363.

11. Luke Booker, *A Moral Review of the Conduct and Case of Mary Ashford in Refutation of Arguments Adduced in Defense of her Supposed Violator and Murderer* (Dudley: John Rann, 1818), 3.

12. Her drowning in a "pit" gave both sides a resonant scene to argue either his extreme villainy or her extreme despair or debauchery. George Cruikshank sketched *A view of the field and pit, where Mary Ashford, was murdered* possibly as early as 1817.

13. *Ashford v. Thornton* 1 (Barnewell & Alderson Reports), 409.

14. Richard Rush, *Residence at the Court of London,* ed. Benjamin Rush, 3rd edn. (London, 1872), 182.

15. *Times* 22 Nov. 1817, 3 a. The figurative use of "literally" and the bodily metaphor of "choking" underscore the representational difficulties of the moment that applied both to popular venues representing the trial, and those figures of representation – lawyers – within the trial.

16. George Neilson, *Trial by Combat* (New York: Macmillan, 1891), 330. Dyer observes that "hardly anyone associated with *Ashford v. Thornton* refers" to the Irish case (Dyer, "Ivanhoe, Chivalry, and the Murder of Mary Ashford," 403).

17. See also *Gentleman's Magazine* Nov. 1817, 464–5, which emphasizes the ancientness of the proceeding: "In pursuance with the old form, he threw [the glove] down for the appellant to take up. It was not taken up."

18. See Hall, *Trial of Abraham Thornton,* 46: "They were merely a kind of bag of white sheepskin with no separate thumbs or fingers. They were attached by a string around the wrists." Neilson suggests the gauntlet's white leather might have been reminiscent of the "sheepskin armour of earlier centuries" (329).

19. *Times,* 30 Jan. 1818, 3 d. Another moment of confusion required Reader rhetorically to become his client: "The prisoner and William Ashford were about to leave the Court ... when Mr. Reader desired that they might return while the appellee delivered his rejoinder in demurrer" (*Times* 18 Nov. 1817, 3 e). The term "appeal" itself heightened the confusion for the public; according to the *Quarterly Review,* of the "great mistakes" made regarding the procedure, the "most common, and perhaps the most natural, is to suppose, that the whole proceeding is an *appeal from the verdict* already given" (Review of *An Argument for Construing largely the Right of an Appellee of Murder, to insist on Trial by Battle,* 18 [Oct. 1817], 181). W.E.K. Anderson, in *The Journal of Sir Walter Scott* (Oxford: Clarendon, 1972) repeats this error; see 241 note 1.

20. See T.C. Hansard, *Parliamentary Debates,* 1st Series, 31 (London, 1815), 1121–2.

21. In 1817, public flagellation of women was abolished; George Ives, *A History of Penal Methods: Convicts, Witches, Lunatics* (Montclair, NJ: Patterson Smith, 1970), 54. Arguments turned on the display of the body as impugning the ideal of femininity and as exciting male passion.

22. See "The British Code of Duel; a Reference to the Laws of Honour and the Character of Gentleman," *Westminster Review* 7 (July, 1825), 20–32. The Wager and Duel were inextricably linked, the Battle being called a "judicial duel," and duels being referred to as "wager of battle," (sometimes with some irony, as in Captain Granow's description of Percy Shelley's "fight at Eaton" as a "wager of battle"; see *Reminiscences and Recollections of Captain Granow* [London: John Nimmo, 1889] 2:79).

23. See R. Gude, *The Practice of the Crown Side of the Court of King's Bench* (London, 1828), in *passim*.
24. The counter-strategy of plain speaking, of addressing the jury man-to-man, prompted certain publishers, such as William Hone, to offer their own defense in libel or sedition trials, unaided by lawyers; see *The Three Trials of William Hone for Publishing Three Parodies* (London: William Hone, 1818). Hone, like Daniel Isaac Eaton (1812), appeared before Lord Ellenborough, who presided over Ashford's Appeal of Murder.
25. See both James Kennedy, *A Treatise on the Law and Practice of Juries as amended by the Statute 6 George IV c. 50* (London, 1826) and, published two years later, R. Gude, *The Practice of the Crown Side* for what Holdworth regards as the most significant accounts of juries in the period (*History of English Law*, 13:456).
26. Holdsworth, *A History of English Law*, 13:90–91 and 304; "why," Brougham asked rhetorically, "do we prize the trial by jury above all the other blessings of our Constitution?" ("Speech on the Catholic Claims" 1812; excerpted in *Opinions of Lord Brougham*, [Paris, 1841], 30).
27. See J Baldwin and Michael McConville, *Jury Trials* (Oxford: Clarendon Press, 1979), Ch.1, "Jury Lore and Jury Learning."
28. For Scottish lawyers and writers, the matter was still more urgent since the entire system of jury proceedings in Scotland was being revamped. For a summary of some of the key issues, see Francis Horner's parliamentary speech 6 March 1815, reprinted in Leonard Horner (ed.), *Memoirs and Correspondence of Francis Horner* (London: Murray, 1853) 2:534–9.
29. Quoted in J.M. Beattie, *Crime and the Courts*, 397. The ability for juries to retire for private deliberations was only about 50 years old, and only available in recently built or improved courthouses. The practice of deliberating on a single case at a time, rather than on the entire day's docket, was introduced into Old Bailey in 1738, while the principal that jurors were to be kept "without meat, drink, fire, candle or lodging" was still in force, and hung juries were not permitted. In some sense, the deprivation of the jurors' bodies insured the verdict, and underscored the sense that the court had produced such a certain truth that deliberation by the jurors was superfluous. See Beattie, 395–9.
30. John Langbein, *Torture and the Law of Proof: Europe and England in the Ancien Regime* (Chicago: University Chicago Press, 1977), 73.
31. The *Quarterly Reviewer*, cataloguing the techniques of Saxon Ordeal in October 1817 – "by fire, by water, by hot iron, by the cross, and by the *corsned* or morsel of execration" – finds they resemble "the more glorious ordeal of arms," rather than trial by jury (186).
32. Quoted in M.I. Zagnay, "Bentham on Civil Procedure," in *Jeremy Bentham and the Law: A Symposium*, ed. G. Keetin and G. Schwarzenberger (London: Stevens and Sons, 1948), 74.
33. Like the *Appeal of Murder*, *Criminal Conversation* was often mistaken for a criminal matter; both are civil suits.
34. Booker's proposed epitaph, reprinted in full in the *Gentleman's Magazine's* review of his book (June, 1818, 535–7), appears as the final page of the treatise, with a double-lined border, multiple fonts, and centered to appear as if on a tombstone (Booker, *A Moral Review*, 55).
35. Quoted in Edgar Johnson, *Sir Walter Scott: The Great Unknown* (New York: Macmillan, 1970), 687. See also Gary Dyer's account of how the authors of dramatic adaptations "felt compelled to revise the scene" (Dyer, "Ivanhoe, Chivalry, and the Murder of Mary Ashford," 405).
36. Scott believed Thornton guilty, since he records that at a dinner in 1826, that Peel "almost" convinces him of "the man's innocence." By this point, Peel was deeply engaged in legal reform. Walter Scott, *The Journal of Sir Walter Scott, 1825–26*, ed. J.G. Tait (London: Oliver and Boyd, 1939), 278. Dyer adds that the "Ashford case was covered by the Edinburgh Weekly Journal, which Scott's associate James Ballantyne edited and published. The lengthy account of the crime, appeal and challenge that appeared in the 26 November 1817 issue (vol. 20, no. 1041, 382) made Thornton's guilt look undeniable" (Dyer, "Ivanhoe, Chivalry, and the Murder of Mary Ashford," 405).
37. "The suggestion that Reader was to appear as Royal Champion must have been a joke for the office was hereditary and at the coronation Henry Dymoke, acting for his father ... appeared

as the Royal Champion." James Corson, *Notes and Index to Sir Herbert Grierson's Edition of the Letters of Sir Walter Scott* (Oxford: Clarendon Press, 1979), 181. In the ceremony, the champion's role was "to ride into the hall at the coronation banquet, and flinging down his gauntlet offer proof by his body that the new crowned king was king by right" (Neilson, *Trial by Combat*, 194).

38. William Forsyth, *History of Trial by Jury*, ed. James Appleton Morgan, 2nd edn. (Jersey City: F.D. Linn & company, 1875), 4. The *Quarterly Review*, in its review of Kendall, argues that the "rude elements of our jury-trials certainly appear to have been derived from the Saxons, but it has required centuries to elaborate them into the form they have now taken. The Saxon trial by jury, *if it may be so called*, was an useful, but very simple and imperfect contrivance" (186, my emphasis).

39. When the Lords abolished the Appeal in 1819, Lord Eldon declared, "It was of little importance in the matters now before their Lordships whether it [Trial by Battle] had been derived from the Normans or the Saxons" (*Times*, 18 June 1819).

40. Adam Smith, *Lectures on Jurisprudence*, ed. R.L. Meek *et al.* (Indianapolis, IN: LibertyClassics, 1982), 283.

41. Sir Walter Scott, *Ivanhoe* (1820; Harmondsworth: Penguin, 1985), 422. All subsequent quotations are from this edition.

42. Thornton's first trial anticipates this tension. In the record, the prosecutor claims that "The prisoner, it seems, when the deceased first entered the house, inquired her name and who she was. On being told by one of the company that she was old Ashford's daughter, he replied, 'I have been connected with her sister, and I will with her, or I'll die by it.'" *The Times* reports the prosecutor's words somewhat differently: "The prisoner was there, admired the figure and general appearance of Mary Ashford, and was heard to say, 'I have been intimate' (I won't use the coarse expression he made use of) 'with her sister, and I will have connexion with her, though it should cost me my life.'" The trial record presents Thornton's claim as at least potentially a statement of chivalric desire: *Unless my efforts of seduction succeed, I will die.* The *Times* emphasizes Ashford's appearance, and presents a different logical structure to Thornton's claim. In the newspaper account, his statement implies a calculated disdain of legal stricture: *I will accomplish my goal, even by rape, for which the legal penalty ['cost'] may be death.* The insinuation of "coarse," not courteous, expression further dislodges Thornton from chivalry. John Cooke, who claimed to have overheard this exchange, is reported to have given this testimony: "I then heard the prisoner say, 'I know a sister of hers, and have been connected with her three times – and I will with her, or I'll die for it'" (Hall, 94).

43. Henry Charles Lea, *Superstition and Force* (Philadelphia: Lea Brothers, 1892), 75.

44. Lord Ellenborough queries Mr. Chitty, pleading for Ashford: "Do you contend that establishing a case of suspicion is sufficient to oust battle? If so, you retire from the high ground you took in the commencement" (*Times*, 7 Feb. 1818, 3 c).

45. Her modernness resembles her father's economic sense, despite the aggressive characterization of him as old fashioned, in ways that align him equally with Cedric and Beaumanoir; for a brief description of the contemporary views on usury law which Isaac echoes, see Holdsworth, *Trial by Combat*, 3:330.

46. At one point, Ellenborough remarks of a legal authority, "In this instance, he seems to be a creator, not a compiler. He does not give a single authority for his statement" (*Times*, 9 Feb. 1818, 3 b).

47. Scott apparently claimed to "owe not a little to [James Skene's] German reminiscences," which detailed contemporary prejudice against the Jews. John Gibson Lockhart, *Memoirs of the Life of Sir Walter Scott* (Boston: Houghton, Mifflin, 1902), 3:423.

48. Lockhart, *Memoirs of the Life of Sir Walter Scott*, 3:423. The death occurs "in the *Outer-house* soon after [Mr. Elphinstone] was called to the bar" and "left a vivid impression on his [Scott's] mind."

49. Even before the battle, Scott prepares conflicting explanations. When the Grand Master asked whom he should assign the task of champion, the preceptor of Goodalicke proposes Bois-Gilbert because he "best knows how the truth stands in the matter" (427). Bois-Gilbert himself, acknowledging Rebecca's innocence in his discussion with Malvoisin, as an

extension of the struggle between Templars and Richard, except that he believes no defender will appear (447).

50. The reverse argument was also made; as Gary Dyer points out, William Barrymore's play, *Trial by Battle* (London, 1818), is meant to illustrate how judicial combat is necessary as a corrective to jury trial where a man's wealth and authority can gain him acquittal so easily (Dyer, "Ivanhoe, Chivalry, and the Murder of Mary Ashford," 403), although the play's tone is skeptical of the entire process: "Here's another pretty bit of business – ...a guilty man found innocent – acquitted – turned lose upon the world, and no other chance left of meeting with his deserts, but getting his head cracked in a trial by battle" (*Trial by Battle,* 21). The "Melodramatic Spectacle," performed 11 May 1818, takes considerable liberties with the law of Battle, including letting the Baron attempt a second battle in his own person after his champion is defeated in the first battle, when the law is clear that he should have been immediately hanged on his champion's defeat. Perhaps more dramatic, his opponent's champion kills him, and his dying glance is at his rival's happy union with Geralda, with whom he is enthralled.

Marianne: Mystic or Madwoman?
Representations of Jeanne d'Arc on the
Parisian Stage in the 1820s

SARAH HIBBERD

France, and indeed Europe, during the first decades of the nineteenth century showed a burgeoning fascination with history. This extended from archaeological projects and the restoration of buildings, to written histories, and historically inspired painting, theater and fiction. A particular interest in medieval and renaissance French history can be seen broadly as an attempt, in the aftermath of the revolution and the defeat of Napoleon, to restore the national image through the recollection of past and glorious episodes which had a resonance with the present.

To this end the accession of Charles VII following Jeanne d'Arc's role in the liberation of Orléans, when the French defeated the English, was an attractive metaphor for the newly restored Bourbons, for all the obvious differences between the events. To all intents and purposes, the defeat at Waterloo grimly echoed that at Agincourt, and the arrival of Louis XVIII on the French throne, like that of Charles VII, meant the restoration of a legitimate monarchy after a long period of war, uncertainty and national humiliation.

Unsurprisingly, Jeanne d'Arc was an extremely popular subject for salon paintings in the early years of the Bourbon restoration. At first she was portrayed in a classical manner, a quasi-masculine figure, armed and bearing the royal flag. Pierre Révoil's troubadour-style painting *Jeanne d'Arc prisonnière à Rouen* (1819), for example, presents Jeanne clad in a tunic, on a raised platform. Expressionless, she presides calmly over a crowd of agitated figures, gently illuminated she looks almost Christ-like. In contrast, Paul Delaroche's *Jeanne d'Arc malade est interrogée dans sa prison par le cardinal de Vinchester* (1824) is a more melodramatic work. Just three figures are represented; the cardinal dominates the picture, while Jeanne, shrinking away from him, is no longer armed or wearing a tunic, but dressed in dark, soft velvet.[1] She is at once more feminine, more vulnerable, with an almost saintly pleading expression in her staring eyes. This more intense, personal, spiritual interpretation was admired by critics as an example of the new, "true" style of historical painting.

The art historian Beth Segal Wright discusses these paintings in the context of the "dramatization" of history in art.[2] Emphasizing the almost theatrical composition and implied movement in each work, Wright maps the developments in French theater during the 1820s onto painting: a shift from the rhetorical to the gestural. She stresses how the immediate visual legibility of pantomime as an expression of emotion, which was transforming all theatrical genres, also came to influence painting, as exemplified by Delaroche's painting.

In the theater this new emphasis on gesture and visual expression came essentially from the popular genres of melodrama and vaudeville, in which mime scenes and *tableaux vivants* summed up emotion and character in an instantly intelligible manner. The royal theaters, regularly criticized for their dry, neoclassical dramas which were dominated by long speeches, felt the pressure to introduce something of the realism, excitement, and visual directness of the popular theaters into their own productions. This immediacy, combined with the growing interest in historical subject matter on stage and in painting, had the potential of bringing the past into the present in a way that was immediately comprehensible to a cross-section of the public.

Given Jeanne d'Arc's significance as a subject for the new type of historical painting developing during the early years of the restoration, one might expect to see her at the center of the concurrent emergence of romantic theater. Yet two issues made such a possibility problematic. First, the political implications of Jeanne's story suggested conflicting and extreme interpretations that were unacceptable to the censor at this politically delicate time. Her association with the "people" so soon after the revolution was one source of anxiety; more importantly, her betrayal by the king and the bishops after her victory at Orléans was another at a time when the church and monarchy were trying to consolidate their power. The second issue was the fact that portrayals of women at this time were increasingly focusing on sexuality, a theme that if allowed to intrude into Jeanne's story would conflict with her supposed purity of purpose.

In spite of these difficulties, there was still a number of successful stage adaptations of the Jeanne d'Arc legend during the restoration. In this article I shall begin by considering how these two problematic issues – politics and the portrayal of women – were treated in the two most popular works. Michele Carafa's *opéra comique Jeanne d'Arc, ou La délivrance d'Orléans* was on the face of it a traditional and classical work, written for a conservative theater by an Italian who had served loyally in the French army.[3] Alexandre Soumet's *tragédie Jeanne d'Arc*, on the other hand was the work of a prominent "romantic" writer, for a theater receptive to "romantic" drama, and promised a more modern interpretation, the equivalent, perhaps, of Delaroche's painting.[4] Yet despite the apparent contrast in the choice of episodes depicted in these works, in the politics of their authors, and in the character of the theaters for which the works were intended, they both approached the political aspect in a cautious fashion, omitting or altering the problematic issues. Significantly, they both focused on Jeanne's emotional state rather than on her physical actions, in ways that, as I shall show, were to characterize the broader cultural treatment of her story in the mid- and late 1820s.

CARAFA'S OPERA

Numerous written histories of Jeanne d'Arc were published in the early years of the restoration. The best known were probably those by Le Brun de Charmettes (1817) and Delavigne (1819), highly detailed, medievalized chronicles of her life which inspired paintings such as that of Révoil (mentioned above) as well as many writings.[5] General histories of France also included episodes in which Jeanne's story was recounted, such as Marchangy's *La Gaule poétique* (1819), in which Jeanne is likened to a phoenix ready to be reborn from the flames of her pyre, and, a little later, Prosper de Barante's *Histoire des ducs de Bourgogne* (1824–26), which was recognized as providing a modern, "factual" account of her story.[6] There was also a number of popular romances, including Madame d'Abany's *L'Amazone française, ou Jeanne d'Arc* (1819) and Augustine Gottis's *Jeanne d'Arc ou l'héroïne française* (1822). Although the stage adaptations of the 1820s were loosely inspired by such works, they were often based on newly invented episodes, and borrowed specifically from Schiller's melodramatic drama of 1802, *Die Jungfrau von Orleans* (itself inspired by Shakespeare's *Henry VI, Part One* and responding to Voltaire's 1755 *La Pucelle*); and also from D'Avrigny's neoclassical tragedy *Jeanne d'Arc à Rouen* (1819).[7]

Carafa's *opéra comique* treats Jeanne's story extremely freely, and, perhaps inspired by Marchangy's version of events, deals only with her victory at Orléans. Jeanne has been sent to live with her uncle near Orléans, as her family in Domrémy suppose her visions to be a symptom of madness, caused by lovesickness. This "folie" continues, however, and her uncle plans to send her back home, believing that her desire to fight confirms her as "folle tout-à-fait" (I, iii). In contrast her aunt, overhearing Jeanne singing about how she has been called upon by God to fight for her country, suggests that she must have been bewitched. In what is ostensibly a love duet with the French soldier Dunois, Jeanne continues to talk of fighting rather than of her feelings, and Dunois concludes "sa raison est égarée" (I, vi).[8] Finally, her uncle tries to trick her into returning to Domrémy by telling her that her father is ill. A sort of mad scene follows in which Jeanne is torn between love for her father and devotion for her country:

> Il faut partir; il faut partir:
> Hélas! je n'ai plus d'espérance.
> O ma patrie! ô noble France!
> Jeanne d'Arc ne peut te servir.
> La vieillesse d'un père
> réclame mon appui:
> La gloire m'est bien chère;
> Mais je vole vers lui.

> [I must leave; I must leave: alas! I have no hope left. Oh, my country! Oh noble France! Jeanne d'Arc can no longer serve you. The old age of a father claims my support: glory is dear to me but I fly to him. (I, ix)]

The stage directions describe her as "still one moment, then suddenly running about the stage with agitation," and the music also switches between strong *fortissimo* descending arpeggios, and quieter, breathless and repetitive fragmentary phrases, accompanied by tremolo chords.[9] Finally, she falls asleep, completely exhausted; at this point a dream sequence is enacted. A young *bergère* – symbolizing, according to the critics, "la patronne de France," a sort of Marianne figure – and a chorus of young girls dressed in white urge, "O chaste fille, à l'éternel si chère!/ Arme ton bras."[10] The act concludes with Jeanne leading a troupe of French soldiers into battle. Following offstage fighting, the French victory is announced and the final scene depicts her planting the French royal flag in the ground, surrounded by light, in a saint-like tableau: "a brilliant halo surrounds her. The king and the whole army kneel on the ground during the last bar of the chorus, and the curtain falls."[11]

The opera is clearly in the tradition of sentimental eighteenth-century opera, depicting Jeanne as a variation on the celebrated mad, pastoral heroine Nina of Dalayrac's 1786 opera (still in the repertory at the Opéra-Comique in the 1820s), who loses her reason when she believes her lover has been killed in a duel.[12] It is Jeanne's visions that effectively provide the cue to introduce the theme of madness into the opera, and although her extraordinary powers are from the start shown to be the result of religious conviction rather than insanity, all the familiar tropes of madness, verging on the supernatural (to which I shall return), are introduced – and are recognized and reinforced by the other characters.

This sentimental mode is combined with an uncomplicated representation of patriotism: victory at Orléans not only confirms Jeanne's sanity, but also provides the opera's happy ending. This focus on French triumph was welcomed on the Parisian stage in 1821 at a time when the nation was still smarting from the indignity of defeat.[13] The critic of *Le Miroir* observed that two phrases were particularly applauded: "Les Anglais sont de bien vilaines gens" and "Nos ennemis sont Anglais, et nous sommes Français."[14] Significantly, the critic for *Le Drapeau blanc* noted that the apparently conflicting elements of the sentimental and the war-like had been captured in the leading actress's performance:

> Although neither the stature nor the gentle features of Mme Regnault-Lemonnier have anything martial or heroic about them, the warmth and exultation that she put into her performance, as into her singing, have replaced the physical illusion and have earned her great and deserved applause. (12 March 1821)[15]

Perhaps most importantly, the critic added, the dream sequence (described above) had *historical* motivation. Thus the sentimental traditions of the Opéra-Comique had been allied to a new interest in the historical – the real – in a way that in fact foreshadowed both the portrayal of historical figures on the Parisian stage generally, and other interpretations of Jeanne's story later in the decade. Visual effects, tableaux and Jeanne's spirituality were emphasized rather than her heroic actions.

SOUMET'S TRAGEDY

By the mid-1820s the French were becoming more interested in the literature and history of northern Europe. Byron was acclaimed as a romantic hero, and his works, together with the historical novels of Walter Scott and the writings of Goethe and Schiller, were inspiring French imitations and stage adaptations. However, the romantic journal *Le Globe* was calling for plays inspired by *French* history, in an attempt to forge a new, "modern" national drama that would not only replace the dull classical repertory, but would also counter the invasion of the French stage by foreign romanticism.[16]

Jeanne's story would seem to be a perfect choice for a prominent romantic writer, and some-time contributor to *Le Globe*. Indeed, in contrast to Carafa's simple pastoral opera, Soumet's tragedy deals with the darker, more complex issues of Jeanne's imprisonment, trial and death. These aspects of her story clearly appealed to the melodramatic (indeed romantic) imagination more than her victory at Orléans, and they echoed the French imitations of English Gothic literature – in the form of popular novels and plays – that were being devoured by the public.[17] However, as suggested above, the political implications of Jeanne's story – her betrayal by the king and the church – were clearly problematic in the political climate of the 1820s. Indeed, as if to forestall awkward questions from the censor, in the first scene of the play she tells her companion Adhémar that it is her own fault that she has been imprisoned:

> Fière et m'environnant de la publique ivresse,
> J'unissais mes accens aux hymnes d'allégresse.
> . . . Je sentis de ma main fuir ma bannière sainte.
> Dieu de mon faible coeur sembla se retirer,
> Je crus voir un moment des flammes m'entourer,
> . . . J'aurais dû, je le sens,
> Poser le glaive après ces signes menaçans.

> [Proud and enveloping myself in the public spirit, I joined in the hymns of elation ... I felt my sacred banner escape from my hand. God seemed to withdraw from my weak heart, for a moment I thought I saw flames surrounding me ... I should, I feel it, have put down my sword after these menacing signs. (I, i)]

The critic Evariste Dumoulin, writing in *Le Constitutionnel*, stated that Soumet had quite blatantly "used only the secular judges, even though everyone knows that it was the bishops, sold to the English, who sentenced Jeanne d'Arc to death."[18] He conceded, however, that this "betrayal of history" was clearly the result of censorship. The critic for *Le Globe*, though, declared that this was no excuse: "the passion for truth and naturalness has made too much progress in France for a poet to be free to violate history ... to put fiction in the place of truth."[19] Moreover, he was clearly uneasy about the way in which Soumet had manipulated his audience by flattering their patriotic feelings, while presenting his own imaginative ideas as truth and leaving out known aspects of Jeanne's story (such as the fact that she apparently dressed as a man). This maneuver was achieved, he suggested, largely through brilliantly conceived scenic effects. Though he did not agree with the method, the critic acknowledged that this was another means of bringing the past into the present in a way that moved the public:

> Jeanne d'Arc, in this play, is the model of a patriot of our age: she expresses our sufferings and our indignation ... France of the nineteenth century is avenging foreign domination and the unhappiness of invasion by applauding.[20]

As well as smoothing out the uncomfortable political implications of Jeanne's story, Soumet also distanced her from her actions as a soldier. She tells us now, "je ne suis plus à craindre: une simple bergère."[21] Indeed throughout the play we are reminded of her humble past, and her fighting is presented as being alien to her, almost as if carried out by someone else. The emphasis is instead placed on her present *emotional* strength, and on her selfless concern for her family.

This effective feminization of her character is developed through the play. The central acts focus on invented episodes, adapted from Shakespeare and Schiller (several critics mention the fact that such fictions have been ruled out by Prosper de Barante in his recent *Histoire*): Jeanne's father has been tricked into declaring that she was possessed by evil spirits, Bedford is so touched by her speech that he tries (in vain) to save her with his own life, and finally, in what was apparently one of the most moving scenes in the play, the Duke of Burgundy is persuaded by Jeanne to return to the French side. According to the critic Martainville, "this scene, in which all the verses seemed to be inspired – like the emotion which raises Jeanne above the mortal state – produced the liveliest impression."[22] Thus the clichés of female susceptibility to the supernatural and an almost seductive (and destructive) persuasiveness are introduced into the play, and indeed form the core of the drama. In the final scene Jeanne urges her sisters not to cry after her death, and to look after their father. For Martainville, "the despair that destroys the hearts of Jeanne d'Arc's father and sisters, and contrasts with her super-human courage and her divine resignation, offers the most touching spectacle."[23]

By moving away from her physical, "masculine," political actions and focusing instead on more personal, emotional, contemporary clichés of femininity, a modern, "romantic" Jeanne is created. While the broad sweep of historical events is maintained, a carefully constructed set of authentic details, which reflect the interests of an 1820s Parisian audience, brings a distant medieval heroine into the nineteenth century.

OTHER JEANNES

It is clear, then, that in both Carafa's opera and Soumet's tragedy the sanitizing of the political implications of Jeanne's story were, in different ways, accompanied by a feminization of her character. Of course this was not a new treatment of the Jeanne legend as such (and it was still apparently based on historical "fact"), but it did respond to the particular political and cultural climate of early 1820s Paris, and foreshadowed the nature of later representations of Jeanne.

A few weeks after the first performance of Soumet's tragedy, the philosopher Alexandre Bertrand took Jeanne as the subject of one of his historically-inspired articles for *Le Globe* that appeared under the title "De l'état d'extase" (28 April 1825).[24] He suggested that her visions, excited by patriotism, were symptoms of "ecstasy" that gave her an assurance that was otherwise alien to her. He thus reclaimed her from the quasi-masculine interpretations of some historians, artists and writers and re-established her spirituality and emotion – in other words her femininity – as the source of her extraordinary powers. In effect, he suggested, her assurance and her fighting were neither characteristic of her, nor were they totally alien to her way of being, rather they were brought about by the state of ecstasy, during which one has the illusion of being outside oneself. Such a description clearly echoes some of the ideas explored by Carafa, Théaulon and Dartois in their opera, and by Soumet in his tragedy. Significantly for the time, Bertrand used an example from history to validate and to explore what was also a modern phenomenon, and thus found another way of bringing history into the present, making it "real."[25]

In a similar vein, as I shall suggest below, Jeanne's visions were more generally linked in the theaters to other related types of "ecstasy" (for which there were also historical as well as contemporary examples): madness, sleepwalking, magnetism, excessive religious devotion and supernatural possession. These were all aspects of a common representation of women in the mid-1820s in which sensuality, even sexual impropriety, was suggested by association with the irrational.[26] These phenomena were being discussed everywhere, by scientists, doctors, and philosophers, by novelists and journalists; indeed clairvoyants and magnetizers were practicing in salons and on the boulevards throughout the city. Unsurprisingly, the "trance" phenomenon also became popular in the theaters. For example, in 1827 Parisians were able to see Harriet Smithson's famous depiction of Ophelia's madness in a production of *Hamlet* staged by a visiting English theater troupe, an opera based on *Macbeth* (in which Lady Macbeth's sleepwalking scene was the highlight), an enormously popular ballet entitled *La Somnambule*, and a series of vaudevilles and *comédies* on the subjects of madness and sleepwalking. All of these works (and indeed Carafa's opera) presented the "entranced" heroine in a similar fashion, derived from Shakespearean drama and fixed in contemporary paintings and engravings by Eugène Delacroix and Achille Devéria:[27] she stands in a long white gown, with flowing, perhaps disheveled, hair, staring eyes, and a gathering of onstage spectators (usually male), who effectively contain her distraction.[28]

In addition to such layering of visual symbolism, theater of the mid-1820s routinely used musical quotation from, and allusion to, other plays and operas to add further suggestions of meaning to a work, and in this way Jeanne is clearly evoked in other works. The practice began partly out of necessity in the eighteenth century at a time when newly composed music was forbidden on many popular stages, and when mime scenes were accompanied by dramatic music that was intended to enhance or clarify gesture. However, it became a valuable resource, particularly in popular theater and ballet, in the first decades of the nineteenth century. A good example of such layering of allusions, and the resulting intermingling of the female susceptibilities described above, is found in Théaulon's *comédie-vaudeville, Héloïse, ou La nouvelle somnambule* (1827, Théâtre du Vaudeville), in which music from a number of operas confirms the visual suggestion of an entranced heroine. Works quoted from include Dalayrac's *Nina*, Rossini's *Armida* (in which the sorceress-heroine leaves the stage at the end of the opera in a mad frenzy), and the ballet *La Somnambule;* and a ballad from Boieldieu's popular *opéra comique, La Dame blanche* (featuring a supposed ghost) is also alluded to. The central sleepwalking scene (in which the heroine dances with a man who is not her fiancée) is introduced by an air from Carafa's *Jeanne d'Arc*. Thus the sleepwalker is subtly embraced by layers of contrasting interpretations of "trance" phenomena, from the pastoral to the threatening, from the supernatural to the lovesick, by musical (as well as visual) suggestion. Although Carafa's opera was not being performed regularly in the second half of the decade, the centrality of Jeanne's music from the work in this *comédie* (and in other works on the same theme), and her importance in discussions about trance, confirm both her importance in the perception of such phenomena, and the degree to which she (unusually for a historical figure) had been drawn into contemporary culture.

Ironically, then, Jeanne's physical actions and leadership, surely the motivation for dramatizing her story at all in the early 1820s, were eroded and replaced by her (still apparently historically grounded) irrationality, instability and emotion, a transformation which became more marked through the decade. As if to confirm this, Hédouville's 1829 play *Jeanne d'Arc, ou la Pucelle d'Orléans* focuses on the jealous rivalry between Bedford and Dunois for Jeanne's affections; she becomes the passive center of the play rather than its driving force.

CONCLUSION

Despite the popularity of paintings depicting Jeanne in the Academy salons, the political implications of her story, outlined above, made her an extremely problematic subject for the censors. Moreover, two weeks after Delaroche's painting was shown at the 1824 salon, Louis XVIII died, and the accession of Charles X effectively marked a return to a more traditional monarchy, a fact reflected in the further tightening of censorship laws in the theater (particularly those relating to the state and the church). Indeed, a Jeanne d'Arc libretto written for the Paris Opéra, the most prestigious and symbolic stage in France, was rejected by the literary jury in 1828, presumably because of its political content.[29]

Another historical opera staged in the same year illustrates the conflicting ideas about what sort of symbolic national figure the Parisian public was looking for towards the end of the restoration. In Auber's *La Muette de Portici*, set during the 1647 Neapolitan uprising, Fenella, the dumb peasant-girl of the title (played by a dancer who mimes her way through the opera), becomes the silent embodiment of a repressed people, a sort of "Marianne" figure. Yet despite her centrality to the opera, driving the plot and sparking the revolt itself, it was her brother Masaniello, leader of the rebels, who was to be embraced as the most symbolically charged figure of the opera. A revolutionary hero, with his Phrygian cap, he recalled the events of 1789, was fêted again in 1830, 1848 and 1870–71, and would sing French revolutionary songs (including "La Marseillaise") in subsequent performances of the opera. In contrast, in 1828 the character of Fenella was imitated and parodied in vaudevilles that exploited her physicality and her silence – her femininity – rather than her political symbolism.[30] Even more than with Jeanne d'Arc, it was the physical and emotional aspects of Fenella's character that were of most interest to contemporaries, and she was almost entirely divorced from her political context.

For the French nation at the end of the restoration, then, male legendary heroes, drawn from medieval and renaissance times, with revolutionary associations, were inspiring public enthusiasm in ways that could easily be channeled into patriotic spirit, as dissatisfaction with the monarchy erupted.[31] Meanwhile the sorts of female characters that were most appreciated were those timeless, entranced heroines, on the boundaries between emotional instability, irrationality and the supernatural. Jeanne d'Arc was unusual in embracing both the historical and the spiritual, thus bringing the past into a non-political present. However, as the evolving depictions of her have shown, her visions were seen increasingly as a means of assimilating her into the voguish depiction of women as irrational and sensual, rather than filling out her historical characterization.

This was not wholly at odds with the new emphasis seen in Delaroche's 1824 painting. However, while it was possible in art to ignore political implications to a certain degree, in dramatic narrative it was more difficult. Thus while Delaroche's painting was and is recognized as an important "romantic" work, Soumet's play was criticized for its "betrayal of history," to the extent that it could never stand as a significant "romantic" work; this was largely owing to the importance of politics, national identity, and dramatic "truth" in the romantic movement in France. Instead, the first "romantic" dramas set events from foreign history, or from less politically charged episodes from France's past;[32] this allowed dramatists to attend more closely to historical "truth" in this new age of romantic realism, while allowing political allusions to be made by the audiences.

NOTES

1. For a fuller description of the painting, and a discussion of its history, see *La Jeanne d'Arc de Paul Delaroche: Salon 1824*, dossier d'une oeuvre, ed. Marie-Pierre Foissy-Aufrère (Rouen: Musée de Beaux-Arts, 1983).
2. Beth Segal Wright, *Painting and History during the French Restoration: Abandoned by the Past* (Cambridge: Cambridge University Press, 1997), 86–9.
3. Premiered on 10 March 1821 at the Opéra-Comique, with a libretto by E.G. Théaulon de Lambert and F.V.A. Dartois de Bournonville.
4. Premiered on 14 March 1825, at the Théâtre de l'Odéon.
5. Philippe Alexandre Le Brun de Charmettes, *Histoire de Jeanne d'Arc, surnommée la Pucelle d'Orléans, tirée de ses propres déclarations, de cent quarante quatre dépositions de témoins oculaires, et des manuscrits de la bibliothèque du roi et de la Tour de Londres* (Paris: A. Bertrand, 1817); Casimir Delavigne, *Deux messéniennes, ou Elégies sur la vie et la mort de Jeanne d'Arc* (Paris: Ladvocat, 1819).
6. Louis-Antoine-François Marchangy, *La Gaule poétique, ou L'Histoire de France considérée dans ses rapports avec la poésie, l'éloquence et les beaux-arts* (Paris: C.-F. Patris, Lecointe & Durey, Chaumerot jeune, 1819); Prosper de Barante, *Histoire des ducs de Bourgogne* (Paris: Ladvocat, 1824–26).
7. D'Avrigny's tragedy was a great success, according to the critic for *Le Corsaire* (6 March 1825), as the audience consisted largely of "citoyens qui avaient versé leur sang pour l'indépendance et la gloire de la France" [citizens who had spilt their blood for the independence and glory of France]. Plays about Jeanne d'Arc produced during the restoration are described in Théodore-Joseph Boudet, Comte de Puymaigre, *Jeanne d'Arc au théâtre, 1439–1875* (Paris: Douniol, 1875), esp. 17–23.
8. "Her reason has left her."
9. "Immobile un moment, et parcourant tout-à-coup la scène avec agitation."
10. "Oh virtuous child, so dear to the eternal one! Take up your arms."
11. "Une auréole brillante l'entoure. Le roi et toute l'armée mettent le genou en terre, à la dernière mesure du choeur, et le rideau baisse."
12. Nicolas-Marie Dalayrac's *Nina, ou La folle par amour*, was adapted by Giovanni Paisiello in 1789 as an Italian opera, and by Louis-Luc Loiseau de Persuis in 1813 as a ballet, and was extremely influential on Italian operas of the 1830s, such as Gaetano Donizetti's *Lucia di Lammermoor* (1835).
13. In the same year a visiting troupe of English actors were booed off the stage of the Théâtre de la Porte Saint-Martin, and Shakespeare was declared an aide-de-camp of Wellington; discussed in Peter Raby, *'Fair Ophelia': A Life of Harriet Smithson Berlioz* (Cambridge: Cambridge University Press, 1982).
14. "The English are really nasty people" and "Our enemies are English, and we are French" (11 March 1821).
15. "Quoique la taille ni la physionomie douce de Mme Regnault-Lemonnier n'aient rien de martial ni d'héroïque, la chaleur et l'exaltation qu'elle a mises dans son jeu comme dans son chant ont suppléé à l'illusion physique et lui ont valu de justes et nombreux applaudissemens."
16. Mme de Staël was central to this interest in north European literature as inspiration for developments in French writing. I discuss some of the ways in which French romanticism was influenced by foreign culture in my dissertation, "Magnetism, Muteness, Magic: Spectacle and the Parisian Lyric Stage c.1830" (Ph.D. diss., University of Southampton, 1998).
17. For example, one of the most popular novels of the period was D'Arlincourt's *Le Solitaire* (1821), in which a young orphan living in a monastery in the Alps falls in love with a mysterious stranger who rescues her from various dangers (storms, fighting, abduction) but turns out to be Charles the Bold, responsible for the death of her parents. It was adapted as a melodrama and several vaudevilles, and Carafa also wrote the music for an opera based on the story in 1822.
18. "[Il] n'a mis en action que des juges séculiers, tandis que personne n'ignore que ce furent des évêques, vendus aux Anglais, qui firent périr Jeanne d'Arc" (21 March 1825).

19. "La passion du vrai et du naturel ont fait trop de progrès en France pour qu'in poète soit libre de violer l'histoire ...de mettre la fiction à la place de la réalité" (17 March 1825).

20. "Jeanne d'Arc, dans cette pièce, est le modèle du patriote de notre âge: elle exprime nos suffrances et notre indignation ... c'est la France du dix-neuvième siècle qui se venge en battements de mains de la dominations étrangère et des malheurs de l'invasion."

21. "I am no longer to be feared: a simple shepherdess" (I, ii).

22. "Cette scène dont tous les vers semblent inspirés comme le sentiment qui élève Jeanne au-dessus d'une mortelle, a produit la plus vive impression," *Le Drapeau blanc* (16 March 1821).

23. "Le désespoir qui déchire le coeur du père et des soeurs de Jeanne d'Arc, et contraste avec son courage plus qu'humaine et sa divine résignation, présentent le spectacle le plus touchant."

24. In another article in the series Bertrand discussed the affair of Urbain Grandier, in which two young nuns with convulsions were said to have been possessed by the devil (30 April 1825).

25. This is discussed in greater detail in Tony James, *Dream, Creativity, and Madness in Nineteenth-Century France* (Oxford: Clarendon Press, 1995), 44–5.

26. While sleepwalking and other dream phenomena were perceived on the Parisian stages as symptoms of sexual impropriety, madness, although represented in a similar way, was increasingly seen as an indication of sexual threat, an interpretation that was to gain ground in the following decades, as for example in the mad scenes of Italian opera. This is discussed in Chapter 2 of my dissertation, "Magnetism, Muteness, Magic." Although Jeanne's sexuality is not really explored at this time, her persuasiveness, mixed with sensual attraction, certainly is.

27. See Lee Johnson, *The Paintings of Eugène Delacroix: A Critical Catalogue,* i: *1816–1831,* ii: *1832–1863* (Oxford: Clarendon Press, 1981–86) for examples including "The Penance of Jane Shore" (plate 81), 1824, "Hamlet Abuses Ophelia" (plate 114), 1849/50, and "Lady Macbeth Sleepwalking" (plate 115), 1849/?50.

28. The sources for, and the significance of, these tropes, deriving above all from depictions of madness, are discussed in Elaine Showalter, *The Female Malady: Women, Madness and English Culture, 1830–1980* (New York: Pantheon, 1985), and, in the context of opera, in Mary Ann Smart, "The Silencing of Lucia," *Cambridge Opera Journal* IV (1992), 119–41.

29. This libretto, written by D'Anglemont and De Feuillade, is referred to in a letter dated 25 July 1828 sent from the Maison du Roi; in which the reading committee judged it "inadmissable" F-Pan, A[13] 120.

30. I consider the interpretation of such mute characters and their reception in Chapter 3 of "Magnetism, Muteness, Magic."

31. William Tell, in Rossini's 1829 opera, was another medieval hero. Some of the complex issues about historical representation in French opera of the first half of the nineteenth century are explored in Anselm Gerhard, *The Urbanization of Opera: Music Theater in Paris in the Nineteenth Century,* trans. Mary Whittall (Chicago: University of Chicago Press, 1998); originally published as *Die Verstädterung der Oper: Paris und das Musiktheater des 19. Jahrhunderts* (Stuttgart: J.B. Metzler, 1992).

32. Indeed during the 1830s at the Paris Opéra, it was the opportunities for the set and costume designers to create beath-takingly authentic scenery and clothing, and the resonances with the present provided by choruses of oppressed peoples, that attracted composers and librettists to medieval subjects, rather than the stories of individual historical figures.

The "Truth" About the Middle Ages: La Revue des Deux Mondes *and Late Nineteenth-Century French Medievalism*

ELIZABETH EMERY

La Revue des Deux Mondes, the preeminent French magazine of the late nineteenth century, dwelt insistently upon the Middle Ages during the 1870s.[1] It published articles praising medieval French art and literature, analyzing medieval law, warfare, economy, and medicine, and describing the life of such famous medieval French characters as King René, Philippe le Bel, and Joinville. In fact, between 1871 and 1876 it devoted nearly 25 per cent of its art and history articles – many of which purported to trace the origins of modern French institutions – to the Middle Ages.[2] But why would the editors of this publication, which appealed to a largely bourgeois readership of 18,000 and which was dedicated to examining contemporary society and its problems,[3] have chosen to focus so strongly upon the Middle Ages at this particular time? In its previous 40 years of publication it had devoted only six per cent of art and history articles to medieval topics.

One could argue that this sudden surge of interest in the Middle Ages occurred purely by chance, but the phenomenon's temporal proximity to the Franco-Prussian war goes beyond mere coincidence. Scholars have linked the late nineteenth-century French attraction for the Middle Ages to a variety of factors including increasing industrialization, the decreasing power of the Catholic Church in French political spheres, the rise of positivism, competition with Germany, and a general European preoccupation with the Middle Ages.[4] This essay contributes to studies about interest in the French Middle Ages by focusing upon the ways in which the periodical press – notably *La Revue des Deux Mondes* – was intrinsically linked to the rise in medievalism after the Franco-Prussian war. Authors used its pages to advocate the scientific study of the Middle Ages as a way of recovering national stability.

The bi-weekly *La Revue des Deux Mondes* is a privileged instrument for examining the ideas that circulated about the Middle Ages after the Franco-Prussian war. As Philippe Régnier has argued, widely read periodicals are valuable sources for studying the constitution and evolution of social trends.

A "revue," by definition, collects essays and articles. By bringing together a wide variety of independent pieces, such magazines seek to provide the reader with a broad panorama of what is being written at a given time.[5] The liberties accorded to editors in France at the end of the century made information about contemporary issues accessible to subscribers and exerted such influence over readers that Eugèn Weber has called the press "the chief site and instrument of public debate ... affecting the public by its capacity to communicate, magnify, and manipulate the notions, scenes, and bits of information that it brought very close to home."[6]

La Revue des Deux Mondes, which was published throughout the war, provides particularly valuable contemporary reactions about the humiliating defeat of Napoleon III and the four-month German occupation of Paris; about the civil insurrection of the Commune; and about the signing of the Treaty of Frankfurt, which gave the provinces of Alsace and Lorraine to the German Empire while requiring France to pay a five billion gold franc ($1 billion) indemnity.[7] By the end of fighting, contributors lamented the nation's state of affairs. Ludovic Vitet, former Inspector of Historical Monuments and a member of the Académie Française, described the defeat as "an abyss of agony and shame" and portrayed France as wounded yet admirable, grieving for "the noble casualty named France."[8] So keen was the sense of injury that 17 years later public figures still spoke of the war as if the wounds were fresh.[9]

Conceiving problems in terms of war wounds provided a convenient metaphor for a distressing, yet reversible state. France's body and soul might be suffering, but its illness could be treated. For leading intellectuals like Vitet, healing the nation's wounds in order to regain power was a priority: "the painful task imposed by our misfortunes is the reconstitution, the renovation of France." In a patriotic *Revue des Deux Mondes* book review of 15 May 1872, he even proposed a course of treatment: reading a new history of France written by former prime minister François Guizot. Vitet's critique summarizes the moral of *L'Histoire de France, racontée à mes petits-enfants* – that France has always completely recovered after periods of invasion and loss – while glorifying the book in no uncertain terms as a "second catechism, which will instill in our children the veritable history of France." Singing the praises of this volume, Vitet stresses the book's therapeutic nature: "It is an instrument of reconciliation, order, peace, and political morals."[10] Vitet lavishes his greatest praise of the book upon its truth and accuracy. He insists that it was not the war, but incorrect ideas about the past that were responsible for the sickness of France: "The false interpretation of the past is, at the present time, the most dangerous of poisons. Give me true ideas about the history of France, spread them in profusion, so that the country can take nourishment from them and soak them up. ... Understanding our history well is the key to all of our problems, the regenerative principle of all order and progress."[11]

The insistence Vitet places upon establishing the "truth" about history in order to heal his country echoes the post-war comments of his contemporaries. Fustel de Coulanges, who held a professorship of ancient history at Strasbourg before the city was lost to the Germans, was one of the leading proponents of historical reform. Though a classicist, he began focusing upon medieval French history after the war, and was one of the first to blame incorrect understanding of the past – especially the Middle Ages – for contemporary historical disputes. He began his crusade to reinterpret France's origins in an 1871 *Revue des Deux Mondes* essay about justice in the feudal world:

> The ancient past ... still exerts over us a domination and an unusual character. There is not one Frenchman, no matter how ignorant, who does not speak of the Middle Ages, who does not think he understands it, who does not pretend to judge it. ... Yet the idea we make of it, true or false, has such a hold on our spirit, that nearly all the stream of our thoughts and opinions comes from it. Observe why two men think differently about questions of government and politics, it is almost always because they have two different ways of judging the Ancien Régime. Two men meet and argue about public affairs, you think they are talking about urgent concerns, – most often they're quarreling about the Ancien Régime, and because they are in disagreement about the way they understand the past, it is impossible for them to agree about the present. ... Thus history forms our opinions.[12]

In this article Fustel assigns an enormous sociological function to the understanding of history, a theme that haunts his 1870s essays. He proposes that France's current moral weakness stems not from the war, but from its inability to come to an agreement about the interpretation of its history. He sees the manipulation of the Middle Ages as responsible for the divisive polemics of his peers.

According to Fustel's reading of documents from the Middle Ages, all of French history as his contemporaries understood it was incorrectly based upon a single assumption about the Germanic invasions of the fifth century. In an 1872 article for *La Revue des Deux Mondes*, entitled "L'Invasion germanique au cinquième siècle," Fustel explained that his contemporaries' beliefs about national identity were founded upon this erroneous theory, which had grown to "enormous proportions" in the national imagination, thus forming a standardized myth about the origin of France:

At the beginning of French history, one usually imagines a great invasion by the Germans. It seems as though it [this event] changed the face of the country and gave its destinies a direction they would not have had without it. It is, for many historians and for the masses, the source for the whole Ancien Régime. The feudal lords pass for the sons of the Germans, and the serfs of the glebe for the sons of the Gauls. A conquest – that is to say a brutal act – is thus posited as the unique origin of ancient French society. All of the great facts of our history are explained and judged in the name of this first iniquity. The feudal system is presented as the reign of the conquerors, the emancipation of towns as the awakening of the defeated, and the revolution of 1789 as their revenge.[13]

Fustel's article clearly identifies his contemporaries' reliance upon the theory of the German invasion for their conception of the long-standing tension between the nobility and the people. This belief had been critical to the French perception of the Middle Ages and their role in French history, and had become even more prevalent in the wake of the recent Germanic invasion.[14]

Fustel sees this *a priori* assumption about the Middle Ages as responsible for a chain reaction of historical interpretation that assumed the inherent weakness of the "vanquished, conquered, enslaved" French, who lost the 1870–71 conflict because of their genetic powerlessness. After stating his disagreement with this interpretation, he uses the rest of this 1872 article to debunk the concept of a German "conquest" of Gaul in the fifth century. He relies upon Gallic and Germanic medieval sources, Sidoine Apollinaire, Grégoire de Tours, and Jornandès, to prove that no one mentioned an all-consuming triumph that would have changed "the destinies of the country." There were invasions by Germanic tribes, he argues, but these people were never able to gain a foothold. He uses other medieval chronicles to prove that the two races never felt the hostility that modern historians attributed to them. Instead, Fustel painstakingly shows the weakness of the Germans – "the debris of a depleted race" – decimated by recurring war with the Romans, and reveals their progressive peaceful waves of immigration into Gaul as workers and soldiers.[15] His essay is a point-by-point refutation of most of the nineteenth-century beliefs about the importance of Germanic tribes in the development of the French nation. Fustel's points greatly influenced contemporaries like writer Barbey d'Aurevilly, whose enthusiasm for these theories is clear: "Here we are, de-Germanized," he notes; "Here we are called back to our origins, which are essentially Roman."[16]

From 1871 to 1872 Fustel published four major articles (one in four installments) in *La Revue des Deux Mondes*. In these essays, he insisted upon the stability of France by linking the nineteenth-century infrastructure of France to the Gallo-Roman period. His articles about the fifth-century "invasions," about the judicial system in Antiquity and in the Middle Ages, about the origins of the feudal order in Rome and France, and about patronage in feudal French society question the importance of a fifth-century invasion and downplay the Germanic influence in the development of French social institutions. He insists, in each article, upon the unbroken links between the Roman Empire and subsequent developments in France, from language to law and medicine. France is, he claims, even stronger than previously thought because the nation's traditions and social structure were adapted from the Romans, the people who had originally conquered the Germans. He returns constantly to the idea that understanding the past will soothe contemporary turmoil because the Middle Ages were a stable time of "simple and just ideas":

> Understanding of the Middle Ages – the exact, scientific, and sincere understanding of them without bias – is, for our society a concern of the highest order. It is the best way to put an end to the insane regrets of some, to the empty utopias of others, to the hatred of all. To reestablish calm in the present, it is not un-useful to begin by destroying prejudices and errors about the past. History imperfectly observed divides us; it is by better understanding history that the work of reconciliation must begin.[17]

For Fustel, an unbiased and universally accepted version of medieval history was therapeutic: learning the truth about the Middle Ages would allow the various factions of French society to see their common heritage and to heal their psychological wounds.

Although Fustel's insistence upon using facts and documents to analyze historical events may seem routine today, the beliefs of this "historian who made objectivity a fetish" were new and controversial at the time. His advice to students – "believe only what documents tell you" – influenced a generation of scholars to reconsider the major tenets of French history.[18] Edward Jenks, a British contemporary, credited the historian's use of authentic documents to confirm or deny commonly held beliefs about the past with spurring a reevaluation of French history.[19] Such theories came at a propitious time, since the Franco-Prussian defeat and subsequent questioning of national identity gave positivist historians an audience, their narrative about a historically strong French nation corresponding to what readers wanted to hear.[20]

Other intellectual figures joined Fustel's quest to reveal the "truth" about the Middle Ages and rallied to convince their contemporaries of the importance of understanding this time. Gaston Paris and Paul Meyer (who formed *Romania,* the review of medieval studies, in 1872, and *La Société des Textes Français* in 1875) and Gabriel Monod, the founder of *La Revue historique* (begun in 1876) all agreed that the scientific reconsideration of French history was of the utmost importance for the health of the country.[21] These scholars had been formally trained in positivist methods and embraced philology – the linguistic and textual analysis of authentic texts – as a scientific and objective way of learning about the traditions of the past.[22] Instead of "making up one's own Middle Ages," scholars after the war argued that it was crucial to hold solid, true and universally accepted ideas about France's past. Joseph Bédier, citing Gaston Paris (who in turn was citing Bossuet), argued that "the greatest depravation of the mind is to believe things because one wants them to be."[23] The Middle Ages, with their wealth of manuscripts, became, for these scholars, the natural starting point for establishing an "objective" or "true" history of France.

Although the desire to reform French methods of studying and teaching history in France would seem to be one of the most unusual aspects of this moment of perceived historical crisis, even more striking was intellectuals' attempt to reach out to the public, to share their concerns with non-erudite specialists. Fustel and Vitet used *La Revue des Deux Mondes* to disseminate their beliefs about the importance of studying the past, possibly because the publication provided contributors with what Régnier has called "journalist platforms."[24] The periodical's editor, Buloz, enjoyed recruiting lecturing professors and members of the Académie Française and l'Institut de France to prove the solid intellectual foundation of his magazine, while the publication gave contributors a highly visible pulpit from which to communicate. This was just the kind of publicity Vitet had demanded to begin the "work of reconciliation" when he asked his fellow historians to give him "true ideas," and "spread them in profusion."

As Claude Bellanger, a specialist on the history of the press in France has demonstrated, such magazines exerted an enormous influence upon the social and intellectual elite of the time.[25] Their dedication to spreading news about a new version of French history, was likely to have convinced many of the 18,000 readers of *La Revue des Deux Mondes* that France was, indeed, strong, superior to Germany, and capable of even greater accomplishments. The periodical's constant comparison of medieval and modern France would have soothed the humiliated nation by showing the ways in which its ancestors had used their strength and resilience to recover from invasion.[26]

The parallels between medieval and modern history unquestionably appealed to contemporaries. Charles Lenient, author of a 1892 book about patriotic medieval poetry, credited scholars with boosting public morale: "At the time when our hearts were most cruelly wrung ... we sought in our souvenirs of the past consolation and hope, more moral comfort than subject of erudite debate." Lenient attributed the idea for his patriotic book of poetry to the siege of Paris, during which he attempted to give his contemporaries spiritual encouragement by insisting upon the "great and virile inspiration" of medieval French literature.[27] The series of lectures Gaston Paris gave at the Collège de France during the war also insisted upon the inherent French patriotism and superiority of medieval texts like *La Chanson de Roland*: "Sweet France! ... The Germans envied us these words, and vainly sought to find their equivalent in their national poetry."[28] As Joseph Duggan has shown, such patriotic sentiment glossed over the strict truth; *La Chanson de Roland* employs the term *Francia* to encompass German lands as well as French.[29] Although scholars planned to explore the "truth" about the Middle Ages, they often fashioned them into a time of "simple and just ideas" that would appeal to contemporaries' need for social and ideological unity.

The appeal to national pride worked. Medieval history, medieval characters, and medieval literature became rallying points for the French; indeed, historian Michel Winock has called this period "the apotheosis" of medieval figures Roland and Joan of Arc.[30] Such sudden enthusiasm for the patriotic texts of the past led to a veritable national furor for epics, notably *La Chanson de Roland*, which became the model, *par excellence* of "virile inspiration."[31] In a *Revue des Deux Mondes* review of *La Chanson de Roland*, Eugène Aubry-Vitet lauds the book as "the history of our national poetry of the Middle Ages." Gautier, himself, had extolled Roland as "France made man," and praised *La Chanson de Roland* as "the national epic," a work that rivaled the *Iliad*.[32] The enthusiasm Aubry-Vitet put into his *Revue des Deux Mondes* review reflects the delirious attraction of the Roland legend during a time of adversity:

> *La Chanson de Roland* is the history of a defeat, but a defeat more glorious, more celebrated, more lauded, more admired than many triumphs. Roland outnumbered, dying proud and Christian with love of the homeland in his heart, and even in those far-off times, with the name of sweet France on his lips – what better-made spectacle to stir a truly French heart, to wake in us a bit of the virtue – love of the homeland! – that people had attempted to kill with ridicule and that alone can fortify men and help the people back to their feet. If the present makes us modest, let us take courage in the past while waiting for the future![33]

Gautier's edition of Roland (helped perhaps by Aubry Vitet's unmitigated praise) was the first hugely successful commercial version of *Roland*: it went through 26 editions between 1872 and 1903.[34]

Joan of Arc was similarly lauded as a model for the modern French nation. She was extolled as "the patron saint of an invaded nation" and the "messiah of nationality."[35] A 12 December 1897 newspaper article from *Le Temps* proposing a school festival in honor of Joan of Arc, underlines the universal appeal of Roland and Joan in the two decades following the war: "Invincible love for the homeland, stronger than death, than discouragement or defeat … , this is what is taught by the humble countrywoman who preached the union of all Frenchmen and who gave her life for France." Innumerable poems, songs, books, plays, school celebrations, and artistic commissions sprang up around their names, while scholars celebrated these heroes' selfless contribution to their communities.[36]

While Roland and Joan might seem ambivalent patriotic figures (their heroic activities ended in defeat and death), after the war their success in failure made them emblems for the French longing for revenge against invaders. Léon Gautier explained such logic in his 1875 edition to *La Chanson de Roland*, "Roland, too, was defeated; but such a loss did not have the slightest diminishing effect on his glory, and, at any rate, Charlemagne avenged him with a brilliant and decisive victory. While waiting for Charlemagne, we console ourselves with Roland." In 1892, he looked back at the post-war period and was proud to have helped his contemporaries "by showing how every Roncevaux can gloriously be put right; if the name of Roland – with that of Joan of Arc, which is even more French – could serve as a rallying point for souls enamored of real patriotism … then my labor will not have been in vain."[37] Models for grace under duress, Roland and Joan were symbolic figures that proved the stability, longevity and supremacy of patriotic pride in France.[38]

By the late 1870s the Roland legend enjoyed such widespread popularity that it became a canonical text for students. *La Chanson de Roland* was placed on the syllabus for the *agrégation des lettres* and *agrégation de grammaire* in 1878 and became a required secondary school text in 1884. Gautier, himself, edited the first student edition and wrote a patriotic introduction for teachers:

> I entreat [teachers] to take care to tell themselves that this poetry is of our race and our fathers, that it is healthy and vigorous, male and proud; that it offers us human types that are one hundred times superior to those of pagan antiquity.

Above all, he noted, the *Chanson* makes the French love France: "This is why I will never regret having restored honor to this masterpiece, which was so long disdained, and to have devoted to it so many years of a life filled and consoled by only two loves: homeland and truth."[39]

Gautier's passion for *La Chanson de Roland* as a model for rebuilding national pride returns to the issues of blood and race addressed by Fustel de Coulanges. In the new history of France, Roland, a true French hero, has become one of the original fathers of the modern French nation: healthy, vigorous, manly, and proud. He, like the "simple and just" Middle Ages praised by Fustel, is a model for France to contemplate as it rebuilds national spirit.

These newly discovered "truths" may never have gained currency had it not been for the war. Gautier and contemporaries Paulin Paris and Francisque Michel had worked tirelessly throughout the nineteenth century to promote public awareness about the Middle Ages and had previously been mentioned in *La Revue des Deux Mondes* (notably by Ludovic Vitet, who had written about *La Chanson de Roland*, Joinville and Saint Louis), but never with great frequency. French historians, especially medievalists, were virtually unknown to the general public in France, and the only journals in which they could publish in France were *La Bibliothèque de l'Ecole des Chartes*, *Le Bulletin du Bibliophile*, *Société de linguistique*, and *Revue des langues romanes*.[40] After the war, however, the public embraced these medieval scholars as they rushed from their ivory tower to join in the fight to rebuild French confidence. The intellectuals who published their works in popularly read periodicals and who gave public lectures suddenly became national heroes. In his enraptured 1872 *Revue des Deux Mondes* review of Gautier's first edition of *La Chanson de Roland*, Eugène Aubry-Vitet presented the scholar as just such a warrior, who had adopted the "arms of a scientist" in order to "take part in the fight against this invading and jealous people, our rival in erudition and in supremacy." "Isn't it," he argues, "serving one's country when one seeks to find for it, at least in the field of science and thought, the place that a disastrous war had made it lose on the fields of battle?"[41]

The extent to which this overwhelming popular embrace of the Middle Ages is inseparable from renewed patriotism is most apparent when compared with pre-war attitudes. As Gautier points out, he had devoted his life to restoring the honor of *La Chanson de Roland,* which had always been scorned by the public. In 1880 he had argued that his contemporaries would persist in refusing to give *La Chanson de Roland* a place in the high school curriculum alongside the classics, yet only four years later he was invited to prepare the schoolchildren's edition. Gautier's surprise and delight in finding that *Roland* had become so popular practically leaps from the pages of his prefaces to subsequent editions, in which he presents it as the French *Iliad*. His many years of anonymous toiling were finally rewarded by the great popularity accorded the Middle Ages in the 20 years following the Franco-Prussian war.

The tone of articles from *La Revue des Deux Mondes* also reveals the extent to which public taste changed nearly overnight. The three essays devoted to the Middle Ages immediately before the war treated the mysterious captivity of "Jeanne la Folle," mother of Charles V (1 June 1869); discussed the influence of sermons in the development of the French language (15 August 1869); and reviewed *l'Histoire des doctrines grammaticales au moyen âge*, by Charles Thurot (1 October 1869). Although all three authors attached importance to the scientific study of the Middle Ages, none glowed with the patriotism of the 1871 and 1872 articles. Both the author of the article about sermons and that of the book review about medieval grammar felt compelled to preface their remarks by defending the books as not too obscure or "pedantic." Where the post-war articles of Fustel, Vitet, and Aubry-Vitet assumed that the public would be fascinated by French history, the earlier authors made no assumption about readerly enjoyment.

Such a sudden shift in attitudes to the Middle Ages reveals not only that the war spurred interest in studies of the Middle Ages, but also that scholars used this event to modify their attitudes toward readers: they went from "pedantic" to popular. Fustel and Vitet had argued that it was crucial to publicize the "truth" about medieval history in order to rebuild national strength, and their insistence upon reaching out to the public through *La Revue des Deux Mondes* put them in contact with a huge audience. Instead of preaching to the converted, they chose instead to present their work to their less erudite contemporaries. Paul Meyer, co-founder of *Romania*, argued that the "best way to make the Middle Ages appreciated is to work to make them known," while Léon Gautier insisted upon the importance of publicizing the Middle Ages for everyone: "It is imperative not to disdain the general public, at the risk of being abandoned by it, and it is particularly important not to transform science into some kind of obscure temple where only priests have the right to enter." "Everything, everything must be put in place to assure the decisive triumph of our national epic: everything, including *La Bibliothèque bleue* books for children and touching images of traditional life for countryfolk and fools; everything including tales and alphabets for children."[42] Medievalist Adolphe d'Avril's 1892 publication of *Les Enfances Roland* in the *Nouvelle Bibliothèque Bleue* series, and Gaston Paris and Joseph Bédier's modern translations of medieval works such as the *Romance of Tristan* and *Les Lais* of Marie de France are products of this grass-roots effort to encourage the study of the Middle Ages. The insistence these medievalists placed upon catering to the people distinguishes the late nineteenth-century vogue for the Middle Ages from others.

It is no coincidence that the confluence of patriotism and positivism, presented through a widely read periodical, resulted in the formation of the institutions and publications that we consider integral to medieval studies today, a veritable body of scholarly works that insist upon the cultural achievements of the medieval French nation. Paul Meyer and Gaston Paris founded *Romania* in 1872 to compete with *Germania*[43] and in 1875 they began publishing medieval works in *La Société des Anciens Textes Français*. In his first speech as president of the society, Gaston Paris presented the project as "a national work," whose objectives were to make medieval France better known. Announcing that "Germany should no longer be the European country where the most monuments of our language and literature are printed," he explained the Society's goals as being "to make the simple language, the heroic dreams, the joyous laughter, and the ancient morals of our fathers come alive again."[44] The years following the war saw the beginning of a number of important publications including Godefroy, *Le Dictionnaire de l'ancienne langue française* (1881); Gaston Paris, *La Poésie du moyen âge* (1885); Petit de Julleville, *Histoire du Théâtre en France* (1880–89) and *L'Histoire de la langue et de la littérature françaises* (1896); and Emile Mâle, *L'Art Religieux du XIIIe siècle en France* (1898). In the meanwhile, Gaston Paris and Paul Meyer were rewarded for their contributions to philology by being elected to chairs at the Collège de France and by being nominated to distinctive positions in the academic and literary circles of France, while the Sorbonne created its first chair in medieval history for Fustel de Coulanges. Michel Espagne has called these careers "a sort of institutional consecration of the discipline."[45]

In an 1892 preface to *Les Epopées Françaises*, Léon Gautier assessed the current state of medieval studies in France and attributed their great popularity to the country's thirst for patriotism after the war.[46] Links between medieval and modern history had sparked enthusiasm for the Middle Ages, thus creating a market for medieval scholars. But they had also turned the Middle Ages into an analogy for modern life, in which the Franco-Prussian war had become "the Roncevaux of the nineteenth-century." Such self-serving uses of the Middle Ages reduced rich political, religious and aesthetic dimensions of *La Chanson de Roland* to a simple reflection of patriotic feeling. As France recovered from its identity crisis, however, it was able to value the Middle Ages as more than a patriotic topic. As Fustel, Vitet, Gautier, Paris, and Bédier continued to present the Middle Ages as a therapeutic activity, their nationalist messages created subsequent waves of interest in the French Middle Ages. In the 1880s and 1890s the increased emphasis scholars placed on philology fueled the public's desire to read medieval texts.

In fact, in the 1890s *La Revue des Deux Mondes* devoted 11 per cent of its art, literature, and history articles to the Middle Ages.[47] This time, however, the focus was not on patriotism, but on medieval French works themselves: their style, content and meaning. In the 1890s Joseph Bédier authored for the *Revue des Deux Mondes* articles about Marie de France, the comic theater of the Middle Ages, the *chanson de geste*, and lyric poetry; while Marcel Schwob wrote about François Villon, Girard de Roussillon and Joinville. Charles Langlois published articles about the Templiers, while Edouard Schuré praised the "celtic genius." René Doumic wrote about Froissart, Ferdinand de Brunetière studied the fabliaux, and numerous authors discussed Joan of Arc. In the second wave of post-war interest in the Middle Ages, scholars used the periodical to study medieval works of art from France in their own right; they did not need to use medieval history as a pretext to shed light upon the "origins" of the French nation.

The interest in the Middle Ages provoked by post-war enthusiasm for medieval history provided the catalyst and the readership necessary to make medieval art and literature popular for a great number of people. In the 1880s and 1890s even best-selling novelists Anatole France, Emile Zola and J.-K. Huysmans incorporated complicated medieval images and themes into their novels. The eponymous hero of Anatole France's *Le Crime de Sylvestre Bonnard* (1881) covets medieval manuscripts; Zola's *Le Rêve* (1888) is set in the shadow of a Romanesque cathedral where his heroine embroiders chasubles and emulates the saints of *The Golden Legend*; and Huysmans' *Là-Bas* (1891), *En Route* (1894), *La Cathédrale* (1898) and *L'Oblat* (1903) chronicle the protagonist's fascination with medieval art, music, history and theology. By the 1890s, the Middle Ages were no longer a pretext for shedding light on the French nation's origins, nor were they intended primarily as a way of soothing national pride. Medieval art, literature and music had become accepted and championed cultural phenomena, capable of holding their own with studies of Antiquity. *La Chanson de Roland* had truly become the "French Iliad."

One can argue, as Janine Dakyns has done, that the late nineteenth-century French interest in the Middle Ages was largely self-serving and reflected France's nationalist needs.[48] While this is true to an extent, and certainly just after the war, France's defeat also began a new era for medieval studies in France. The post-war period should thus be distinguished from other medieval revivals of the nineteenth century in France. The sheer popularity of the Middle Ages during the *fin-de-siècle* – regardless of whether it stemmed from nationalist or aesthetic needs – brought medieval art, civilization and culture to the forefront of the national imagination as a field worthy of study. The large volume of articles devoted to medieval themes in *La Revue des Deux Mondes* engendered real interest in them, thus creating a demand for serious medieval scholarship. Moreover, the phenomenon was not isolated to largely Republican periodicals such as *La Revue des Deux Mondes*. The same surge of interest in medieval literature, celebrations, history and art is reflected in other publications. *Le Temps*, the French equivalent of the London *Times*, discussed new medieval purchases by the Louvre, evoked the exhibits devoted to medieval stained glass and tapestry at the 1889 and 1900 World's Fairs, and consecrated yearly articles to pilgrimages in honor of Joan of Arc. Although it is easy to condemn late nineteenth-century French medievalism as a fad created to build national confidence and to compete with the Germans, it was an integral movement in the creation of modern medieval studies in France. The humiliating defeat against the Germans and a desire to rebuild national pride provided the catalyst necessary for the French to mend their self image and to examine their past in a new way, thus discovering yet another truth about the Middle Ages: it was an accessible, fascinating, and indispensable component of French history.

NOTES

1. According to Claude Bellanger, *Histoire Générale de la presse française. Tome III: De 1871 à 1940* (Paris: Presses universitaires de France, 1970). The *Revue* had 18,000 subscribers in 1874 and was the model for other magazines (391).
2. This figure comes from an analysis of the rubrics "art" and "histoire" in the tables of *La Revue des Deux Mondes*. Only 5.89 per cent of articles in these rubrics discussed the Middle Ages from 1831 to 1870. 22.8 per cent of the art and history articles from 1871 to 1876 treat medieval topics.
3. An anonymous article from February 1832 (probably the work of Sainte-Beuve) stated the magazine's goals: "For thirty years now Germany and England have possessed periodicals, journals that serve as rostrums for people of the greatest intelligence, for the most active and supple spirits, who follow and dominate history as it is made. ... France has come late to this method of thought and teaching, which partakes of the nature of newspapers and of the serious discussion of books." Cited in Simon Jeune, "Les Revues littéraires," *Histoire de l'édition française*, ed. Roger Chartier and Henri-Jean Martin, Vol.3 (Paris: Fayard/Promodis, 1990), 455. Unless otherwise indicated, all translations are mine.
4. Laura Morowitz, "Consuming the Past: The Nabis and French Medieval Art" (Ph.D. diss., New York University, 1996), discusses the increase in medievalism as a reaction against industrialization; Richard Griffiths, *The Reactionary Revolution* (New York: Frederick Unger Publishing Co., 1965), links Catholicism and Medievalism; Janine Dakyns (*The Middle Ages in French Literature 1851–1900* [London: Oxford University Press, 1973]), suggests relationships among political, scientific and cultural movements and the rise of interest in the Middle Ages; and Peter Frankl (*The Gothic: Literary Sources and Interpretations through Eight Centuries* [Princeton: Princeton University Press, 1960]) provides information about general European trends in Medievalism.
5. Philippe Régnier, "Littérature nationale/littérature étrangère au XIXe sièle. La Fonction de la *Revue des Deux Mondes* entre 1829 et 1870." *Qu'est-ce qu'une littérature nationale? Approches pour une théorie intercultrelle du champ littéraire*, ed. Michel Espagne and Michael Werner (Paris: Editions de la Maison des sciences de l'homme, 1994), 289–314 (289).

6. Eugen Weber, *France, Fin de Siècle* (Cambridge, MA: Harvard University Press, 1986), 240.
7. See J.M. Gobert, "L'Itinéraire intellectuel et politique de *La Revue des Deux Mondes* (1848–1893)" (Doctoral thesis, L'Institut d'Etudes politiques de Paris, 1984–85) for more about the analysis of Franco-Prussian relations in *La Revue des Deux Mondes* before, during, and after the war.
8. Ludovic Vitet, "Une Nouvelle Histoire de France, de M. Guizot," *La Revue des Deux Mondes* 95/2 (15 May 1872), 439–49 (439).
9. An 18 December 1897 article in *Le Temps* refers to the memory of the war as a still unhealed wound: "Plus se prolongera l'attente, plus risquera de se refermer et de guérir la blessure faite à notre honneur de nation; or, il ne faut pas que cette blessure guérisse, si l'on veut que la fête du patriotisme garde toute son efficacité et toute sa vertu."
10. Vitet, "Une Nouvelle Histoire de France," 440–42
11. Ibid., 441.
12. Fustel de Coulanges, "L'Organisation de la Justice dans l'Antiquité et les temps modernes. III. La Justice royale au Moyen Age," *La Revue des Deux Mondes* 94/2 (1 Aug. 1871), 536–57 (536–7).
13. Fustel de Coulanges, "L'Invasion germanique au cinquième siècle," *La Revue des Deux Mondes* 99/2 (15 May 1872), 241–59 (241).
14. See Colleen Beth Hays for a lengthy discussion of the development and dissemination of these issues of origin from the sixteenth to the nineteenth centuries. "Literary History and Criticism of French Medieval Works in the Nineteenth Century: The Phenomenon of Medievalism." (Ph.D. diss., University of Oklahoma, 1993).
15. de Coulanges, "L'Invasion germanique au cinquième sièle," 241–3.
16. Article in *Le Constitutionnel* (20 July 1875). Cited in François Hartog, *Le XIXe siècle et l'histoire: le cas Fustel de Coulanges* (Paris, 1988), 79. Hartog also discusses the perennial debates between Germanists and Romanists that accounted for some of Barbey's glee. These discussions were critical to the establishment of a new story about national identity (83–95). See also Gonthier-Louis Fink, "Classique et Romantique, Critères du génie national," in *Images de soi, image de l'autre* (Strasbourg: Presses universitaires de Strasbourg, 1994), 71–86.
17. From the third installment of "L'Organisation de la Justice dans l'antiquité et les temps modernes" (1 Aug. 1871), 538.
18. See Jane Herrick, *The Historical Thought of Fustel de Coulanges* (Washington, DC: The Catholic University of America Press, 1954), 4 and 120–1.
19. See "Fustel de Coulanges as an historian," *English Historical Review* XII (April 1897), 209–24. Thirty years later Marc Bloch also admitted that French historians would not be studying the history of France as they were if Fustel had never existed. He called Fustel "the historian of French origins" (*Revue internationale de l'enseignement* LXXXIV [15 July 1830], 178). Both historians are cited in by Jane Herrick in *The Historical Thought of Fustel de Coulanges*, 95.
20. See Gonthier-Louis Fink, "Classique et Romantique, Critères du génie national." Fink argues that in order to better assert their identity following the war, the French felt the need "purge" all foreign elements from their self image (82).
21. In his inaugural preface for the journal, Gabriel Monod described the importance of history: "L'étude du passé de la France ... a aujourd'hui une importance nationale. C'est par elle que nous pouvons rendre à notre pays l'unité et la force morales dont il a besoin" (*Revue historique*, i [1876], 4).
22. After the death of Gaston Paris, in 1903, scholars Joseph Bédier, Mario Roques and Paul Meyer paid homage to their mentor by insisting upon the extent to which his dedication to philology, which he had discovered while studying in Germany, had influenced medieval studies in France. Bédier defined the work of philologists as "donner sur l'analyse linguistique et sur l'interprétation des textes littéraires la connaissance vraie du passé." Joseph Bédier, "Hommage à Gaston Paris" (Paris: Honoré Champion, 1904), 9. Michel Espagne's valuable comparative studies of European philology have shown that French philology did not function effectively as a discipline until after the war and that it was not until the mid-1870s that the works of Gaston Paris and Paul Meyer began to create a true discipline. These authors are considered the founders of French philology. See Michel

Espagne, "A Propos de l'évolution historique des philologies modernes: l'exemple de la philologie romane en Allemagne et en France" (Paris: Editions de la maison des sciences de l'homme, 1990), 174–5.

23. Bédier, "Hommage à Gaston Paris," 11.

24. Régnier, "Littérature nationale/littérature étrangère au XIXe siècle," 293.

25. Bellanger, *Histoire Générale de la presse française*, 391.

26. Although Fustel drew parallels between modern and medieval France, he preferred study of the past: "je préfère les études d'histoire à des travaux sur le temps présent" (cited in Hartog, *Le XIXe siècle et l'histoire*, 272). See Hartog, pages 56–7, for more about Fustel's collaboration with Buloz.

27. Charles Lenient, *La Poésie patriotique en France au Moyen Age* (New York: Burt Franklin, 1971), vii–viii.

28. In a 7 December 1870 lecture for the *Collège de France* entitled "La Chanson de Roland et la nationalité française," later published in *La Poésie du Moyen Age* (Paris: Hachette, 1885).

29. Joseph Duggan, "Franco-German Conflict and the History of French Scholarship on the Song of Roland," *Hermeneutics and Medieval Cluture*, ed. Patrick J. Gallagher and Helen Damico (Albany: State University Press of New York, 1989), 102.

30. Michel Winock, "Joan of Arc," *Realms of Memory: The Construction of the French Past*, vol. 3, ed. Pierre Nora and Lawrence D. Kritzman (New York: Columbia University Press, 1997), 433–82 (443).

31. Joseph J. Duggan calls this period the "apogee of the *Roland*'s use as an offensive intellectual weapon." See his "Franco-German Conflict and the History of French Scholarship on the Song of Roland," 103. Christian Amalvi's study of the "consecration" of the *Roland* legend in the years from 1880 to 1914, traces the erudite, patriotic, political, religious and moral debates that led to the work's adoption as a text for secondary school students. *De l'art et la manière d'accomoder les héros de France* (Paris: Albin Michel, 1989).

32. Léon Gautier, "Roland, c'est la France faite homme," *La Chanson de Roland* (Tours: Alfred Mame et fils, éditeurs 1872), vii. Gautier used the concept of *La Chanson de Roland* as l'épopée nationale" and as a rival for the *Iliad* in nearly every preface he wrote after the war. See, for example, *Les Epopées Françaises*, vol. II (Paris: Société Générale de librairie catholique, 1892), 794 and vol. ii, xv-xvi.

33. Eugène Aubry-Vitet, "Nouvelle Edition de la Chanson de Roland," *La Revue des Deux Mondes* 99/2 (15 June 1872), 956–61 (958).

34. Duggan traces the nationalist and anti-German rhetoric linked to *La Chanson de Roland* throughout the nineteenth century and describes the impact of Gautier's edition upon his contemporaries (Duggan, "Franco-German Conflict," 100–101).

35. Paul Déroulède and Henri Martin, respectively. Cited by Winock, "Joan of Arc," 441.

36. For a discussion of the flowering of Roland as a moral and patriotic figure after the war see Christian Almavi, op. cit. See Harry Redman, *The Roland Legend in Nineteenth-Century French Literature* (Lexington, KY: The University Press of Kentucky, 1991), for more about the literature dedicated to Roland, and see Duggan, "Franco-German conflict," for the ways in which Roland was used as a way of competing with the Germans. For the flowering of Joan of Arc imagery in the post-War period see Winock, "Joan of Arc," Marina Warner, *Joan of Arc: The Image of Female Heroism* (New York: Random House, Inc., 1981), and Rosemonde Sanson, "La 'Fête de Jeanne d'Arc' en 1894: Controverse et Célébration," *Revue d'Histoire moderne et contemporaine* (1973), 444–63. The sheer volume of entries in Pierre Lanéry d'Arc's 1894 bibliography of Joan, *Le Livre d'or de Jeanne d'Arc*, makes abundantly clear the overwhelming popularity she enjoyed between 1870 and 1894.

37. Gautier cited his Roland preface in *Les Epopées Françaises* (II, 746) and praised Roland and Joan in his preface to *Les Epopées* (II, viii).

38. Such attention to the vitality of the French nation and its virile roots would continue to thrive in the nationalist discourse of Maurice Barrès and Charles Maurras and would culminate in the foundation of ultra-nationalist factions such as L'Action française and La Ligue des patriotes français.

39. *La Chanson de Roland*, 15e édition pour les élèves de seconde (Tours: Alfred Mame et fils, éditeurs, 1884), vi.

40. In the inaugural issue of *La Revue historique* (1876), Monod pointed out the relative obscurity of French scholars, especially when compared to the celebrity of those in Germany (4). Similarly, Paul Meyer remarked upon the lack of venues open to medieval scholars before he had begun publication of *Romania*. "Notice sur Gaston Paris (1839–1903), Extrait du tome XXXIII de *L'Histoire littéraire de la France*" (Paris: Imprimerie Nationale, 1906), xiii.

41. Aubry-Vitet, "Nouvelle Edition de la Chanson de Roland," 956 and 958.

42. Paul Meyer made his statements about the Middle Ages in the July 1880 issue of *Romania*: "Le meilleur moyen de faire apprécier notre vieille littérature, c'est de travailler à la faire connaître" (477). Gautier's comments are from *Les Epopées Françaises*: "Il ne faut pas dédaigner le grand public, sous peine d'être abandonné par lui, et il convient surtout de ne point transformer la science en je ne sais quel temple où les prêtres seuls ont le droit d'entrer" (II, 748). "Tout, tout doit être mis en oeuvre pour assurer le triomphe décisif de notre épopée nationale: tout, jusqu'à la Bibliothèque bleue et aux images d'Epinal pour les campagnards et les ignorants; tout jusqu'aux Contes et aux Alphabets pour les enfants ..." (II, 779).

43. The introductory article by Paris establishes the opposition between Roman and German literature. See also Paul Meyer, "Notice sur Gaston Paris," and Maurice Croiset, "Notice sur la vie et les travaux de M. Gaston Paris." *Bibliothèque de l'Ecole des chartes,* Année 1904, t. LXV (Paris, 1904).

44. Cited in Meyer, "Notice sur Gaston Paris," xix.

45. Gaston Paris was nominated to the Collège de France in 1872, to the Académie Française in 1896, and to the Académie des Inscriptions et Belles-lettres in 1876. Meyer became a professor at the Collège de France in 1876, director of the Ecole des Chartes in 1882, member of the Académie des inscriptions et Belles-lettres in 1883. Fustel received his chair in medieval history in 1878 (Herrick, *The Historical Thought of Fustel de Coulanges*, 8). See Espagne, "A Propos de l'évolution," 175.

46. "Les désastres de 1870 ont donné soudain à l'Epopée française et aux études dont elle est l'objet un caractère résolument patriotique. *La Chanson de Roland* a pris alors les apparences et les proportions d'une manifestation contre les vainqueurs, et le cor de Roland a été le clairon qui a rallié les amis de la France. Rien n'a été plus sincère, rien n'a été plus sain. De toutes parts on s'est mis à publier de nouveaux textes épiques" (II, 791).

47. Between 1890 and 1896.

48. Dakyns, *The Middle Ages in French Literature*, 291.

Medieval Religion, Victorian Homosexualities

FREDERICK S. RODEN

For too long in the academy the study of "Medievalism" has been associated with quaint fixations on the Arthurian and the courtly in the romanticization of a medieval past. More recently scholars have looked critically at the construction of the Middle Ages in modern (and indeed postmodern) discourse. We have engaged the subject of nostalgia, the mythologization of a past that never existed. We have become conscious of the "Middle Ages" as a cultural Other to us as moderns: a space requiring the anthropologist's self-consciousness of the difference of the material we encounter when we read (and therefore define) the medieval.

Concurrent with scholarly inquiries into Medievalism in modern and postmodern works are more incisive definitions by professional medievalists – in literary studies, history, religion, and disciplines outside the humanities – of how we might date that period called the "Middle Ages." Increasingly, that moment of the "Early Modern" is being pushed back, to the point that even the "twelfth-century renaissance" can no longer claim the birth of a "modern" consciousness. Rather, categories such as "late Antiquity" and the "early Middle Ages" are blurring the boundaries between ancient, classical culture and modernity. In the process, whatever may be defined as the Middle Ages becomes more liminal, making it all the more powerful for forming that articulation of a "Modern" which is not rebirth but construction.

This essay concerns modernity, and the role of the medieval in making modernity: in shaping those categories and constructions we consider modern. In recent years, the study of religion has gained greater favor among medievalists. However, this has not necessarily been the case among "Medievalism-ists." I suggest here that we may invigorate the religious medieval that has been ignored while also interrogating the scholarly project of Medievalism. Medievalism is historicism. As we may practice a New Historicism by bringing contemporary critical and cultural theory to the study of history and historiography, we also need to revive medievalism. We cannot simply look at the way we make the medieval – how moderns have constructed the Middle Ages. We also must question how the medieval has made us: how we are constructions of the Middle Ages, and its subsequent Medievalisms.

Mark Jordan's recent *The Invention of Sodomy in Christian Theology* and Carolyn Dinshaw's *Getting Medieval* make clear the power of the past in creating the present.[1] Both Jordan and Dinshaw are conscious of the medieval's sexual resonance in contemporary culture. As a Victorianist, I am concerned with Foucault, who claimed the late nineteenth century as definitive in constructing modern sexual identities.[2] Constructions of a self do not, however, operate outside of historical – or historicizing – frameworks, as Foucault was well aware. Linda Dowling has demonstrated this phenomenon in *Hellenism and Homosexuality in Victorian Oxford*, where the role of ancient models in articulating categories of same-sex desire in the nineteenth century is carefully evidenced.[3]

I will argue here for the role of medieval religion in constructing late Victorian homosexual identities. In this essay, I take "Victorian" as precursor to "modern," following Foucault, as a period that created categories which twentieth-century individuals would inhabit. Our more secular scholarly culture tends to neglect the power of Christianity and Christian history, with its types and typologies, to provide a matrix for individual and collective definitions of a self. I maintain that religious culture in the nineteenth century, such as "medieval"-modeled, single-sex monastic communities revived in England at that time, offered spaces for persons of same-sex desire to live separate from a heteronormative society and, through devotion and friendship, explore their homoeroticism in both spiritual and mundane contexts.

The subject of this essay is the use of medieval religious referents in sexology's articulation of homosexual desires and identities. However, the literary, devotional and imaginative spaces in Victorian culture that I do not explore here exist as complementary to these medical, theological and philosophical declarations engaging medieval religion. They are the "affective piety" companion to the "systematic theology" in this nineteenth-century epistemology of same-sex desire and identity. It is important that "New Medievalism" examine, as New Historicists have been doing, documents and texts that may be considered "non-literary." For if we are to fully explore the cultural phenomenon of Medievalism, we must broaden our frame of reference.

To make another argument, if contemporary religious feminists may admire and be moved by Hildegard of Bingen's songs, the theology of her *Scivias* and other prose texts must also be read and understood. I cite Hildegard here because she is a fine example of our *fin-de-siècle*'s appropriation of medieval religion. She has become a favorite among Christian feminists. The Hildegard phenomenon is both justifiable and understandable. The prolific twelfth-century theologian, musician, poet – "Renaissance" woman, if that phrase can be used in this article – was until recently relatively unknown. However, she also speaks to a particular audience in our own time and place: one that is culturally-specific and has chosen to read her in particular ways for certain reasons. It is this "medievalism" – one that is emotional and affective, while strategic and articulated – that I wish to examine in my essay on late Victorian culture.

In 1896, Marc-André Raffalovich, a French-Russian-Jewish-Catholic convert who had fled England to avoid the perils of the Oscar Wilde trials, published *Uranisme et Unisexualité: Étude Sur Différentes Manifestations de L'Instinct Sexuel*. In this work, Raffalovich discusses "uranism," from the Greek *uranos*: "unisexuality," what we might call "homosexuality." He defines it through the Greeks, drawing on Plato. In Raffalovich's discussion of sexual "inversion," as the sociological models of the period named it, special attention is given to what he calls "superior inverts" – those who accomplish Plato's transcendence to spiritual love and in the Christian world inhabit the religious life. According to Raffalovich,

> Christianity naturally did not change uranism, but over a very long time it permitted superior inverts to follow enthusiastically and devoutly the principle of Plato. In a world that had witnessed Saturnalia of every kind, debauchery, and scandal, religion greatly attracted superior inverts. Virginity was placed so very high, and the love of one's fellow man turned so sacred and so tender, in the love of its young God naked and bleeding, disfigured and transfigured, torn and tearing. This filled uranists ... with an enthuasiasm easy to understand, that has not been extinguished even today; and for the good of men perhaps it will never go out. The soul of man, made the fiancée of Christ, has expressed over the centuries its desires and its adoration in poetry and prose. Angelus Silesius, Friedrich Spe, Saint John of the Cross, Saint Teresa, and so many graceful and illustrious others have languished in love on the breast of the Divine Lover. Hafiz [the homoerotic Islamic poet] may be compared with the "dark night" of Saint John of the Cross. One could read such poems and ignore what is in the spirit of the man who cries and kisses the feet, the hands, the merciful side, in a way that one does not ignore a lover that [the nineteenth-century theorist of sexuality] Krafft-Ebing places in *Psychopathia sexualis* as suffering from sadism, masochism, and unisexuality. Only in such moments of sensual and sentimental defiance does the literature of today dare what the poets of divine love have cooed about and moaned over with great delights.[4]

Raffalovich firmly places same-sex desire in a religious context. He sets it in a historical framework: in relation to the Christianization of Europe, western and non-western mysticism, and the development of monasticism.

The celibate with his duties, occupations, and devotions was a vocation for these ardent and desirous souls to elevate themselves to wisdom.

If one has studied the mystics, the sectarists, the doctors of the Church, one sees for the superior invert a wisdom, an elevation and a practice absolutely comparable to Plato, but with greater devotion, and for the weak invert discipline.

The history of the great founders, the great religious, whatever their age or flavor of faith ... teaches us much about the psychology of inversion and education. (31–2)

In Church history, inversion was neither neutral nor evil, but rather was a positive good. Elsewhere in his work, the sexologist develops this point further.

Raffalovich does not, however, argue that Christianity was without intolerance of homosexuality:

If Christianity opened itself to receive inverts, to help them, absolve them, save them, it became at the same time a pretext for persecution. Each sect that broke away was accused of sodomy. After having themselves been accused of every excess, after having thundered against the excesses of the pagans, the Christians helped themselves to this reproach against every sect, and against every heretic without exception. (32)

Raffalovich came to England as a young man, corresponded with Walter Pater, and set up shop as an Aesthete. From a wealthy banking family, Raffalovich never lacked the capital to establish himself in society. He published several volumes of poetry, but did not succeed in making a mark on London. He and Wilde were enemies and rivals – perhaps because of Wilde's own marginal status as an Irishman. Raffalovich has the distinction of being the butt of one of Wilde's biting one-liners. Wilde said that he "came to London with the intention of opening a *salon*, and he has succeeded in opening a saloon."[5] Raffalovich excelled in society later in life, after Wilde's death. He maintained a famous salon in Edinburgh blocks away from the church that he had built for his lifelong friend, John Gray – once "Dorian" Gray to Oscar Wilde, but for 30 years after a Roman Catholic priest.

Scholars of both gay and medieval studies might easily agree and accept as a given that the religious matrix in the Middle Ages cannot be minimized in any cultural analysis of same-sex desire. However, what I seek to demonstrate in discussing Raffalovich here is the degree to which historical periods different from our own, postmodern culture likewise sought and found queer desires in the Middle Ages. I am concerned not only with theological arguments about the articulation of homosexuality in relation to medieval religion, but indeed sites, as Raffalovich posits here, where same-sex desire is located in a historical context and then used in addressing one's own culture's definition of homosexual identity.

Perhaps the first Victorian space in which this phenomenon can be demonstrated is monasticism. That institution returned to England with the Catholic revival of the 1830s and 1840s, having disappeared with the Reformation. In 1844, John Dalgairns published a *vita* of Aelred of Rievaulx in a series edited by the future Cardinal Newman (perhaps the greatest icon of Victorian homosocial religious life). While here I will not belabor details from Dalgairns's biography of the saint whom John Boswell calls the "gay abbot" of the twelfth century, I wish to stress the importance of what I call the "Aelredian" model for religious friendship in the nineteenth century.[6] Monastic historian Peter Anson demonstrates such identification in his biography of a turn-of-the-century abbot who took the name of Aelred.

As a London youth in the 1880s and 1890s, the future Abbot Aelred Carlyle attended St. Alban's, Holborn, an Anglo-Catholic parish notorious for the large number of homosexual men who worshipped there. Clothed as a Benedictine oblate in 1893 at St. Austin's Priory, a site favored by Pater, Carlyle adopted the name Aelred after reading Dalgairns's biography. Anson, who at one time lived in Carlyle's community, analyzes the abbot thus:

> As he read he came to many a passage which proved that he had found a canonized saint who was a kindred spirit. For Aelred of Rievaulx "went about the world seeking for objects on which to expend his affection, and feeling pained if his love met with no return." ... This twelfth-century abbot was "always looking for someone to love." ... Carlyle discovered that "Cistercians do not seem to have been so jealous of particular friendships in their communities as were other orders," and that their "monastic system was an expression of the love of the domestic circle upon a large community." ... This little book revealed a world in which natural and spiritual relationships were just what the would-be Anglican monk craved for, and he must have felt that it would be possible to emulate this saint in almost everything.[7]

For Carlyle, who, according to Anson, "seemed to live from boyhood in a romantic dream," was a "devotee of friendship and affection," and who took "delight in friendships with 'charming young men'," there was much to be found in Dalgairns's *vita* (10,7).

The following extracts illustrate Anson's memories of Carlyle's sense of community:

> I cannot help feeling that many of the vocations in the Caldey community depended largely on personal affection for the Abbot; in fact, it would have been difficult, if not impossible, to remain in the monastery without a real love for him as a man ... in this respect there was a certain affinity between the spirit of our community and that of the twelfth-century Cistercian monasteries.

> Aelred of Rievaulx, as is clear from his writings, could conceive of nothing so perfect as to love and to be loved. It must be admitted that "he was inclined to favouritism and the joys of spiritual friendship with charming young men." ... Our Abbot, like his patron, generally had his "Simon," "Hugh," "Ivo," or "Little Ralph." It was not only the twelfth-century Cistercian abbot who chose a young monk who soothed him, when he was worried, and refreshed his leisure. ... If any specially favoured novice or professed monk decided that he was not called to the cloister and left the Island, Aelred of Caldey would mourn his loss in much the same words as Aelred of Rievaulx used in the famous lamentation for Simon ... which must have been inspired by David's lament for the death of Jonathan.

> Spiritual friendships were not discouraged in our community, and their expressions sometimes took a form which would not be found in any normal monastery to-day, but which appears to have been common enough in the early Middle Ages. Embraces, ceremonial and non-ceremonial, were regarded as symbolical of fraternal charity, so our variant of the Roman rite permitted a real hug and kisses on the cheek ... the Caldey ceremonial had medieval precedent, because a kiss on the mouth was expressly stipulated in the earlier forms of the Cistercian and Premonstratensian rites. (124–6)

The institution of friendship – whether or not same-sex desire is articulated – not surprisingly appears in numerous late-nineteenth and early twentieth-century discourses of homosexuality. While I am not suggesting that every spiritual friendship contained a sexual component, I do maintain that the homosociality of religious life enabled erotic and affective possibilities to be explored, even in a celibate context.

The English homosexual writer Edward Carpenter historicizes male-male relationships in his 1902 *Iolaus: An Anthology of Friendship*. He concludes by suggesting that such relationships survived quietly in medieval monasticism:

The quotations we have given from Plato and others show the very high ideal of friendship attained in the old world, and the respect accorded to it. With the coming of the Christian centuries, and the growth of Alexandrian and Germanic influences, a change began to take place. Woman rose to greater freedom and dignity and influence than before. The romance of love began to centre round her. The days of chivalry brought a new devotion to the world, and the Church exalted the Virgin Mother to the highest place in heaven. Friendship between men ceased to be regarded in the old light – i.e., as a thing of deep feeling, and an important social institution. It was even, here and there, looked on with disfavor – and lapses from the purity or chastity of its standard were readily suspected and violently reprobated. Certainly it survived in the monastic life for a long period; but though inspiring this to a great extent, its influence was not generally acknowledged.

The special sentiment of comrade-love or attachment (being a thing inherent in human nature) remained of course through the Christian centuries, as before, and unaltered – except that being no longer recognized it became a private and personal affair, running often powerfully enough beneath the surface of society, but openly unacknowledged, and so far deprived of some of its dignity and influence.[8]

Carpenter here makes the same argument that Raffalovich had made a few years earlier. He finds an unbroken line of same-sex desire from antiquity to the present that simply found a different means to flower when relationships were no longer publicly affirmed. For Carpenter, the decline of male-male relationships parallels the rise of women in western culture. His creation of a continuum of homosocial desire and suggestion of male-male affection as an open secret is reminiscent of the pioneering work of Eve Sedgwick in this field.[9]

Carpenter also quotes from Augustine's *Confessions*, on his deep friendships in youth, and Anselm's affectionate letters that discuss love in monastic life. For both Raffalovich and Carpenter, the importance of religious vocations in preserving affective bonds between people of the same gender cannot be underestimated. However, both are also very conscious of the transformation brought about by modernity. If Carpenter imagines that a renaissance of publicization of homoerotic desire is possible at the turn of his new century, Raffalovich exalts the power of religion to foster the "inverted," homoerotic sensibility. Where Carpenter historicizes , Raffalovich looks to the past as a means of advocating religiously-sanctioned spaces for the safe expression of same-sex desire.

Strong evidence of the role of medieval religious models in shaping Victorian definitions of homosexuality are also found in Havelock Ellis's *Sexual Inversion*, first published in 1897. The celebrated social scientist begins his work with a historical analysis:

> In the Penitentials of the ninth and tenth centuries, "natural fornication and sodomy" were frequently put together and the same penance assigned to both; it was recognized that the priests and bishops, as well as laymen, might fall into this sin, though to the bishop nearly three times as much penance was assigned as to the layman. Among the Normans, everywhere, homosexuality was markedly prevalent; the spread of sodomy in France about the eleventh century is attributed to the Normans, and their coming seems to have rendered it at times almost fashionable, at all events at court. In England William Rufus was undoubtedly inverted, as later on were Edward II, James I, and, perhaps, though not in so conspicuous a degree, William III.[10]

Like Caryle and Anson, Ellis also draws conclusions from Anselm, noting that when Anselm advises the Archdeacon William on how "to deal with people who have committed the sin of sodomy," he

> instructs him not to be too harsh with those who have not realized its gravity, for hitherto "this sin has been so public that hardly anyone has blushed for it, and many, therefore, have plunged into it without realizing its gravity." So temperate a remark by a man of such unquestioningly high character is more significant of the prevalence of homosexuality than much denunciation. (40)

Ellis then discusses the less cosmopolitan clerics:

> In religious circles far from courts and cities, as we might expect, homosexuality was regarded with great horror, though even here we may discover evidence of its wide prevalence. Thus in the remarkable *Revelation* of the Monk of Evesham, written in English in 1196, we find that in the very worst part of Purgatory are confined an innumerable company of sodomists (including a wealthy, witty and learned divine, a doctor of laws, personally known to the Monk), and whether these people would ever be delivered from Purgatory was a matter of doubt; of the salvation of no other sinners does the Monk of Evesham seem so dubious. (40–41)

Ellis's reading of history is comprehensive. His development of an understanding of homosexual activity and later identity rests on essentialist assumptions. Like Carpenter and Raffalovich, Ellis maintains that same-sex behaviors have always been practiced. The three writers grapple, as have contemporary theorists, with the question of the fixedness of homosexual identity in differing historical periods. If our intellectual culture is more conscious of the social construction of the self and its desires, these writers were more likely to attempt to name stable categories. While the association of actor with act is ambivalent and ambiguous in Ellis, Carpenter and Raffalovich, the place of the medieval in their claims is equally central. They argue that if such actions and individuals could exist in a period as different from their own as the Middle Ages, there is something transcendent, universal and therefore identifiable about inversion.

Ellis includes in *Sexual Inversion* a case study of a young man, "aged 31, American of French descent," who sublimates his homoeroticism through religious desire. An intellectual, R.S. enjoys "'metaphysical and theological subjects … and certain forms of mysticism'" (111). R.S.'s comments echo Raffalovich's evaluation of the place of same-sex desire in mysticism:

> "I possess only a slight knowledge of the particulars of erotic mysticism, but it is likely that my notions are neither new nor peculiar, and many utterances of the few mystical writers with whose works I am acquainted seem substantially in accord with my own longings and conclusions." (Ellis 114–15)

According to Ellis, the subject is psychologically healthy, with no taste for the occult, spiritualism, or the supernatural. Rather, literature led him to join his sexuality to his spirituality, since he informs Ellis,

> "Three or four years ago a little book by Coventry Patmore fell into my hands, and from its perusal resulted a strange blending of my religious and erotic notions. The desire to love and be loved is hard to drown, and when I realized that homosexually it was neither lawful nor possible for me to love in this world, I began to project my longings into the next. By birth I am a Roman Catholic, and in spite of a somewhat skeptical temper, manage to remain one by conviction." (114)

Although Patmore is best remembered for his long poem *The Angel in the House*, which celebrates Christian marriage in a contemporary setting, he and his wife translated medieval religious writers, and to some extent his mystical approach to "marriage" as union between the Christian believer and Christ has homoerotic overtones. In his correspondence with the poet Gerard Manley Hopkins on mystical love, Patmore offered the idea of intimate relations with Christ/God as the end of belief and meditation. In the case study, R.S.'s thoughts, inspired by Patmore, are theological:

> "From the doctrines of the Trinity, Incarnation and Eucharist, I have drawn conclusions which would fill the mind of the average pietist

with holy horror; nevertheless I believe that (granting the premises) these conclusions are both logically and theologically defensible. The Divinity of my fancied paradise resembles in no way the vapid conceptions of Fra Angelico or the Quartier San Sulpice. His physical aspect, at least, would be better represented by some Praxitilean demigod or Flandrin's naked, brooding boy." (114)

Eros and devotion circulate here through imagination. This case history demonstrates the exchange between the ancient and the Christian. The appropriation of the Greek inflects the spiritual life while devotion is designated as a site for erotic play, as Raffalovich also suggests. R.S. rejects the Christian art of the Middle Ages and early Renaissance in favor of the classical male body.

> "While these imaginings have caused me considerable moral disquietude, they do not seem wholly reprehensible, because I feel that the chief happiness I would derive by their realization would be mainly from the contemplation of the loved one, rather than from closer joys. ... I possess only a slight knowledge of the particulars of erotic mysticism, but it is likely that my notions are neither new nor peculiar, and many utterances of the few mystical writers with whose works I am acquainted seem substantially in accord with my own longings and conclusions. In endeavoring to find for them some sanction of valid authority, I have always sought corroboration from members of my own sex; hence am less likely to have fashioned my views after those of hypersensitive or hysterical women." (114–15)

R.S., like Raffalovich, places same-sex desire within a mostly celibate religious context. He also sees his desires as part of an historical tradition: not unusual or unhealthy. R.S. is anxious lest he be labeled a male hysteric. He wants to dissociate himself from the female ecstatic mysticism (presumably of the Middle Ages or Counter-Reformation) that was considered pathological in his secular age. However penetrated he may be by Christ, R.S. is concerned about being feminized. This gesture is not surprising, since sexual inversion was defined as a woman's soul in a man's body (a particularly appropriate gender-bending for mysticism as well, since the soul is almost always feminine in relation to the Judaeo-Christian Divine). R.S. had put himself in danger of being judged insane by speaking of his proclivities. His self-assertion must be viewed as strong evidence of acceptance of his sexuality.

> "You rightly infer that it is difficult for me to say exactly how I regard (morally) the homosexual tendency. Of this much, however, I am certain, that, even if it were possible, I would not exchange my introverted nature for a normal one. I suspect that the sexual emotions

and even inverted ones have a more subtle significance than is generally attributed to them; but modern moralists either fight shy of transcendental interpretations or see none, and I am ignorant and unable to solve the mystery these feelings seem to imply." (115)

R.S. validates his orientation, and indeed spiritualizes it. Being inverted is a "mystery": not unlike faith in that regard. As with mystical experience, reason fails in trying to explain inversion. R.S. locates his beliefs with respect to other writers:

"Patmore speaks boldly enough, in his way, and Lacordaire has hinted at things, but in a very guarded manner. I have neither the ability nor opportunity to study what the mystics of the Middle Ages have to say along these lines, and, besides, the medieval way of looking at things is not congenial to me. The chief characteristic of my tendency is an overpowering admiration for male beauty, and in this I am more akin to the Greeks." (Ellis 115)

Like Carpenter, R.S. turns to Hellenism, although it is Christianized. For R.S., the "medieval" is failure, as Wilde claims in "The Soul of Man Under Socialism," where the aesthetic of the medieval Christ is flawed because he glorifies pain rather than pleasure.[11]

For both self-preservation and self-definition, R. S. cannot accept this. He puts forth his own religious-erotic aesthetic:

"I have absolutely no words to tell you how powerfully such beauty affects me. Moral and intellectual worth is, I know, of greater value, but physical beauty I *see* more clearly, and it appears to me the most *vivid* (if not the most perfect) manifestation of the divine ... as time goes on I find that I long less for the actual youth before me, and more and more for some ideal, perfect being whose bodily splendour and loving heart are the realities whose reflections only we see in this cave of shadows. ... God grant that after the end *here*, I may be drawn from the shadow, and seemingly vain imaginings into the possession of their never-ending reality *here after*." (115)

R.S.'s theology is the Neo-Platonism of the medieval Church, before Scholasticism. It is fully incarnational, as unembodied, Reformed Christianity holds no attraction for him.

R.S. demonstrates a powerful process of sublimation of desire for men into longing for an ideal, embodied Divinity. He is one of the "types" of inverts Raffalovich depicts: he is "superior." "Sublimation" here is not pejorative, as it glorifies transcendence. While R.S. denigrates the absence of male beauty in medieval art, he nevertheless re-enacts in his own body the very medieval mystical relationship between man and Divine Lover. He articulates the process which I suggest was practiced on various levels throughout the nineteenth century.

R.S., however, engages in this transformation of desire with an awareness of identity. He is not a sinner; his desires are not impure. Rather, to act on such desires would make the sin. Hence their transference to God is the proper course to take. R.S. is aware of his same-sex desire and conscious of the repertoire such feelings may be played out on. When he makes the decision to sublimate, he comes from a different position than those earlier spaces where no stable identity or homosexual subculture offered such choices, when same-sex desire could only be conceived broadly, not in terms of fixed orientations.

Nineteenth-century discussions of homoeroticism in religious history are not limited to either esoteric, intellectual inquiries among social scientists and practitioners or to known homosexual writers. The following analysis in the *Westminster Review* of a volume of poetry by an Anglican clergyman, entitled *Passing the Love of Women* (referring to the love between David and Jonathan that also inspired Aelred Carlyle) demonstrates the pervasiveness of these allusions.[12]

> Friendship between man and man, and even more, the friendship between man and youths, form the theme of many of Dr. Bradford's poems. He is as alive to the beauty of unsullied youth as was Plato. If his religion is Christianity, tinged by Platonism, we must remember that Neo-Platonism was the philosophy of Christianity until the Middle Ages, when Aristotle came in with the Schoolmen and banished it from the theology of the Western Church.[13]

Between the lines, the critic argues for the presence of same-sex desire in western Christianity from antiquity to the late Middle Ages, a philosophical complement to Carpenter's social analysis. This position is used as justification for the homoerotic themes of Bradford's poetry. A stanza from the title poem of one of Bradford's books, *The New Chivalry*, is representative of the tone of much nineteenth-century uranian verse. Its homoeroticism is checked by Christian referents.

> Is Boy-Love Greek? Far off across the seas
>   The warm desire of Southern men may be:
> But passion freshened by a Northern breeze
>   Gains in male vigour and in purity.
> Our yearning tenderness for boys like these
> Has more in it of Christ than Socrates.[14]

English anxiety over same-sex desire is built into such male-male love, which recoils from classical antiquity in favor of Victorian "muscular Christianity." Of course, the social possibilities in this era of traveling to the Mediterranean or North Africa for homosexual experiences contribute to this xenophobia. Bradford's poem is not exclusively a Christian triumph over pagan history.

The works discussed in this essay are neither obscure in the literature of the period nor insignificant in socio-medical discourse. However, for a better-known poet, one could analyze Gerard Manley Hopkins's discussion of Bernard of Clairvaux or his translations of the *"Adoro te devote"* hymn on the Eucharist attributed to Aquinas. Hopkins's homosexual tendencies and the importance of Christ's body in his devotional life and works are well-established. The significance of writers such as Ellis, Carpenter and Raffalovich in shaping modern definitions of homosexuality has been acknowledged. My concentration here has been upon prose writings, where my consideration almost exclusively addresses male homoeroticism. Works such as Eliza Keary's 1874 "Christine and Mary," a long dialogue poem between a Catholic-convert nun and the friend she left behind in the world demonstrate the degree to which historical religion pervaded Victorian literary discourses of desire. Teresa of Avila figures prominently in this poem, as simultaneously a soul longing for the Divine – who may not be inflected as exclusively a biological male – and as a heteronormative regulator of anxieties over female-female desire in the convent.

While another essay would discuss an array of poets who utilize medieval religious imagery and references to address same-sex desire, I will briefly evaluate two representative figures as exemplary of the relationship between the non-fiction prose and poetry of the period. Frederick Rolfe, Baron Corvo, is perhaps best known for his gender-bending novel, *The Desire and Pursuit of the Whole* (alluding to Aristophanes in Plato's *Symposium*). His tales of romps with naked Italian boys appeared in the Decadent journal, *The Yellow Book*. Corvo's desire to be ordained a Roman Catholic priest and his avowed two decades of celibacy have often been caricatured. This homoerotic, indeed pederastic, writer was drawn to religious typology to express same-sex desire. Many of his poems are set in the Middle Ages.

Corvo's favorite poetic trope is the boy-martyr. He wrote a pseudo-Middle English "Sestina yn honour of Lytel Seynt Hew who was crucyfyed by ye Jewys atte Lincoln on ye Eve of Seynt Peter ad Vincula yn ye yeare of our Lord MCCLV." The Jews "seysed ye fayre syr Hew, / And yn theyr dwellynges baryd hys youthfulle bloome" (17–18).[15] The narration of Hugh explores the body in mortification. "On hys whyte fleyshe theyr scourge made roses bloome, / A thornye wreathe they bounde upon hys browe" (19–20). Rolfe writes of Saint William in "A.M.D.G." (the abbreviation of the Jesuit motto, "*Ad Maiorem Dei Gloriam*"), "Nailed to his cross the fair boy hangs alone – / *Sancte Guilielme ora pro me*" (3–4). The boy-martyr is compared to Christ, since imagining Christ as a boy enables the speaker to invert the *erastes/eromenos* (lover/beloved) relationship with the Lord. If in standard devotion Jesus is lover of the soul – the Divine *erastes* – by making Him a child (comparing a child to Him), Christ plays an *eromenos*, a beloved youth. He is submissive rather than dominant. This fantasy permits a variant of religious mastery: to make love to Christ rather than receiving love from him. Rolfe also composed three sonnets on that icon of gay male devotion, Saint Sebastian.

Besides the role of invention on the medieval, there is also the important question of translation. During the nineteenth century, numerous medieval religious works were reprinted for the first time in centuries, and many were made available in translation. John Gray, later Catholic priest and canon in Edinburgh and intimate friend of Raffalovich, published a collection called *Spiritual Poems* in 1896. That same year Raffalovich's *Uranisme et Unisexualité* was released in France. Gray's poems include translations of Bernard of Clairvaux, Jacopone da Todi, John of the Cross, and other mystics. At this time, Raffalovich was financing Gray's publications and otherwise supporting him. He had hired an attorney to protect Gray's interests at the Oscar Wilde trials. That Raffalovich, who probably introduced Gray to mystical writers, should incorporate them into his own sociological argument concerning homosexuality makes clear the importance of medieval religious history in the sexologist's definitions of same-sex desire. Gray, who had been a favorite of Oscar Wilde, sued a newspaper for libel when he was named as *the* Dorian Gray. He had signed a letter to "My Dearest Oscar" with "Yours ever, Dorian." However, when befriended by Raffalovich – some would say "rescued" – Gray embraced his Roman Catholicism, the religion to which Raffalovich converted. Gray's epistolary signature to Raffalovich while he studied for the priesthood at Scots College in Rome was "Jacopone." He was no longer "Dorian," abandoning both its Wildean and Greek resonances. This new signifier of a thirteenth-century ecstatic mystic in love with Christ suggests a different mediation of homoerotic desire, one that is religious. In a post-Wilde era of articulated homophobia, this role was permissible in its creation of a queer religious space in a way that avowed homosexuality was not and vague suggestions of homoeroticism were no longer possible.

If Gray's medievalism is best represented by his translations – 30 years later he translated works by Gertrude and Mechthilde on the Sacred Heart – he also wrote on the influence of medieval models. In an 1897 short story called "Light," Gray depicts a woman whose life is turned upside down by reading the translation of a Jacopone poem. In his story, Gray comments on the power of mystical literature:

> Johann Scheffler has shown the nativity in sentences of tenderness which human speech has poor hope ever to excel, so frail that they cannot be stirred from the tongue in which they were first set; Friedrich Spe has expressed physical contact with Christ in words which swoon upon his lips; the English language holds the pomp and glory of song in Crashaw's poem on the circumcision.[16]

Gray's reading of devotional writers was not limited to the medieval period. Like Raffalovich and later Evelyn Underhill, the historical array of mystical literature is acknowledged in Gray's work.[17]

I began and now end my discussion of Victorian sexology with the Raffalovich/Gray pairing. These two writers triangulate a relationship with the foremost literary and cultural representation of homosexuality of the period, Oscar Wilde, who was indeed definitive for modernity in shaping homosexual identity. Wilde, who wrote about Christ from his earliest poetry to his *magnum opus*, *De Profundis*, reconsidered his previous views on the limitation of medievalism. Imprisoned for gross indecency, he celebrated the "medieval" suffering Christ. He had once declared in "The Soul of Man Under Socialism" that "Medievalism, with its saints and martyrs, its love of self-torture, its wild passion for wounding itself, its gashing with knives, and its whipping with rods – Medievalism is real Christianity, and the medieval Christ is the real Christ."[18] This medievalism was limited in its imaginative sympathy, for art could not spring forth from pain alone: "Christ had no message for the Renaissance" (1103). But by the end of his life, Wilde was quoting Francis of Assisi and concluding:

> Still, I am conscious now that behind all this Beauty, satisfying though it be, there is some Spirit hidden of which the painted forms and shapes are but modes of manifestation, and it is with this Spirit that I desire to be in harmony. ... The Mystical in Art, the Mystical in Life, the Mystical in Nature – that is what I am looking for. (955)

In *De Profundis*, Wilde adopts the Neo-Platonism – and, indeed, mysticism – of Ellis's subject R.S.

The same Raffalovich and Gray who were preoccupied with medieval religious figures were also the Raffalovich who fled to the Continent during Wilde's trials, having his hairdresser (who was also Wilde's) wire him the verdict, and Gray who reputedly spent days on his knees in church while the trials were in progress. Hence we cannot view their interest in medieval religion as separate from the sexual lives of these writers. The sexological texts considered here articulate the relationship well. We find a range of experience in late nineteenth-century writing on medieval religion and same-sex desire: from religious typologies to queer appropriations, from historical readings of the role of homoeroticism in the Christian West to assertions that ancient Greek and medieval Christian can be reconciled. Regardless of the particular inflections on this range, it is crucial to note that at that important moment of homosexual definition, medieval religious history, not simply the Greek, shaped identities. While recently the medieval *as* queer has been considered, I suggest that we take note of the significant role of readings of the Middle Ages in *defining* the queer – in Victorian as well as postmodern culture. In the process, I believe we have the ability to practice New Medievalism, as we bring contemporary theory and cultural practice to this field of inquiry.

NOTES

1. Mark Jordan, *The Invention of Sodomy in Christian Theology* (Chicago: University of Chicago Press, 1997); Carolyn Dinshaw, *Getting Medieval: Sexualities and Communities, Pre- and Postmodern* (Durham: Duke University Press, 1999).
2. Michel Foucault, *Introduction to the History of Sexuality*, trans. Robert Hurley (New York: Vintage, 1990).
3. Linda Dowling, *Hellenism and Homosexuality in Victorian Oxford* (Ithaca: Cornell University Press, 1994).
4. Marc-André Raffalovich, *Uranisme et Unisexualité: Étude Sur Différentes Manifestations de L'Instinct Sexuel* (Lyon: Storck, 1896), 30–31. All translations in this essay are mine.
5. *The Letters of Oscar Wilde*, ed. Rupert Hart-Davis (New York: Harcourt, Brace & World, 1962), 173, n. 4.
6. John Boswell, *Christianity, Social Tolerance, and Homosexuality: Gay People in Western Europe from the Beginning of the Christian Era through the Fourteenth Century* (Chicago: University of Chicago Press, 1980), 221–6.
7. Peter Anson, *Abbot Extraordinary: Memoirs of Aelred Carlyle* (Leighton-Buzzard: Faith Press, 1958), 29–30.
8. Edward Carpenter, ed., *Iolaus: An Anthology of Friendship* (London: Swan Sonnenschein, 1902), 97–9.
9. Eve Kosofsky Sedgwick, *Between Men: English Literature and Male Homosocial Desire* (New York: Columbia University Press, 1985).
10. Havelock Ellis, *Sexual Inversion: Studies in the Psychology of Sex*, Volume One, Part Four (New York: Random House, 1942), 39–40.
11. *Complete Works of Oscar Wilde* (New York: Harper & Row, 1989), 1102.
12. "Thy love for me was wonderful, passing the love of women" (2 Sam. 1.26 KJV).
13. E.E. Bradford, *The New Chivalry and Other Poems* (London: Kegan Paul, 1918), 160.
14. Ibid., 31.
15. All quotations from Baron Corvo are taken from Frederick Rolfe, *Collected Poems*, ed. Cecil Woolf (London: Cecil and Amelia Woolf, 1974) and are parenthetically cited by line number.
16. John Gray, *The Selected Prose of John Gray*, ed. Jerusha Hull McCormack (Greensboro, NC: ELT Press, 1992), 121.
17. See Underhill's 1911 *Mysticism* (New York: Image, 1990).
18. *Complete Works of Oscar Wilde*, 1102.

Heraldry and Red Hats:
Linguistic Skepticism and Chesterton's Revision of Ruskinian Medievalism

CHENE HEADY

In her foundational study of Medievalism, *A Dream of Order*, Alice Chandler asserts that her subject, for all serious purposes, died with the nineteenth century. She briefly acknowledges that in some twentieth-century Catholic circles Medievalism retained a certain currency, but views this phenomenon more as an eccentric tangent than as any real exception to her rule.[1] To Chandler, John Ruskin is the height of Medievalism, and the movement tapers off as his heirs grasp only the periphery of his thought, abandoning its central impetus. Ruskin, she claims, possessed a grand vision of an elaborately and perfectly ordered universe, ordered from God down to the Gothic, but his heirs took hold only of his aesthetics and a rather mis-perceived notion of his class politics. However, nowhere does Chandler discuss the Ruskinian Catholic G.K. Chesterton, a highly popular and influential early twentieth-century author, and an enthusiastic medievalist. The other major crafters of the master narrative of Medievalism (Mark Girouard, Lee Patterson, etc.) also ignore Chesterton, causing the only scholarship on his responses to medieval themes to take the form of a defensive soliloquy by the *Chesterton Review*. Writing Chesterton out of the history of popular Medievalism creates a contained narrative that asserts or implies that no "dream of order" could survive World War I and the intellectual complexities of the twentieth century. Chandler ends her look at Ruskin with Henry Adams desperately attempting to work through Ruskin's reasoning, and finding that the task ends only in "the impossibility of such coherence."[2] But Chesterton would accept neither Adams's conclusion nor Chandler's sense of historical inevitability. Chesterton's Medievalism is a vision of metaphysical order both highly influenced by Ruskin's sense of coherence[3] and deeply aware of the problematic nature of meaning.

In his strongest writing, Chesterton preserves Ruskin's attempt to find metaphysical order in the medieval by altering the focus of the search. More than a social or a natural order (though at times it is both), Chesterton's medieval vision is of a distinctly linguistic paradise of order, the only moment in history when sign systems work perfectly, when the signifier stands in an exact relation to the signified. Deeply affected by the nihilism of the 1890s, Chesterton radically revised and revitalized Ruskinian Medievalism as a way of historicizing his difficulties in creating meaning. This may help explain why Chesterton's medievalist religious polemics (like *Heretics* or *Orthodoxy*) were widely popular and influential, though his attempt at creating his own Guild of Saint George, the medievalist social and political movement Distributism, was a dismal failure. His Medievalism most resonated with the age where it was furthest from the typical purposes of the tradition that he inherited.

Admittedly, this essay approaches a deconstructive reading of Chesterton's Medievalism, based largely on his discussion of heraldry in *Chaucer*. Born into the Victorian age, Chesterton often writes like a Victorian medievalist, depicting the medieval as a near-ideal social and religious state whose pillars, the guild system and the Catholic church, should be restored as the pillars of modern society. I am in a somewhat paradoxical position as I attempt to deconstruct Chesterton to reveal one of his less apparent strategies for creating meaning. But "deconstructive" is perhaps too strong a term for my reading; "structuralist" might be a better term. For the concept of the Middle Ages as the high point of human expression is one of Chesterton's prime intellectual debts to Ruskin and one of the main areas where he pushes Ruskin's thought further than anyone had previously thought to take it. For most readers of *Chaucer*, this theme is lost behind the louder rhetorics of Catholicism, Distributism and Thomism, but as we shall see, it resonates throughout the work.

Chesterton develops his sign theory through a complicated revision of Ruskin's model of art history, so it is fitting to begin our study by briefly discussing Ruskin. Ruskin's influence on Chesterton has been noted by scholars of Medievalism and culture at least since the time of Marshall McLuhan.[4] Maureen Corrigan goes so far as to dub Chesterton and his friend Eric Gill "the most outspoken disciples of Ruskinian Medievalism in the twentieth century."[5] For the sake of brevity and clarity, I will focus my discussion of Ruskin on "The Nature of the Gothic," a portion of *The Stones of Venice* published as a freestanding essay during the nineteenth century, and perhaps his most popular work. As Chesterton alludes to *The Stones of Venice* in his *The Victorian Age in Literature*,[6] and echoes "The Nature of the Gothic"'s view of art history throughout his work, it is reasonable to claim this essay as a direct influence.

In "The Nature of the Gothic," Ruskin outlines his famous model of art history: civilized antiquity created art that was beautiful but limited in subject by allowing its craftsmen no artistic freedom; the Middle Ages created art both beautiful and diverse in subject by allowing its craftsmen great freedom; and the modern age creates art exact but unbeautiful and limited in subject by dehumanizing and enslaving its workers in factories.[7] Ruskin also stresses the idea that Gothic art near-perfectly "unites fact with design," the abstract with the concrete, the ideal with the real.[8] The medieval is the high water mark of human expression, a Ruskinian idea that will be more important for Chesterton than it was to Ruskin.

The philosophical basis for this view of history is a kind of Romantic primitivism (whether Ruskin's schema is inherently primitivistic has been sharply debated by scholars; that he posited it based on primitivistic assumptions is indubitable). For Ruskin, the art of the Middle Ages is superior to that of classical antiquity not because culture had progressed in the interval, but rather because it had collapsed. As primitives, medieval craftsmen have no "artistic laws" and so represent "natural objects for their own sake, frankly."[9] In Ruskin's early work, "children and primitive artists" are inherently able to perceive and represent the divine order of reality, and the dictums of cultured society, whether ancient or modern, only obscure it.[10] Medieval workers achieve ideal expression because, in their primitivism, they possess a closeness to humanity's idyllic original state; they are devoid of the culture that now corrupts England's art and work. This culture causes true aesthetics to be deliberately "hidden from us ... by false teaching," preventing Gothic art, the art which best reflects reality, from being made in Victorian England, even though its principles are "self-evident."[11] In response, Ruskin, throughout his writing, challenges the British populace to regain the medieval Eden by rejecting the false artifice of their culture.[12]

If the medieval is an ideal moment for expression because it embodies a return to humanity's original state, it follows that accurate expression is a natural property of humanity, albeit a property now diminished by corrupt and artificial societal laws. And, further, if accurate expression is an innate part of humanity's original nature, it follows that even the societal laws of a corrupt culture cannot completely suppress this property; sign systems can be rendered limited, but they cannot be rendered dysfunctional. Hence, Ruskin does not complain that modern artistic representation possesses no meaning or an unclear meaning, but that its meaning is inherently limited. It says "the same thing over and over again."[13]

While Ruskin is famous for seeing the modern age as morally and artistically corrupt, his essentially primitivistic and optimistic sign theory thus limits the extent to which he can see signs themselves as corrupted. For, even in the decadent modern age, all signs can be read, provided that they are read by such an astute reader as John Ruskin. This principle is illustrated throughout Ruskin's work, but I will here give just two examples. Both occur within the space of one page. Ruskin can easily read the "ugly goblins, and formless monsters, and stern statues" of a Gothic cathedral;

they are "signs of the life and liberty of every workman who struck the stone; a freedom of thought, and rank in the scale of being" with no modern equal. But he can with equal facility view a modern English room and see that the "accurate mouldings, and perfect polishings, and unerring adjustments of the seasoned wood and tempered steel" are "Alas! if read rightly ... signs of a slavery in our England worse than that of the scourged African, or helot Greek."[14] He can read meaning in both Gothic and modern signs from the political to the metaphysical level. In the words of Jeffrey Spear, "Through the various stages of his religious belief Ruskin held firmly to the conviction ... that somehow ... he could read both the face of the sky and the signs of the times; indeed, each in the other."[15] As a good Victorian sage, an omnicompetent "Understanding Eye" for the "mysteriously encoded,"[16] Ruskin never considers the possibility that there could be such a thing as a floating signifier, a sign that, perhaps, signifies nothing definite at all.

Yet Chesterton's Ruskinian Medievalism is triggered by precisely such a realization, by the sense that in modern England floating signifiers haunt the streets like ghouls. A major figure in the Edwardian reaction against the aesthetes of the 1890s and their (real and perceived) nihilism, Chesterton possesses an awareness of unstable or uncertain meaning which is just as intense as his desire to drive it from Britain. In the 1890s he was a nihilist himself, and almost committed suicide as a consequence. From our current vantage point, this difference in both opinion and level of concern about signification may be the most interesting difference between Ruskin and Chesterton, and Chesterton's response the most original aspect of his Medievalism.

To Chesterton, the modern era is virtually synonymous with unmeaning. For him, such a common object as the corner post box represents the breakdown of sign systems, the disjunction between signifier and signified. The exchange of mail possesses a poetry to Chesterton, the conveying of "a thousand secrets" across the country, yet the modern age has almost conspiratorially chosen an unmeaning concrete form to represent this concept.[17] The mail box's "shape is the most unmeaning of shapes, its height and thickness just neutralising each other ...[;] one of the most beautiful ideas under one of the most preposterous of forms."[18] Chesterton's letterbox oddly resembles Lacan's "letter," the signified becoming subsumed, distorted, lost under the signifier. If Chesterton manages in this case to escape the full consequences of the breakdown of sign systems, knowing somehow what the sign should mean even though the sign fails to represent it, this is still more disjunction than Ruskin ever encounters. But this is not the end of Chesterton's problems. Heir of the Victorian sages, Chesterton is even more disturbed to find many of the modern signs simply unreadable.

If like Ruskin's signs they show the horror of the modern age, they show it only in that they fail to signify successfully. This surfaces particularly in the context of his discussions of heraldry. In a description that seems disturbingly like that of the mail box, Chesterton sees a modern "dull dumpy woman, with an expressionless face ... in a hat ... of flaming crimson like a Turner sunset." While he is inclined to think her and her clothes a sign, as they give him "a weird complex of thoughts," he cannot interpret this sign, other than to suggest that possibly it does not signify.[19] Here meaning is lost because the signified cannot correspond with the fixed meaning of the signifier. Because this image of a woman seems incompatible with her distinguishing sign, a "color of blood and fire" fit to inspire Ruskin, whatever meaning she may possess is lost, or at least indiscernible. Any meaning Chesterton can invent for her smacks of the absurd. He wishes he could ask the woman "as if she were at a masquerade ball, what she is meant to be," basically what she thinks she *means* (*Chaucer* 59).

Chesterton's Medievalism arises partly as a strategy for historicizing these breakdowns in sign systems. Strangely, he historicizes them in the context of Ruskin's art history, a history that ignores the very problem which drives Chesterton toward historicism. Chesterton explicitly endorses Ruskin's art history in his essay "On Gargoyles," and implicitly accepts it in *Chaucer*'s discussion of literary history. In both works he performs a reading of Ruskin that scrupulously preserves the most famous elements of the Ruskinian position, while quietly destroying their philosophical foundations. He divides art exactly into Ruskin's three "great stages," an antiquity beautiful but limited in subject, a medieval which could beautifully depict even the ugliest aspects of reality, and the modern, which is a collapse.[20] "Paganism," Chesterton says, "was in art a pure beauty; that was the dawn. Christianity was a beauty created by controlling a million monsters of ugliness; and that in my belief was the zenith and the noon." Then comes the modern, and with it decline, "the disruption and the decay."[21] Similarly, in the literary sphere, pre-Chaucerian literature is beautiful but limited and overly abstract in its subject matter; Chaucer accurately translates reality into verbal terms; yet modern literature, obsessed with "the chaotic and the incomplete," again fails to express the fullness of reality (*Chaucer* 135–6).

Less apparently, Chesterton shifts the meaning of Ruskin's stages slightly but significantly in its consequences for his sign theory. Two differences will prove crucial. In Chesterton's three stages of art, there is legitimate cultural progress between the ancient and the medieval (paganism, not Medievalism, is the primitive system, the "dawn"), and the modern is not merely a period of repetition, but of lingual breakdown and chaos amongst sign systems. If the medieval was a "beauty created by controlling a million monsters of ugliness ... [m]odern art and science practically mean having the million monsters and being unable to control them." Chesterton consistently sees the modern world as a place where external forms are generally random and meaningless, though he psychologically needs a world where every visible thing is a sign, and every signifier possesses a clear signified. In the modern world he sees just random colors, though he would like to see "a language of colours," ordered and purposeful (*Chaucer* 58). He is conscious that when he perceives a meaningful pattern in modern phenomena he is usually creating meaning where there is none, but he longs for "designs to appear by design, and not by accident" (*Chaucer* 58). He finds these longings fulfilled in the medieval, a paradise of sign systems, where every thing means and means exactly. Whereas in the modern era what seem to be signs are really meaningless "externals," medieval signs are true "emblems" of what they purport to represent (*Chaucer* 57).

To return to our earlier examples of unmeaning, Chesterton is certain that if the medievals had had a postal system and a mail box, the mail box would have received a meaningful form, one deferring the meaning of the postal system back to the deity: "If the medieval Christians had possessed it [the post box], it would have had a niche filled with the golden aureole of St. Rowland of the Postage Stamps."[22] Unlike the red of the "dull dumpy woman'"s horrifyingly unmeaning clothes, the sign which Chesterton cannot read, "red robes ... on a Cardinal ... have this extra glow or intensity of having a meaning" (*Chaucer* 59).[23] Chesterton's comparison between the medieval and the modern is best seen in one short but stark contrast. The flowers on the clothing of Chaucer's Squire "do express the Squire," but the flowers on "the flowered waistcoat of a fat stockbroker in 1860 ... did not express anything at all" (*Chaucer* 58). Meaning fails, since for Chesterton, flowers can't possibly signify "crass materialism," as in this case they must, if they are to signify "anything" related to their wearer "at all." For Chesterton the medieval is idyllic not for, as in Ruskin, possessing the right meaning, but rather for possessing any meaning. The elements of medieval culture praised are praised for meaning something, and their modern foils are not evil but meaningless.

It is important to note here that Chesterton could have possessed these insights about the modern and opinions about the medieval and still retain a rather simple Ruskinian sign theory if he, like Ruskin, envisioned the medieval as a return to an original human state (though, to be sure, it is psychologically likely that if Chesterton were temperamentally hopeful enough to accept such an essentially optimistic idea, he would not possess the anxieties about meaning we have been discussing). Were Chesterton a primitivist, he could posit the modern as a radically fallen state, and retain belief that humanity's natural tendency is toward accurate expression, that the normal relation between signifier and signified is correspondence. He would need to revise Ruskin only minimally. Chesterton does not, however, see his medieval paradise of accurate expression as due to a Ruskinian closeness to the original human state. Ruskin's rather arbitrary, though culturally common, conflation of the medieval and the primitive was always unacceptable to Chesterton. Original human innocence and perfection were ideas no more palatable to Chesterton's Catholicism than to his readers between the wars. He was relentless in his attacks on the primitivistic assumptions of many British medieval scholars. The modern critic, he remarks, "has made up his mind that Chaucer's mind must have been more simple than his own, merely because Chaucer lived at the most complicated and entangled transition time in European history, and drew on the traditions of about four European literatures instead of one" (*Chaucer* 19). In fact, for Chesterton, the Renaissance is a "revolt" against the "rationalism" of the Middle Ages, a "monomaniac" revolt arising out of a desire for a more simple and less logical view of life than the highly developed medieval culture will permit (*Chaucer* 240, 242). Yet if medieval people were not primitives, then Chesterton's contrast between the medieval and the modern sign systems implies that the natural order of things does not provide for a connection between signifier and signified, but that this is a fortunate occurrence which can easily slip away, as it has in the modern era.

As inherent nature provides no solution for Chesterton's problems with meaning, he seeks for a solution in artifice. He looks at the chaos of the "modern world" and wishes "that there were some way of ordering the externals of life, so as to make them appropriate; and, above all, so as to make them expressive" of internal states and deeper levels of reality (58). In other words, he wants an elaborate cultural system which will artificially and forcefully weld the signifier to the signified, the external to the internal, the surface to the reality. The entirety of medieval culture, he then alleges, is such a system, of which heraldry is the subset which he finds most emblematic, a subset giving even clothing and color, which clearly have no inherent meaning, the ability to "mean something" (59). This creation of meaning is an end in itself. "The ultimate justification of heraldry ... lay in the fact that it was a sort of pattern or standard of significance, by which even slighter and more trivial things tended to be significant" (56). For this reason, even the medieval Sumptuary Laws are not to be entirely condemned, as they quite forcefully and arbitrarily perform this "ordering [of] the externals of life" (58). Chesterton wants to believe that the medieval cultural system was a result of the medieval "passion for significance," that medieval culture was constructed for the same reasons as his Medievalism (59–60).

Chesterton's view of modern sign systems, then, borders on the basic principles of structuralist linguistics (or even, at points, Lacan), and he constructs his medievalism in response to his observations about signification, as a way of proving to himself that the disjunction between signifier and signified which he perceives as the usual state of sign systems is not inevitable. As George Levine has similarly observed of Newman,[24] Chesterton's faith in the divine permits him to go further in recognizing the arbitrary character of human meaning than many (though certainly not all) of his contemporaries. Because he writes with the intent of defending medieval faith, Chesterton is willing to grant as surely as Derrida that the coherence of the medieval system of meaning is entirely dependent on the relation of every term in the system back to a central term both inside and outside the system, the incarnate deity (the Transcendental Signified). In a key passage he discusses what Derrida would consider the limited "play" of the medieval system, asserting that the "decorative allegories" of medieval literature "seem so dead to us" but were "once alive like a dance with the balanced morality of the Middle Ages" (*Chaucer* 157). By the end of this passage, he has extended this simile to cover the whole medieval order. The medieval sign systems and the medieval world function because they dance, moving in perpetual variations and permutations, but always around God as a central term. "There might be any amount of movement, but it was movement around this central thing ... the Incarnation," so the system stayed in "balance." By contrast, in the modern age, the dance around God has broken up, and attempts to construct meaning or significance are, in the end, unsuccessful. The terms Chesterton uses to describe the modern here eerily anticipate Derrida. As modernity does not recognize the incarnate God, the ultimate referent from which a modern sign system (or modern life in general) derives meaning can only be an "alleged object ... a flying object ... a disappearing object" (*Chaucer* 159).

We have seen that, most probably as a way of containing his nihilistic tendencies, Chesterton constructed a linguistically skeptical Medievalism. How, one must wonder, could Chesterton, of all people, posit such a pessimistic Medievalism, one which seems to contradict both his aggressively orthodox Catholicism and his Ruskinian medievalist inheritance? As early a critic as Borges saw in Chesterton's work a Christian veneer unsuccessfully imposed on a nihilistic, "nightmarish" psychological world,[25] but this is, at best, only a partial answer, if, in fact, it is an answer at all. The full answer is less paradoxical than inevitable: Chesterton's Catholicism causes him to reject the central pillar on which Ruskin's more positive Medievalism was based.

As a Catholic, as an opponent of capitalism and industrialism, and as a lifelong lover of a well-wrought compound-complex sentence, Chesterton would naturally applaud Ruskin's early writing and its model of artistic history, under which the Middle Ages mark the high point of civilization. However, as we have seen, Chesterton, as not only a Catholic, but also, by the time of his study of Chaucer, a devoted Thomist, could not possibly accept Ruskin's assertion that the Middle Ages were a primitive time, when people thought and expressed themselves more truly because of their lack of knowledge of abstract systems. For the post-conversion Chesterton, the work of St. Thomas Aquinas marks the high point of human thought, and forms the summit towards which all medieval culture consciously or unconsciously tends. To Chesterton, even Chaucer's artistic genius is ultimately derived from his tendencies toward Thomism. "We shall get no further," he argues, "till we allow for this central and civilized character in the medieval poet; for the fact that he knew his philosophy" (*Chaucer* 19). That Chaucer "had a clear philosophy" is "the general thesis of this book" and "that philosophy was a Christian philosophy" (*Chaucer* 52). The great virtue of Chaucer's writing is his broad-minded humanism, and "he got his broad-mindedness from his [Thomistic] theology; though it was not what is now generally meant by a broad theology" (*Chaucer* 294).

Given how consistently Chesterton praises Ruskin (except for his views on religion and his opposition to democracy), it is doubtful that Chesterton realized how much he had problematized and destabilized the basic model from which he drew his Medievalism. He seems strangely unable to even recognize Ruskin's primitivism, asserting instead that Ruskin had convinced the world that the Middle Ages were a refined civilization.[26] However, Ruskin's primitivism is the central element on which the whole of Ruskinian sign theory rests, and Chesterton's Catholic rejection of this concept by a merciless logic requires his linguistic pessimism (this is probably not how Chesterton, biographically speaking, developed his position, but the logic does follow). If the medieval state is, as Ruskin asserted, the time when concrete facts and abstract truth stand in the best relation to each other, and when symbolic representation most accords with the real, but is not, as Ruskin assumed, a return to an original state, then any correspondence between the symbolic and the truly real, between the signifier and the thing signified is merely (in the Thomistic sense) accidental. The medieval is not the norm from which the modern has sadly veered, but the only period in history when signifier and signified accurately correspond. It follows that the typical relation between the signifier and signified is disjunction, and that the medieval is a miraculous, unstable moment when this condition is reversed.

But despite all his linguistic skepticism, Chesterton is not an unorthodox Catholic, just a little less orthodox than he would have liked to believe. For he is not merely uprooting the foundations of language and of Ruskinian Medievalism; he is (to use Steven Helmling's observation about Newman) deconstructing the "materialist world picture as prelude to the 'construction' of alternatives answering better to [his] desire."[27] If Chesterton were responding to his nihilistic tendencies merely with a "Nietzschean affirmation," he would have no need to construct a Medievalism at all. To understand why his writings prompted so many conversions to Catholicism in the skeptical 1920s and 1930s, we must not be satisfied with sketching the pessimistic basis of his dream of order; we must look at how this dream manages to stand on its improbable foundation. To do so, we must look again at his ideas about the nature of sign systems. Paradoxically (but where should we expect to find paradox if not in discussing Chesterton?), Chesterton's view of language may be less essentialist than that of Lacan and Derrida. Lacan believes that there must be floating signifiers; Derrida believes that the Transcendental Signified could never really be both outside and inside the sign system. Chesterton's ideas would seem to coincide with Lacan and Derrida's analysis of sign systems, but imply that sign systems do not possess such traits inevitably. Chesterton's history of art, when analyzed closely, suggests instead that sign systems function unsuccessfully "usually" rather than "normally," that they possess no "normal," organic state, positive or negative, at all.

Instead, Chesterton suggests that how well a society's sign systems work is entirely dependent upon how totalistic a society's dominant philosophy is. As antiquity's philosophy is incomprehensive, and can relate only a limited number of terms to the Transcendental Signified, antiquity's sign systems are troubled mostly by repression, by the limited number of things they can properly express. Antiquity's sign systems express only the beautiful because their philosophy, lacking the principle of the material incarnation, can only relate "godlike things to … their god."[28] Modernity's philosophy, as discussed above, lacks a God-concept to center its system, so modernity's sign-system problems are fragmentation and meaninglessness, as there is ultimately no accepted fixed term from which the others derive meaning. For Chesterton, only medieval Thomistic philosophy is totalistic enough to permit both full expression and the accurate correspondence of signifier and signified, avoiding the problems of sign systems both ancient and modern. He feels it and it alone to be the Bakhtinian impossibility of an "impermeable monoglossia." Unlike modern philosophy, Thomism ties every conceivable term back to the deity, guaranteeing coherence for medieval society's sign systems. Unlike ancient philosophy, Thomistic philosophy is comprehensive enough to contain and control even its own negation, making everything expressible within its society's sign systems. Heteroglossia is impossible, as there is nothing, no fact or rival system of signification, which the Thomistic system cannot successfully contain; the parodic itself is subsumed by the system. He hence argues that

> The Schoolman always had two ideas in his head; if they were only the Yes or No of his own proposition. The Schoolman was not only the schoolmaster but the schoolboy; he examined himself; he cross-examined himself; he may be said to have heckled himself for hundreds of pages. Nobody can read St. Thomas' theology without hearing all the arguments against St. Thomas' theology. ... The essential point is that it was not a simple theology. (*Chaucer* 293–94)

As discussed earlier, Chesterton considers Chaucer to be the high point of verbal expression, and Chaucer derives the perfection of his expression, its unlimited subject matter and perfect correspondence between the abstract and the concrete, from his inherited Thomism (*Chaucer* 282–4).

Thus the difficult and arbitrary nature of the construction of meaning becomes, surprisingly, the very basis for the appeal of Chesterton's medievalist religious apologetic. "Any free-minded and imaginative man," Chesterton plausibly alleges, will be unhappy that signifiers and signifieds do not accord in the modern world, that the external and the internal are disjunct (*Chaucer* 58). As sign systems possess no inherent state or nature, positive or negative, acceptance of this state of meaninglessness and disjunction is not a necessary act of intellectual honesty or of resignation to reality. It is, rather, an arbitrary choice. Modernity's misery and unmeaning are, then, unnecessarily self-inflicted. Consequently, modern society could choose for its philosophy the totalism of Thomism as easily as it has chosen the disjunctions of atheism, and thereby render its sign systems functional and its sense of meaning restored. What those optimistic about human nature, such as Ruskin, have considered the organic, normal human state could, through a complex series of artificial cultural constructs, be regained, but only through a Thomistic Catholicism. The dreams of both competing schools of popular Medievalism Patterson discusses, the institutional and the primitivist,[29] are combined in this latter day Medievalism, as the ideal expression belonging to Ruskin's medieval primitives can be regained only through the divine institution recommended by Kenelm Digby's *Broad Stone of Honor*. This hope, which Chesterton implicitly offers the reader throughout *Chaucer*, comes to the surface in the otherwise strange combination of institutional and organic language in the book's concluding paragraph. Only due to "medieval philosophy and culture," Chesterton says, was it possible for Chaucer to utter "the shout that normality had been found" (*Chaucer* 303). The hope that Ruskin had formerly offered England is still available, but is now a gift of grace rather than nature, of Incarnation rather than Eden.

To return to our original theme, Chesterton's Medievalist apologetic shows that, counter to Chandler's assertion, a Ruskinian dream of order that intelligently responds to twentieth-century concerns is possible. Chesterton revises Ruskin's Medievalism as a way of historicizing nihilism, and a way of asserting that if, as he has realized, meaning is arbitrary, meaninglessness is equally so. Both meaning and unmeaning require a cultural leap of faith; at this level Chesterton, a Thomist in belief but a fideist at heart, reads like a less individualistic Kierkegaard. The idea of the medieval as a paradisaical lingual moment may be the key to understanding how Chesterton, despite his own skeptical tendencies, kept a Medievalist faith alive in skeptical times, triggering even the "Catholic Revival" of the 1920s and 1930s. It may also be Chesterton's most original contribution to Medievalism. As Kevin Morris notes, religious Medievalism began early in the nineteenth century as a quest for "a communal language" in an age of individualism.[30] Chesterton prolonged religious Medievalism well into the twentieth century by making it a quest for any language at all.

NOTES

1. Alice Chandler, *A Dream of Order: The Medieval Ideal in Nineteenth-Century English Literature* (Lincoln, NE: University of Nebraska Press, 1970), 183.
2. Ibid., 195.
3. Cf. Maureen Corrigan, "Gill, Chesterton, and Ruskin: Medievalism in the Twentieth Century," *Chesterton Review* 9 (1983), 18.
4. Marshall McLuhan, "The Origins of Chesterton's Medievalism," *Chesterton Review* 1 (1975), 49–50.
5. Corrigan, "Gill, Chesterton, and Ruskin," 15.
6. Gilbert Keith Chesterton, *The Victorian Age in Literature* (Oxford: Oxford University Press, 1966), 25.
7. John Ruskin, "The Nature of the Gothic," in Clive Wilmer, ed., *Unto this Last and Other Writings* (London: Penguin Books, 1985), 82–5.
8. Ibid., 100–101.
9. Ibid., 99.
10. Chandler, *A Dream of Order*, 197–8.
11. Ruskin, "The Nature of the Gothic," 94.
12. Cf. Jeffrey Spear, *Dreams of an English Eden: Ruskin and His Tradition in Social Criticism* (New York: Columbia University Press, 1984), 2.
13. Ruskin, "The Nature of the Gothic," 94.
14. Ibid., 85–6.
15. Spear, *Dreams of an English Eden*, 40.
16. This is one way George Landow defines the Victorian sage in his definitive *Elegant Jeremiahs: The Sage from Carlyle to Mailer* (Ithaca, NY: Cornell University Press, 1986), 43.
17. G.K. Chesterton, "William Morris and His School," in *Twelve Types* (London: Arthur Humphreys, 1902), 19–20.
18. Ibid.
19. G.K. Chesterton, *Chaucer* (New York: Farrar and Rinehardt, 1932), 59. Subsequent references are cited in the text as "Chaucer."
20. G.K. Chesterton, "On Gargoyles," in Raymond Bond (ed.), *The Man Who Was Chesterton:*

The Best Essays, Stories, Poems, and Other Writings of G.K. Chesterton (New York: Dodd, Mead, and Company, 1937), 3.

21. Ibid., 6.
22. Chesterton, "William Morris," 20. Rowland Hill devised the penny postage stamp system in the 1840s. Anthony Trollope claimed credit for the invention of the pillar box.
23. Surprising as it may be, communism is one meaning for red which Chesterton does not even consider, William Morris notwithstanding. This may be because he refused to take Morris seriously. In *The Victorian Age in Literature* (89), he sardonically remarks that Morris was essentially a "shopkeeper" and that "the importance of his Socialism can easily be exaggerated."
24. George Levine, *The Boundaries of Fiction: Carlyle, Macaulay, Newman* (Princeton: Princeton University Press, 1968), 264.
25. Jorge Borges, "On Chesterton," in *Other Inquisitions*, trans. Ruth Sims (Austin: University of Texas Press, 1984), 84.
26. Gilbert Chesterton, "John Ruskin," in Dorothy Collins, ed., *A Handful of Authors: Essays on Books and Authors* (New York: Sheed and Ward, 1953), 151.
27. Steven Helmling, *The Esoteric Comedies of Carlyle, Newman and Yeats* (Cambridge: Cambridge University Press, 1988), 28.
28. Chesterton, "Gargoyles," 6.
29. Cf. Lee Patterson, *Negotiating the Past: The Historical Understanding of Medieval Literature* (Madison, WI: University of Wisconsin Press, 1987), 9–11.
30. Kevin Morris, *The Image of the Middle Ages in Romantic and Victorian Literature* (London: Croon Helm, 1984), 223.

The Return of the King:
Medievalism and the Politics of Nostalgia in the Mythopoetic Men's Movement

SUSAN ARONSTEIN

Often, when a new era begins in history, a myth for that era springs up. The myth is a preview of what is to come... In the myth of Parsifal's search for the Holy Grail we have such a prescription for our modern day. The Grail myth arose in the twelfth century, a time when many people feel our modern age began; ideas, attitudes and concepts we are living with today had their beginnings in the days when the Grail myth took form...

The Grail myth speaks of masculine psychology.[1]

The preface to Robert Johnson's *He: Understanding Masculine Psychology* makes explicit the mythopoetic men's movement's debt to medieval narrative, particularly the legends of King Arthur and the Holy Grail.[2] While Johnson is the only writer to base his analysis of the masculine psyche solely on the Arthurian tales, the movement's other primary texts – Robert Bly's *Iron John: A Book About Men*; Robert Moore and Douglas Gillette's *King, Warrior, Magician, Lover: Rediscovering the Archetypes of the Mature Masculine*; and Sam Keen's *Fire in the Belly: On Being A Man* – also draw from medieval narrative patterns and locate the models for the "mature" and "deep" masculine within an idealized medieval past.[3] However, in spite of these authors' obvious debt to medieval romance, most critics relegate the mythopoetic men's movement's medievalism to a quick aside, focusing instead on its Jungian methodology. While the movement's Jungian roots certainly influence its particular version of medievalism, I would argue its use of medieval narrative, its link to the original audiences of Arthurian romance, and the ideological implications of its medievalism are central to understanding its seemingly confused politics and the surprisingly prominent role that it played in American culture in the late 1980s and 1990s.[4]

In the following article I explore the role played by medievalism in shaping both the narratives and the politics of the mythopoetic men's movement. I will begin by exploring the ideological implications of medievalism and its politics of nostalgia. I will then discuss the mythopoetic men's movement, its cultural context, and the popular and critical reaction to it, analyzing the ways in which the ideological implications of both medievalism and Jungian psychoanalysis framed the movement's "unconscious" politics. After this analysis, I will discuss the ways in which both the Arthurian romances' original audience (the French aristocracy in the late twelfth and early thirteenth centuries) and the mythopoetic men's movement use the legend to create a nostalgia for a past that reinscribes them at the center of cultural privilege.

MEDIEVALISM AND THE POLITICS OF NOSTALGIA

The mythopoetic men's movement, as it looks to the medieval past for its model of the ideal masculine, participates in what Umberto Eco calls our collective cultural "dreaming" of the Middle Ages.[5] This dreaming, according to Morton Bloomfield, "clothes our deepest dreams and hopes ... in medieval garments."[6] While Bloomfield is unalarmed by the implications of disguising modern ideals in a medieval costume drama, Eco warns us that "since the Middle Ages have always been messed up in order to meet the vital requirements of different periods" it is critical that we should ask "which Middle Ages one is dreaming of" (68). The ideological implications of medievalism are all the more profound, in Eco's view, because a return to the Middle Ages represents a quest for our origins; "looking at the Middle Ages means looking at our infancy, in the same way that a doctor, to understand our present state of health, looks at our childhood, or in the same way that a psychoanalyst, to understand our present neuroses, makes a careful investigation of the primal scene" (65).

Eco's analysis of this continual state of return to the primal scene alerts us to the fact that the medieval past exists only as a modern construct or dream; however, it glosses over what I see as one of the most profoundly and dangerously ideological implications of medievalism. To "dream the Middle Ages" is not merely to construct what Bloomfield recognizes as an idealization of the era, but to present that era as the ideal, as, to extend Eco's psychoanalytical analogy, the site of our original cultural and psychological unity, lost in the fragmentation of modern culture, to which we must return. Thus, when we clothe "our deepest hopes and dreams in medieval garments," we engage in a politics of nostalgia, arguing for the return to a lost ideal that is paradoxically portrayed as both ahistorical and universal.

THE MYTHOPOETIC MEN'S MOVEMENT AND
ITS CULTURAL CONTEXT

The mythopoetic men's movement's attempt to recover the "lost" ideal of masculinity moved into the cultural limelight in 1991, at the end of a period characterized in America by a persistent dream of our own past – a politics of nostalgia exemplified in Lucas's and Spielberg's blockbusters, Reagan's rhetoric, and political neo-conservatism.[7] *Iron John* and *Fire in the Belly* topped the bestseller list for most of that year and the movement itself became the subject of derisory media sound bytes and academic and feminist alarm.[8] The media was unable to resist the vision of white, middle-aged corporate employees capering naked in the woods to the beat of "primeval" drumming or sobbing lustily in Sheraton conference rooms, a vision that culminated in Murphy Brown's summation of the movement on primetime television, "You rent a room, read some Viking poems, and CPAs all over America are having cathartic breakthroughs."[9]

While the popular media implicitly criticized the movement as the silly, but harmless, overindulgence of a privileged class with too much money to spend, feminist and cultural critics condemned it as one more example of what Susan Faludi had characterized in the same year as American culture's "backlash" against women.[10] Early reviews of the movement's primary texts (mostly of *Iron John*) stigmatized the movement as, at best, "incoherent" and "programatically hollow" and, at worst, a movement in which "the powerful separate themselves in order to regroup and recoup what they believe has been stolen from them."[11] Gail Collins, writing in the popular press, sums up both media and academic reactions to the phenomenon as she advises *Working Woman* that *Iron John* "explains quite a bit ... those hostile memos, that nasty scene at the water cooler. Next time you feel yourself choking up ..., simply remind yourself that this is only a large primitive being covered with hair down to his feet, out of the pond again and wandering down mainstreet."[12] This early critique culminated in *Women Respond to the Men's Movement*, in which popular and academic feminists outlined their major objections to the mythopoets; these objections are most strongly and succinctly stated in Caputi and MacKenzie's contribution to the collection, "Pumping Iron John": "The men's movement, as epitomized in Bly's writing (is) a manifestation of authoritarian backlash ... reinforcing separatism, hierarchy, contempt for the "other" and invidious distinctions between men and women" (72).[13] In addition, they argue, the movement's characteristic "yearning for political authority figures smacks not of therapeutic healing but of fascism" (74).

This scornful feminist critique is understandable. The written texts of the mythopoetic men's movement *are* alarmingly misogynist, in spite of their authors' claims that they are discussing archetypes, not "real" women. However, there is more to the cultural context of the men's movement than the backlash phenomenon, as has recently been argued by Michael Schwalbe and Micheal Kimmel, who both place the mythopoetics in the context of a general "crisis in masculinity" rooted in the 1960s and reaching its peak in the 1980s and early 1990s.[14] This crisis, as chronicled by Schwalbe and Kimmel, confronted the participants in the movement, whom Schwalbe describes in his ethnography as white, middle-to-upper-middle-class men between 35–60, with a situation in which they had been figuratively displaced from their central position in American culture. This displacement occurred, according to Kimmel, on several levels. First, "all the marginal groups whose suppression had been thought necessary for men to build secure identities began to rebel" as women and minorities refused to be defined as extensions of or in opposition to white men (Kimmel, 262). Second, the cultural conditions that had allowed manhood to be constructed in traditional icons, such as the soldier and the frontier man, changed; the frontier had disappeared and, in the wake of the Vietnam War, the soldier was no longer valorized but, rather, pitied and demonized. Finally, feminism, in addition to insisting that women had the right of self-definition, offered a scathing and pointed critique of men which characterized the traditional masculine ideal as distant and violent – an emotional cripple, a potential killer, rapist, abuser.

If most of these white, American, middle-class men retained their positions of social and economic privilege, their loss of figurative power left them without secure identities and in the position of having to reconstruct a positive masculine identity. One response to this challenge was that taken by the feminist men – whom Bly later stigmatizes as the "soft men" of the 1960s – who themselves engaged in a critique of and escape from limited conservative definitions of masculinity. Another response, the dominant response of the 1980s, the decade which saw the birth of the mythopoetic men's movement, was "the reassertion of pride, the retrieval of political and metaphorical potency for America and, hence the American man" (Kimmel, 291). This response sought not to redefine the masculine but to reinscribe the old ideal into the center of cultural and figurative power.

The mythopoetic men's movement, in spite of its self-declared apolitical status and in direct opposition to the stated politics of most of its members, belongs in this second category. How did a group of men whom Schwalbe describes as "gentle and decent, acting on good intentions, and trying to cope with life without hurting anyone" – men who, on the whole, were supportive of the feminist movement and at odds with the neo-conservative politics of the 1980s – end up associated with a movement that was rhetorically in tune with those politics (Schwalbe, 232, 135)? The answer to this question is complex; it lies in a combination of its leaders' Jungian methodology and their choice of medieval romance to shape the movement's founding narratives.

JUNGIAN PSYCHOLOGY AND MEDIEVAL NARRATIVE

The mythopoetic men's movement's reliance on Jungian psychoanalysis has been widely noted, although, according to Schwalbe, Jung himself was "kept out of sight" at the gatherings because the men were "allergic to doctrine" (26). He is also often kept under wraps in the textual tradition. But whether they explicitly refer to Jung or not, the movement's writers all base their "map" to a new manhood on the assumptions of Jungian psychoanalysis. They each posit an original psychic unity – wounded or fragmented in childhood, a psyche made up of archetypes which must be activated and ordered to recreate that unity, and a narrative blue print for the proper disposition of these archetypes to be found in ancient stories.[15]

Jungian psychoanalysis contains within its assumptions and methodologies a definite tendency towards conservatism, as does any system that posits an essential, ahistoric, universal self. In addition, and more importantly to what came to be seen as the backlash politics of the mythopoetic men's movement, Jung claims that this self – this ideally unified and ordered series of archetypes – is *different* for men and women. Psychological disorder occurs when either gender "activates" the wrong archetypes. Indeed, the mythopoetic men's movement focuses on this assumption; it argues that what ails modern men is their misplacement of – or subservience to – feminine archetypes. Bly's "soft men," who "have learned so well not to hurt anyone that (they) cannot lift the steel, even to catch the light of the sun on it" and are so engulfed by the mother that "they have no male face or no face at all" (4, 17), Keen's questing knights who must "take leave of WOMAN and wander for a long time in the wild and sweet world of men" (16), and Johnson's Grail Knights who fail because "so long as a man is encased in his mother complex, he cannot appreciate the Grail or, worse yet, ask the right question to heal the Fisher King" (48), all need, in Bly's metaphor, to steel the key from under their mother's pillow and become "real men." While all of these writers earnestly argue that they are referring to archetypes, not "real" women, the line between the two not only has the potential to become dangerously blurred, it often does so in their own writings. Bly tells the story of the teenager who knocks his mother across the room when she asks him to come to dinner, an act that Bly fondly affirms as a release of "Zeus" energy. Similarly, in the original version of *He*, Johnson states, "the new feminism scares me out of my wits because so much of it is women demanding to come out of her traditional feminine role of serving man" (Bly 19; Johnson, 1988, 48).

The mythopoetic men's movement's Jungian roots advocate universal gender-specific models of psychological unity. This assumption about men's and women's roles in the psychological world, combined with the movement's desire to reinvest the (white) male with a positive moral valence – a reinvestment that within their writings is concomitant with a redemption of patriarchy – dictated their choices from what Bly calls the universal "reservoir of stories" that will lead us to psychological (and social) truth (x). While the mythopoets' assumption that both stories and psychological truths exist independently of historical and cultural context leaves them free, in the words of Kimmel, "to wander through anthropological literature like post-modern tourists, as if the world's cultures were arrayed like so many ritual boutiques in a world shopping mall," these writers "buy" a very specific set of stories on their shopping spree (319).

Why do these writers choose medieval romance, particularly the Grail legend, to provide their essential myths of masculine psychology? First, they suit their Jungian assumptions about the dangers posed to the masculine psyche by the feminine archetypes, especially the mother. Second, these tales provide narratives that satisfy the mythopoets' not-so-unconscious longings for the simpler gender roles of a pre-feminist era, before the "alarming feminists" whom Johnson complains about in the original version of *He* (a comment he diplomatically removes from his revised version) had questioned both masculine identity and male cultural dominance. As Bly wistfully states in his discussion of the Princess, "during the twelfth and thirteenth centuries all this was understood" (136). In fact, as Schwalbe argues, the mythopoets chose only narratives that "portrayed gender roles and power relations between men and women in traditional ways ... There was little in the stories to disrupt the expectations about gender roles and gender inequality that the men had brought with them from the literal world of late twentieth century America" (94). I would further argue that these tales appealed not merely because they did not disrupt gender expectations but also because they reaffirmed them in the wake of the feminist challenge. By turning to the Middle Ages, the mythopoetic writers found a narrative world which ran smoothly along the hierarchical and essentialist lines advocated by Jungian psychoanalysis, a world now lost.

In their analyses, these writers divorce the medieval narratives from their historical context, employing a method of textual interpretation that is an English professor's nightmare. They focus on an image as it "speaks" to the individual and use that image as an occasion to spin out into additional personal and literary stories. Bly employs this method to maddening effect in *Iron John*, a book where "interpretation" involves personal experience, anecdote, literary and mythological analogues and even, as Jane Tompkins notes, "quotations from the author's own poems and argumentative clinchers."[16] In both their assumptions about the nature of stories and their interpretive methods, the mythopoets insist that narrative transcends both history and politics. Thus, any attempt to question the political implications of a tale is derailed and the questioner "reminded that stories (have) to be interpreted mythologically, not literally." Besides, as Schwalbe was tartly informed by one of the movement's teachers, "these stories have been around for ages and haven't caused any harm" (Schwalbe, 94, 177).[17]

The mythopoet's sacralization of medieval social structures as they are inscribed within the narratives upon which they base their "quest" to find the "Grail" of "deep masculinity" reveals their ideology. By reinterpreting medieval narratives with not only the idealism of typical medievalism – here is our cultural ideal past – but also the universalism of Jungian psychoanalysis – here is our ideal psychological past – they present the view of ideal masculinity and women's role in the creation of masculinity found in these tales as a psychological *fait accompli*. Thus, the mythopoets inscribe in their "truth" a vision of social order that itself was the "backlash" response of a displaced social class trying to reinscribe itself at the center of cultural and political power and privilege.

ARTHURIAN ROMANCE AND ITS ORIGINAL AUDIENCE

It is not surprising that the mythopoetic men's movement's authors, in their attempt to redefine (or rediscover) ideal manhood in the midst of a cultural crisis, should have turned to these medieval romances. The similarities between the audiences for the original romances (the French aristocracy in the late twelfth and early thirteenth centuries) and the mythopoetic men's movement's rewriting and interpretation of those romances are striking. Each audience was, or saw itself as, displaced from a former position of political and social power; each had to deal with a cultural redefinition of the ideal masculine; each felt threatened by a perceived increase in women's power and agency.

The political and social displacement of the French aristocracy in the late twelfth and early thirteenth centuries has been discussed by many historians and literary critics, most notably Georges Duby, Erich Kohler, Howard Bloch and Gabrielle Spiegel.[18] As Duby notes, this period, 1180–1220, represents a time of progress and change unequaled until the mid-eighteenth century (*France*, 96). Much of this progress and change, however, came at the expense of the aristocracy as a program on the part of both monarch and church to centralize authority, aided by the move to a money economy, eroded their traditional power base. This program resulted in: the displacement of the aristocratic knight by a new class of mercenary soldier, paid and armed by the King; a new King's council, which included the lesser nobility and non-noble members of the new moneyed classes; the continual elimination of intermediary lords as legislation declared more and more vassals held their fiefs directly from the king; marriage redefined as a sacrament, placing it under the church's control, which now had a right to meddle in aristocratic "dynasty building" by barring marriages within an ever-widening circle of consanguinity and strictly limiting divorce; and the switch from feudal justice to a system of centralized law courts answering to the King. Furthermore, the literature of this period also chronicles a perceived increase in the power of women through the rise of *fin amor* as, at least in literary and social fictions, women were endowed with the power to judge and reward masculine prowess.[19] The result of all these power shifts, accompanied by an increasing need for hard cash, was an aristocracy who found (or felt) themselves alienated from the centers of power which they saw as their traditional prerogative and, furthermore, unable to economically "buy" their way back into power or, sometimes, even to support themselves.

While this displaced class employed several means in their attempts to regain social and political status, including warfare, judicious marriages, sale of land, and the manipulation of language to preserve class distinctions, Arthurian romance stands as their most important ideological tool. These romances, by reinscribing aristocratic power into an ideal past reaffirm, for their displaced audience, their own superior place in the scheme of things, and argue for a return to the "good old days" when Arthur (idealistically) functioned merely as a figurehead to provide a court for his feudal lords.[20] These larger political implications are couched within the genre's central narrative of a knight's quest for what the mythopoets would later call "mature" or "deep" masculinity.

Given the confines of this article, my analysis of the ways in which Arthurian romance functioned to side-step social and political reality and both reinscribe aristocratic privilege and redefine "ideal manhood" for the medieval French aristocracy, will be necessarily general. I base my discussion on Chrétien's work, particularly *Yvain, Erec and Enide*, and *Perceval or the Story of the Grail*, and later Grail continuations. In the first two romances, which chronicle Chrétien's own codification of ideal manhood, the knight's quest begins with a series of adventures through which he proves his physical prowess by defeating and either killing or imprisoning (at Arthur's court) various renegade knights. This first series ends in the acquisition of a "lady," whose approval of the knight signifies his successful negotiation of the path to manhood. However, the lady also poses a threat to this manhood, as the knight's infatuation with her separates him from the homosocial order in which he should be participating. This precipitates a second set of adventures in which the knight must reclaim his masculine identity by relegating the lady back to her proper place as symbol and adjunct.[21] Several things are key in these expositions of aristocratic masculine identity. First, what the mythopoets call the "warrior archetype" stands at their center. Second, that archetype, while technically in the "service" of the King, is actually vital to the monarch's political survival. Third, and most crucial to the neo-conservative backlash inherent in the mythopoetic movement, women must function only as a signifier of masculine achievement. The moment they step out of that role, masculine identity falls apart and can only be reasserted by relegating women back to their symbolic function, a crisis which is central to Chrétien's *Lancelot*.[22]

In these early tales, Chrétien reinscribes aristocratic privilege, presenting it – with its physically aggressive warrior values – as central to Arthur's idealized court. Chrétien's final romance, *Perceval or the Story of the Grail,* and its continuations present an alternative to this pattern in which ideal masculinity is increasingly defined as something in opposition to political power and privileged over it. In *Perceval*, Chrétien follows a nameless boy from the isolation of his mother's forest on his quest to become a knight. As he does so, he presents both his most explicit warning about the dangers that women pose to the construction of the masculine self and an attempt to redefine that self as something apart from the political structures of the Arthurian court.[23] Chrétien's exploration of alternative discourses of masculinity, combined with *Perceval*'s lack of closure, paves the way for his continuers to introduce, in the Grail tradition, a world in which spiritual or moral prowess trumps physical prowess and the quest for "true" knighthood signals the end of the political court.

The introduction of the Grail into the Arthurian cosmos strengthened the legend's pull towards conservative, authoritarian and masculine values. To seek the Grail is to seek God and a single ultimate meaning. To find the Grail is to find the "Father" whom your masculinity serves. Furthermore, the Grail tales specifically eliminated women from this quest and then went to great lengths to justify that elimination, portraying women as cleverly disguised fiends sent to lure the knights from their true purpose or, at best, as misguided virtuous women who end up dead. The history of the Grail stories is the history of women's progressive threat to the formation of masculine identity and their consequent exclusion from the courtly world.[24]

ARTHURIAN ROMANCE AND THE MYTHOPOETIC MEN'S MOVEMENT

These tales, for their original medieval audiences, first imagined a world in which they had been returned to political power and, later, redefined "true" power as necessarily separate from the court. Furthermore, in both versions, the masculine identity through which this power was achieved depended upon the subordination and displacement of women. Since the mythopoetic men's movement brought these narratives, with their authoritarian assumptions and gender roles intact, into their texts and presented them as the lost map to true manhood, "understood" by our ancestors and inscribed into our psychological unconscious, it is not surprising that the movement, in spite of its own conscious intentions (although in keeping, I would argue, with their unconscious and less politically-correct longings), participates in its culture's larger neo-conservative backlash. When Sam Keen identifies himself as "on a quest to find the Grail" of manhood (5), when Bly claims that the healing of the Fisher King will heal our wounded society, when Gillette and Moore argue for the release of warrior energy in the service of the King, and when Johnson advances the Grail myth as the tale of "masculine psychology," the movement's major authors carry the political and cultural baggage of the original narratives into their texts.

All of these authors try rhetorically to escape this baggage by arguing that the texts themselves are much older than their literary manifestations and attempting to construct the "true" story out of various renditions of the tales. Because of this, their narratives – even Johnson's, who actually claims to be using Chrétien's version of *Perceval* because "it is simpler, more direct, and nearer to the unconscious" (x) – represent a hodgepodge of motifs and stories in which every scene refers to a similar motif in another story, and all the pieces are put together in the service of rediscovering the psychological "ur" myth. In this way, the mythopoetic writers are "medievalist" in their critical methodology as well as their choice of stories. The narratives presented in their books, interspersed with psychological interpretations (which become the real story), resemble the criticism of early Arthurian scholars such as Roger Sherman Loomis and Jessie Weston more than they do any recognizable medieval romance.[25]

These author's revisions and analyses of medieval narratives highlight and reinforce both the original romances' gender politics and their vision of ultimate authority. These retellings lead to a reinscription of the masculine and patriarchy – and, by extension, traditional gender roles – through the restoration of their positive moral valence. The mythopoets use these stories to argue that what feminists have objected to is not patriarchy but "puerarchy" and "poisoned patriarchy," and that what our culture desperately needs is the return of the "true King" or "true Father." This figure, narratively portrayed by Christ, Arthur, and the healed Fisher King, lives as a potential archetype in all men and is activated, as the legends show us, when a boy leaves his mother, finds a male mentor, accesses his warrior archetype, and subjugates (either by abandonment or marriage) the feminine. The activation of the King archetype will, first, heal modern men and, ultimately, restore familial and social order.

Each of the mythopoetic men's movement's four major texts rewrite medieval narratives to illustrate the restoration of the king and offer him, the "mature masculine," as a cure for our modern culture. Johnson in *He* explicitly identifies "Crétien's *Parsifal*'s [sic] search for the Holy Grail" as "a prescription for our modern day" (ix). In Johnson's analysis of this myth, the key to curing modern men lies in the healing of the Fisher King. "With the wounded Fisher King presiding at the inner court of modern western man we can expect much outward suffering and alienation. And so it is: the kingdom is not flourishing; the crops are poor; maidens are bereaved; children are orphaned" (9).

Johnson's masculine quest to heal this "wounded archetypal underpinning" is outlined in his story of Parsifal (9). In his telling and exposition of this story, Johnson rewrites Chrétien's original romance to emphasize the crisis of the male psyche, the dangers posed to the development of the male self by the "mother," the crucial role of male mentors, and the need to subjugate the interior feminine. According to Johnson, modern men are going through a dark time brought on by their original failure at the Grail Castle; these ills can be cured by a successful return to the Grail Court. In order to succeed on the Grail Quest, however, a man must leave the feminine (represented by Parsifal's mother and, to a lesser extent, by Blanchflor) and acquire a male mentor (represented by Gournemand and the hermit).[26] While Chrétien's text does indeed argue that the masculine order needs to take precedent over the feminine, Johnson's rewriting emphasizes this theme. In particular, his retelling further demonizes the mother. Chrétien merely accuses Perceval's mother of enclosing him in her female world, denying him his patrilinear heritage and removing him from the homosocial order that is his birthright. Johnson compounds this crime by shifting the responsibility for Parsifal's failure at the Grail Castle from Gournemand to his mother. In Chrétien, Perceval leaves his mother's garment behind when Gornemant knights him. Gornemant then tells the young knight to stop referring to his mother and to follow his new mentor's advice, which includes the admonition to only speak when he's invited to. This advice, which Perceval obeys in spite of his desire to ask the Grail question, precipitates his failure at the Grail Castle. In Johnson's version, however, Parsifal arrives at the Grail Castle still wearing his mother's garment and heeding her advice never to ask questions (advice she does not give in the actual text Johnson claims to be retelling). According to Johnson, Parsifal's mother's robe, "prevents him from appreciating the Grail when he sees it. So long as a man is encased in his mother-complex, he cannot appreciate the Grail or, worse yet, ask the right question to heal the Fisher King wound" (48).

Once a man has shed his "mother complex," he can return to the Grail Castle. Johnson acknowledges that this return does not occur in Chrétien's romance. "Here the great French poem by Chrétien stops! ... The great story from the collective unconscious had gone thus far in its evolution and the author had the humility to stop when he had nothing further to say" (76). Johnson then informs his audience that their quest is to finish the story, offering them a conclusion in the final chapter that emphasizes the Grail legend's ultimately conservative, authoritarian ideology:

> The Grail serves the Grail King. ... Translated this means that life serves what a Christian would call God, Jung would call the Self and we call by the many terms we have devised to indicate that which is greater than ourselves. ... All Grail quests are to serve God or the Grail. If one understands this and drops his idiotic notion that the meaning of life is personal happiness, then one will find that elusive quality immediately at hand. (Johnson, 79)

In *He* Johnson retells Chrétien's *Perceval*, embellished eclectically with other Grail traditions from writers as diverse as Jessie Weston and Wolfram von Essenbach, and reread through his own Jungian lens. In this version not only is the "mother" demonized as the cause of male failure but also all women – even Blanchflor's romance ideal – are put back in their place as secondary to the male quest, which ultimately leads Parsifal to an idealized version of the "Father" in the Grail.

Similarly, Bly offers his tale of "Iron John" as a model for "soft men" suffering from "The Hunger for the King in a Time with no Father" (93–102). He uses this tale to outline the path that men must follow as they search for positive masculine "Zeus" energy and connection with the King. These men, like Perceval, must leave their "mothers" (in Bly's tale "steal the key from under the mothers pillow"[1–27]) and wander into the forest, where they will be re-educated by a male mentor (the Wild Man, standing in for Gornemant). A part of this re-education involves an initial failure that propels the boy away from the site of potential bliss (the Wild Man's stream or the Grail Castle) and into the "dark" or "ashes" time, during which the young man grows up, accesses his inner-warrior, and is given a second chance to heal the Fisher King or transform the Wild Man. It is here that Bly's narrative turns away from the outline of the Grail story and to the narratives of more traditional medieval romances. Unlike Perceval, who must leave Blanchflor once he's earned her and turn to the Grail Quest, Bly's golden-haired hero is allowed to retain the princess he earns by feats of arms. Like any lady of medieval romance, she passes from father to knight as a symbol of his social status and military prowess:

> "If you can perform feats of that magnitude you are obviously not a gardener's boy. Who is your father? ..."
>
> "My father is a notable King, and I have a great deal of gold, as much as I will ever need."
>
> "It is clear ... that I am in great debt to you. Whatever I have in my power that will please you, I will give."
>
> "Well, ... I'd suggest that you give me your daughter as my wife." (Bly, 220)

Although the King's daughter, a good romance lady, acquiesces to this exchange, the message is clear: knights earn women; fathers bestow them; and the women recognize the "natural rightness" of the system.

The wedding which ends this tale in proper romance fashion shows that the boy's successful negotiation of the path to manhood has restored harmony in both the natural and social orders as both the boys parents and the "Wild Man," a baronial king mysteriously freed from his enchantment by the youth, attend the ceremonies. The boy has become a man, escaping from the mother, accessing the warrior, and earning the princess; both he and the dominant social order are healed.

Sam Keen also tries to show modern men the way to a healed self and a healed social order. Unlike Johnson and Bly, however, he does not specifically retell a tale as a way into his pilgrimage. However, he casts his quest in the narrative form of the Grail quest: "Hidden in his young heart was a craving to discover his own definition of manhood. ... He did not know it, but he had already set out ... on a quest to find the Grail" (Keen, 6). This quest, as Keen chronicles it, takes the form of both the hero's journey with its forest of adventures and the later Grail quests of the medieval French prose tradition, handed down to our own culture via Malory's Arthurian works. For Keen, as for Malory's Grail knights, the quest for the Grail of "true manhood" involves a double displacement of perspective. First, in order to achieve the Grail, the knight must leave the feminine behind. In Malory, the knights are informed: "None in this quest (may) lead lady nor gentlewoman with him for it is not to do in so high a service as they labour in."[27] Keen also admonishes his would-be Grail knights: "We begin to learn the mysteries unique to maleness only when we separate from WOMAN'S world," an admonition that goes on for two pages (15). Once both medieval and modern questors have separated from the feminine, they must access a redefined warrior archetype. Medieval knights must learn to read and act not chivalrically but spiritually, and modern men must submit themselves to the "logic of the imagination.[28] As we pass through the looking glass our values and visions of who we are change; a reversal of figure and ground occurs" (Keen, 129). Through this reversal of figure and ground, the medieval knights achieve ideal knighthood and a vision of God; the modern man, according to Keen, achieves not God, but what displaces God in his vision, "inner masculinity." This inner-masculinity, in turn, becomes the ideal father, "a new kind of leader who seeks to empower others" (Keen, 153).

Moore and Gillette's work also advocates a redefinition of the warrior archetype that revolves around the maturation of the hero. This hero comes of age in the romance world, leaving the mother, fighting the dragons, and winning the princess. However, the activation of the archetype who can win the princess is not, as it is in Bly, enough. As Gillette and Moore observe, "he doesn't know what to do with her" (39); the hero must find the "generative, affirming, empowering father" (Arthur) and access his mature archetypes – Warrior: Perceval; Magician: Merlin; Lover: Lancelot (Gillette and Moore, 49–63; 80–88;106–10; 121–6).

While Gillette and Moore discuss all of these archetypes as they can be positively enacted in the mature masculine, their major focus is clearly on the King and his centrality to both psychological and cultural health. They slide alarmingly from a discussion of the King as archetype to his inscription at the center of social order, arguing:

> It is the mortal king's duty to receive and take to his people this right order of the universe and cast it in societal form, but even more fundamentally to embody it in his own person, to live it in his own life. If the king does not ... the realm will languish. ... On a more immediate note, we see in modern dysfunctional families that when there is an immature, a weak, or an absent father and the King energy is not sufficiently present, the family is very often given over to disorder and chaos. (56, 58)

Gillette and Moore's call for the "return of the king" is typical of the mythopoetic men's movement's use of Arthurian romance. In their emphasis on overpowering mothers, rescued princesses and transcendent Grails, these tales valorize a restored patriarchy in which the threat posed to male identity by feminist critique is silenced and women, if allowed to remain at all, are relegated to the sidelines as symbols of male success. These contemporary Arthurian tales inscribe a politics of nostalgia; through them, the mythopoets dream the middle ages, presenting the gender politics and authoritarian values of a medievalized past as the answer to the confused present of modern America.

NOTES

1. Robert Johnson, *He: Understanding Masculine Psychology* (New York: Harper and Row, 1988, revised 1989). Subsequently cited in the text as "Johnson."

2. The mythopoetic men's movement is only one of several contemporary men's movements. Other men's movements, as outlined in Kenneth Clatterbaugh, *Contemporary Perspectives on Masculinity: Men, Women and Politics in Modern Society* (Boulder, CO: Westview Press, 1997) include: the profeminists, men's rights, socialists, gay men, African American Men, and the evangelical Promise Keepers.

3. Robert Bly, *Iron John: A Book About Men* (New York: Addison-Wesley, 1990), subsequently cited in the text as "Bly." Robert Moore and Douglas Gillette, *King, Warrior, Magician, Lover: Rediscovering the Archetypes of the Mature Masculine* (San Francisco: Harper Collins, 1990); Sam Keen, *Fire in the Belly: On Being a Man* (New York: Bantam, 1991). Although Bly claims the Grimm Brothers' "Iron John" as his founding narrative, Jack Zipes, in "Spreading Myths About Fairy Tales: A Critical Commentary on Robert Bly's' *Iron John,*" *New German Critique* 55 (1992), 3–19, notes that the tale Bly tells is Wilhelm Grimms' adaptation of Stith-Thompson's type 314, "The Golden-Haired Youth at the King's Court," which developed in medieval Europe. Furthermore, the tale derives from the literary tradition of the twelfth-century romance, *Robert der Teufel.*

4. This movement was a peculiarly American phenomenon; as Nick Lawson mused in his review of the mythopoetics, "The Wild Man Mystique," *World Press Review* (Dec. 1991), 40, "will 'masculinism' follow McDonald's and *Twin Peaks?*"

5. Umberto Eco, *Travels in Hyperreality*, trans. William Weaver (New York: Harcourt Brace, 1986).

6. Morton Bloomfield, "Reflections of a Medievalist: American Medievalism and the Middle Ages," in *Medievalism in American Culture*, ed. B. Rosenthal and P. Szarmach, Medieval and Renaissance Texts and Studies (New York: State University of New York Press, 1989), 13–27.

7. For a discussion of neo-conservatism, Reagan, and Lucas and Spielberg see Douglas Kellner and Michael Ryan, *Camera Politica: The Politics and Ideology of Contemporary Hollywood Film* (Bloomington: Indiana University Press, 1987), Robin Wood, *Hollywood from Vietnam to Reagan* (New York: Columbia University Press, 1986) and Peter Biskind, "Blockbuster: The Last Crusade," in *Seeing Through Movies*, ed. Mark Crispin Miller (New York: Pantheon Books, 1990), 112–49. I have discussed Medievalism in the Lucas-Spielberg blockbusters in "'Not Exactly a Knight': Arthurian Narrative and Recuperative Politics in the *Indiana Jones* Trilogy," *Cinema Journal* 34 (1995), 3–30.

8. Michael Kimmel, *Manhood in America: A Cultural History* (New York: Free Press, 1996), 315.

9. Michael King, "Male Call," episode of *Murphy Brown* aired 30 Sept. 1991, program #187164.

10. Susan Faludi, *Backlash: The Undeclared War Against American Women* (New York: Crown Publishers, 1991).

11. Daniel Seligman, "Men in Trouble," *Fortune* (2 Dec. 1991), 184; Garth Baker-Fletcher, "Escape Artists," *Christianity and Crisis* (13 Jan. 1992), 419–20.

12. Gail Collins, "Warning: Vikings in the Office," *Working Woman* (Oct. 1991), 114. Other notable early reviews include: Carol Bly, "The Charasmatic Men's Movement: Warrior Wannabes, Unconscious Deals and Psychological Booty," *Omni* (March 1992), 6, and Diane Johnson, "Something for the Boys," *New York Review of Books* (16 Jan. 1992), 13–17.

13. Jane Caputi and Gordene MacKenzie, "Pumping Iron John," in *Women Respond to the Men's Movement*, ed. Kay Hagan (San Francisco: Harper, 1992), 69–82.

14. Michael Schwalbe, *Unlocking the Iron Cage: The Men's Movement, Gender Politics and American Culture* (New York: Oxford University Press, 1996); Michael Kimmel, *Manhood in America: A Cultural History* (New York: Free Press, 1996).

15. I am indebted to Schwalbe and Clatterbaugh for the general outline of Jungian methodology.

16. Jane Tompkins, "Saving our Lives: *Dances with Wolves, Iron John* and the Search for a New Masculinity," in *Eloquent Obsessions: Writing Cultural Criticism*, ed. Marianna Torgovnick

(Durham: Duke University Press, 1994) 96–105, p.105.

17. Schwalbe's discussion here, which stems from his own questioning of one of the "fairy stories" told at a gathering, which included a date rape, is fascinating.

18. For an overview of the plight of the French aristocracy during this time see, Howard Bloch, *Medieval French Literature and Law* (Berkeley: University of California Press, 1977); Georges Duby, *The Knight, the Lady and the Priest: The Making of Modern Marriage in Medieval France*, trans. Barbara Bray (New York: Pantheon, 1983) and *France in the Middle Ages: 987–1460*, trans. Juliet Vale (Oxford: Blackwell, 1991); Ernst Kohler, *L'Aventure Chevaleresque: Idéal et Réalité dans le Roman Courtois* (Paris: Gallimard, 1974); and Gabrielle Spiegel, *Romancing the Past: The Rise of Vernacular Historiography in Thirteenth Century France* (Berkeley: University of California Press, 1993).

19. For a discussion of *fin amor* as a social and literary phenomenon see Jane Burns and Roberta Krueger, "Introduction," *Romance Notes* 25 (1985), 205–19.

20. Kohler, Bloch and Duby (*Marriage*) all discuss the aristocracy's use of Arthurian romance as an ideological tool.

21. A discussion of this formula (without the feminist inflection) can be found in James Schultz, *The Shape of the Round Table* (Toronto: University of Toronto Press, 1983).

22. Roberta Krueger discusses the role of women in the formation of male identity in *Women Readers and the Ideology of Gender in Old French Verse Romance* (Cambridge: Cambridge University Press, 1993).

23. I discuss Chrétien's exploration of ideal knighthood in "'Chevaliers Estre Deüssiez:' Power, Discourse and the Chivalric in Chrétien's *Conte du Graal*," *Assays* VI (1991), 3–28.

24. For a further discussion of the exclusion of women in the Grail stories, see my article, "Rewriting Perceval's Sister: Eucharistic Vision and Typological Destiny in the *Queste del San Graal*," *Women's Studies* 21 (1991) 211–30.

25. It is not my purpose here to enumerate the inaccuracies in these authors' presentations of medieval narratives. They are indeed numerous. However, the only difference between their rewriting of Arthurian legend and other cultural retellings, such as Tennyson's *Idylls of the King* and Lerner and Lowe's *Camelot*, is their claim that they are relating the original medieval version and their use of that claim to establish their tale's authority.

26. In my discussion of the two tales I will use Johnson's spelling of proper names when referring to his text and Chrétien's spellings when referring to the medieval version.

27. Thomas Malory, *Le Morte D'Arthur*, vol. II, ed. Janet Cowen (New York: Penguin, 1986).

28. For discussions of the changed perspective required of medieval Grail knights see Jane Burns, *Arthurian Fictions: Re-Reading the Vulgate Cycle* (Columbus: Ohio State University Press, 1985) and Laurence de Looze, "A Story of Interpretations: The *Queste del San Graal* as Metafiction," *Romanic Review* 76 (1985), 129–46.

Abstracts

Samuel Daniel's Defense of Medievalism *by Kelly A. Quinn*

Samuel Daniel's 1603 *Defence of Ryme* is ostensibly a rejection of a 1602 argument put forth by Thomas Campion in support of quantitative verse. In fact, the *Defence* is more concerned with addressing the anti-medievalism which informs Campion's argument – and the humanist movement generally. Using humanist techniques of argument and playing upon humanist sympathies, Daniel mounts an attack on anti-medievalism. Nationalist humanists, he suggests, ought to embrace, rather than reject, the medieval heritage.

Chivalry and Romance in the Eighteenth Century: Richard Hurd and the Disenchantment of *The Faerie Queene by Kristine Louise Haugen*

Hurd's best-remembered work, *Letters on Chivalry and Romance* (1762), called on the medieval era as part of a bold reinterpretation of Spenser's *The Faerie Queene* and other postmedieval epic poems. Rejecting not only the critical method of identifying literary texts' parallels and sources, but also the received notion of Spenser as an inventive fabulist, Hurd read *The Faerie Queene* as a direct reflection of medieval social life. The theoretical program Hurd thus advanced presented new problems that Hurd exploited argumentatively rather than solved. Hurd's enterprise and its difficulties recall eighteenth-century notions of realistic fiction, as well as an established ecclesiastical tradition of scholarly debunking.

Waging Battle: *Ashford v. Thornton, Ivanhoe,* **and Legal Violence** *by Mark Schoenfield*

In 1817, the trial of Abraham Thornton for the murder of Mary Ashford forced English law to acknowledge that legal chivalry, with its stress on the body as a locus for truth, survived as part of contemporary law when her brother lodged an Appeal of Murder calling for a Wager of Battle against the suspect. The implied challenge to the effectiveness of the jury system as a means of achieving justice prompted widespread debate over law's real and imagined medieval heritage and continuing role of this heritage in modern law. In *Ivanhoe*, Rebecca's final recourse against charges of witchcraft is Wager of Battle. By constantly juxtaposing medieval and modern points of view in this episode, Scott is able to explore the gaps in the coherence of the medieval sense of law, yet simultaneously to question whether modern law has really replaced the legal violence of the Middle Ages with a model based on eighteenth-century rationality.

Marianne: Mystic or Madwoman? Representations of Jeanne d'Arc on the Parisian Stage in the 1820s *by Sarah Hibberd*

During the Napoleonic era Jeanne d'Arc was frequently portrayed as a "Marianne" figure, leading the French into battle against the English. However, during the Bourbon restoration the abandonment of Jeanne by the king and the church during her trial were seen as problematic by the authorities at a time of great political sensitivity. Thus although she remained a popular figure, the subject of many writings, paintings and dramas, her significance in the theater as a symbol of nationhood was downplayed. Instead, her visions were a cue both for exploring the melodramatic ideas about female madness and the supernatural that were growing during the 1820s, and for bringing the past into the present in a way that was recognizable to a modern audience.

While Carafa's 1821 *opéra comique* presents her as a sentimental heroine, on the brink of madness, Soumet's 1825 *tragédie* focuses on her emotional and spiritual strength and persuasiveness. This shift from the political to the spiritual was continued in plays of the second half of the decade which exploited more explicitly the visual and musical tropes of female madness and entrancement associated with her visions.

The "Truth" About the Middle Ages: *La Revue des Deux Mondes* and Late Nineteenth-Century French Medievalism *by Elizabeth Emery*

After the French defeat of the Franco-Prussian war (1870–71), scholars Fustel de Coulanges, Ludovic Vitet and Eugène Aubry-Vitet used *La Revue des Deux Mondes*, the leading periodical of their time, to boost patriotism. Their essays exalted the Middle Ages as the birthplace of France and called upon contemporaries to reconsider ideas about the past. They argued that discovering "the truth" about medieval France – that it was never barbaric, but always strong, independent and resilient – would speed recovery of war wounds. These intellectuals' dedication to rewriting French history sparked contemporary interest for all things medieval while creating a market for medieval scholarship.

Medieval Religion, Victorian Homosexualities *by Frederick S. Roden*

This essay suggests the potential for reading medieval religion (rather than the more-often studied courtly literature) in understanding one aspect of Victorian fascination with the Middle Ages. I argue here that medieval religion as a discourse facilitated the formation of homosexual communities in the nineteenth century. Medieval religious models of mysticism and monasticism created a space for the expression of same-sex desire in the literature of the period. The late Victorian sociological/sexological writings (which defined modern homosexual identity) in turn utilized medieval religious history in articulating a fixed and essential model of same-sex desire. Writers such as Raffalovich, Carpenter, Ellis and Wilde demonstrate this phenomenon in the prose of the period, as Gray and Corvo reflect it in poetry.

Heraldry and Red Hats: Linguistic Skepticism and Chesterton's Revision of Ruskinian Medievalism *by Chene Heady*

In *A Dream of Order*, Alice Chandler depicts Ruskinian Medievalism as dying upon contact with the complexities of the twentieth century. The work of the Ruskinian Catholic G.K. Chesterton, especially his *Chaucer* (1932), belies this conclusion. Aware that in modern England he often encounters floating signifiers, Lacanian "letters," and signs which he simply cannot read, Chesterton historicizes his difficulties in creating meaning by envisioning the medieval as a time when, due to an elaborate and arbitrary cultural system, every sign signified and signified exactly. As all sign systems are artificial, Chesterton suggests, meaning could be regained as artificially and easily as it was lost if England would only return to medieval religion.

The Return of the King: Medievalism and the Politics of Nostalgia in the Mythopoetic Men's Movement *by Susan Aronstein*

The mythopoetic men's movement uses the Arthurian legend to create a politics of nostalgia for a past that reinscribes its white middle-to-upper-middle class members at the center of cultural privilege and reinvests traditional masculinity with a positive moral valence. By choosing medieval narratives as the basis for their "map" to true manhood, the mythopoets import the gender politics and authoritarian values of those narratives. Furthermore, their retellings emphasize overbearing mothers, warrior knights and ideal fathers. These values, coupled with its essentialist Jungian roots, place the movement – in spite of its apolitical stance and in direct opposition to the stated politics of most of its members – within the larger neo-conservative backlash of the late 1980s and early 1990s.

Notes on Contributors

Susan Aronstein is Associate Professor of English at the University of Wyoming. She is the author of numerous articles on Arthurian adaptations in literature, popular culture, and film, and is working on a book on Arthurian cinema.

Elizabeth Emery is Assistant Professor of French at Montclair State University. She is the author of *Romancing the Cathedral: Gothic Architecture in Fin-de-Siècle French Culture* and co-author of a nearly completed book entitled *Consuming the Past: The Medieval Revival in Fin-de-Siècle France*. Other publications focus on the links between medieval and nineteenth-century French literature and culture.

Kristine Louise Haugen studies early modern and eighteenth-century intellectual history at Princeton, where she is completing her doctorate in English. Her dissertation reappraises literary canonization and professional criticism in eighteenth-century England, focusing on Richard Bentley. She has published articles in the *Journal of the History of Ideas* and *Sixteenth-Century Journal*.

Chene Heady is a doctoral student in Victorian and Edwardian literature at the Ohio State University, where he obtained the degree of Master of Fine Arts in Creative Writing. His primary area of research is sage discourse.

Sarah Hibberd is a Junior Research Fellow in the Music Department at Royal Holloway, University of London. Her doctoral dissertation (University of Southampton, 1998) examined the relationship between popular theater and opera in Paris around 1830. She has published on grand opera in Paris and on French adaptations of the *Faust* legend for the theater in the 1820s. She is currently exploring historical representation on the Parisian stage.

Kelly A. Quinn is a doctoral candidate at the University of Toronto, writing a dissertation on the writings of Samuel Daniel. Her previous degrees are from the University of Toronto and the University of Cambridge. She has published on Sir Thomas North's marginalia.

Frederick S. Roden is Assistant Professor of English at the University of Connecticut. He has published essays on Christina Rossetti, Oscar Wilde,

Judith Butler, Aelred of Rievaulx and Hildegard of Bingen. He is at work on a book entitled *Same-Sex Desire in Victorian Religious Culture.*

Mark Schoenfield is Associate Professor of English at Vanderbilt University. He is the author of *The Professional Wordsworth: Law, Labor, and the Poet's Contract* and articles on nineteenth-century British literature and law. His current book-length project is provisionally titled *Voices Together: Romantic Identity and the British Periodical Industry.*

Clare A. Simmons is Professor of English at the Ohio State University, Columbus. The Co-Editor of *Prose Studies*, she is the author of *Reversing the Conquest: History and Myth in Nineteenth-Century British Literature*, *Eyes Across the Channel: French Revolutions, Party History and British Writing 1830–1882*, and articles on nineteenth-century literature and history. She is working on a study of the common-law tradition in Romantic-era Britain.

Index

For Product Safety Concerns and Information please contact our EU
representative GPSR@taylorandfrancis.com
Taylor & Francis Verlag GmbH, Kaufingerstraße 24, 80331 München, Germany